T0355722

BULLDAGGERS, PANSIES,
AND CHOCOLATE BABIES

TRIANGULATIONS
Lesbian/Gay/Queer ▲ Theater/Drama/Performance

Series Editors
Jill Dolan, Princeton University
David Román, University of Southern California

BULLDAGGERS, PANSIES, AND CHOCOLATE BABIES

Performance, Race, and Sexuality in the Harlem Renaissance

James F. Wilson

THE UNIVERSITY OF MICHIGAN PRESS
ANN ARBOR

First paperback edition 2011
Copyright © by the University of Michigan 2010
All rights reserved
Published in the United States of America by
The University of Michigan Press
Printed and bound by CPI Group (UK) Ltd, Croydon, CR0 4YY

2014   2013   2012   2011   5   4   3   2

A CIP catalog record for this book is available from the British Library.

Library of Congress Cataloging-in-Publication Data

Wilson, James F.
    Bulldaggers, pansies, and chocolate babies : performance, race,
and sexuality in the Harlem Renaissance / James F. Wilson.
        p.   cm. — (Triangulations: lesbian/gay/queer
theater/drama/performance)
    Includes bibliographical references and index.
    ISBN 978-0-472-11725-3 (cloth : alk. paper)
    1. American drama—African American authors—History and
criticism.   2. American drama—20th century—History and criticism.
3. African Americans in the performing arts—New York (State)—New
York—History—20th century.   4. Theater—New York (State)—New
York—History—20th century.   5. African Americans—New York
(State)—New York—Intellectual life.   6. Harlem (New York, N.Y.)—
Intellectual life—20th century.   7. Harlem Renaissance.   8. African
Americans in literature.   9. Race in literature.   10. Sex in the
theater.   I. Title.
    PS338.N4W555   2010
    812'.5209896073—dc22   2009050344

ISBN 978-0-472-02696-8 (e-book)
ISBN 13: 978-0-472-03489-5 (pbk. : alk. paper)
ISBN 10: 0-472-03489-8 (pbk. : alk. paper)

Cover illustration: Program cover for production of *Harlem* at the
Majestic Theatre in Chicago ca. 1930. (Billy Rose Theatre Division, The
New York Public Library for the Performing Arts, Astor, Lenox and
Tilden Foundations.)

For my parents,
John and Mary Wilson

Acknowledgments

This book, over ten years in the making, would not have been possible without the guidance, support, and inspiration of some truly remarkable individuals. I am indebted to them all, and I wish I had the space to pay more than just passing tribute in these introductory pages. I must first thank Jill Dolan, who has been a constant source of intellectual sustenance over the years. Even when she wasn't directly prodding me to dig more deeply and challenging me to think beyond immediate impressions, I could hear her voice urging me to complete the book. My admiration for her political, theoretical, and pedagogical commitment is immense, and I am honored and proud that I have had the opportunity to work with one of the trailblazers in the profession.

Thanks must also go to James Hatch, who introduced me to the rich field of African American theater and performance. With his encouragement, my enchantment with Florence Mills and the Broadway musical revues of the 1920s soon became a paper, subsequently a conference presentation, then the basis for a doctoral dissertation, and now this book. My association with Florence Mills, whom I first encountered in James Hatch's seminar, soon led to intense archival relationships with Ethel Waters, Gladys Bentley, and a host of supporting figures of the Harlem Renaissance.

Daniel Gerould and Alisa Solomon provided generous feedback in various stages of the project as meandering thoughts morphed into full-blown ideas. Dan offered a limitless source of knowledge and suggestions, particularly about the blues, and Alisa pushed for clear, jargon-free English while exhorting for scholarly rigor throughout. I have also benefited greatly from my other mentors and colleagues at CUNY Graduate Center, and because of them, I cannot think of a more academically stimulating place than the third floor suite of offices on Thirty-fifth Street in Manhattan. Marvin Carlson, Jean Graham-Jones, Judith Milhous, David Savran, and Maurya Wickstrom are my academic role models, and they have, by their example, stoked my passion for theater scholarship. It is fair to say that such passion would all be for naught were it not for Lynette Gibson's and Rob Hume's respective administrative and technological assistance.

I am also grateful for my colleagues at LaGuardia Community College, especially Terry Cole and Eleanor Q. Tignor, who generously shared their knowledge and expertise on African American literature and offered feedback and guidance as I wrestled with texts and theoretical claims. Additionally, Sandra Hanson, J. Elizabeth Clark, Marian Arkin, and Phyllis Van Slyck provided intellectual and emotional support. I am enormously fortunate to work in a department that not only gets along famously (a rarity in academia, I understand), but also revels in the accomplishments of others.

Directly and indirectly, my students at the Graduate Center and LaGuardia have contributed to the development of the ideas in the book. While teaching African American and gay and lesbian literature and theater courses, I have benefitted from the knowledge generated in class discussions. Furthermore, my work has been enriched by the feedback I have received from colleagues and audience members at conferences, invited lectures, and panel discussions. Kim Marra and Robert A. Schanke, editors of *Staging Desire: Queer Readings of American Theater History* (University of Michigan Press, 2002), in which a version of my Lulu Belle chapter appeared, offered excellent advice. I am also thankful for the extensive and incredibly detailed reports by the outside readers of this project. Scott Ham and Marcia LaBrenz at the University of Michigan Press have provided their editorial expertise in all aspects of the production of this book. Brad Krumholz was enormously helpful on the index.

I appreciate the financial assistance I have received from the City University of New York, especially for the grants and fellowships bestowed upon the project. The Geoffrey Marshall Dissertation Fellowship in the Humanities, Richard C. Wade Dissertation Prize, and a Professional Staff Congress Project Grant all allowed me time and space to research and write. I would like to extend my deep gratitude to the staffs of the libraries and archives that provided outstanding and efficient research support, in particular the New York Public Library, and the various collections in the Schomburg Center for Research in Black Culture, the New York Public Library for the Performing Arts, Stephen A. Schwarzman Building. I must also thank the individuals at the Beinecke Rare Book and Manuscript Library at Yale University; Columbia University Library, especially Anne Marie Menta; the staff of the Institute of Jazz Studies at Rutgers University; the Lesbian Herstory Archives; and the Museum of the City of New York. Bruce Kellner, the Successor Trustee of the Carl Van Vechten Estate, authorized permission to use a photo of Gladys Bentley, and he kindly offered suggestions for pursuing other images. Thomas Wirth and the late Marvin Smith shared their memories and historical knowledge of the period with me.

My friends and family have provided crucial support throughout the process. My parents, John and Mary Wilson, never doubted the importance of the work and were always my greatest publicists (at least among their friends in Schenectady, New York). My father died before the book was completed, but I know that he would have been elated. I met my partner, Kevin Lustik, on a walking tour of Harlem thirteen years ago, so he is an integral part of this project. Kevin has been a constant source of inspiration and reinforcement throughout the process, and I am profoundly beholden to him for his unflagging endorsement and support. I am also appreciative of the help from Kevin Winkler, who offered archival assistance and close readings of several chapters in the early stages. Similarly, Charles Kloth directed me to little-known musical treasures, and raised interesting points about the work.

Finally, this book would not have been possible if it were not for LeAnn Fields, who has patiently shepherded this project and neophyte author from proposal to publication. Even when I harbored doubts about my own abilities to address the challenging issues raised by the editorial board and the anonymous readers, she never did. LeAnn's expert counsel has been transformative, and indeed, the book would not have evolved to its current form without the assiduous attention to structure, content, and style that she has generously offered throughout the undertaking.

Contents

Introduction: "It's Getting Dark on Old Broadway"

It's getting dark on Old Broadway,
You see the change in ev'ry cabaret;
Just like an eclipse on the moon,
Ev'ry cafe now has the dancing coon.
Pretty choc'late babies
Shake and shimmie ev'rywhere
Real dark-town entertainers hold the stage,
You must black up to be the latest rage.

—"IT'S GETTING DARK ON OLD BROADWAY"
FROM THE *ZIEGFELD FOLLIES OF 1922**

"WHAT IS SHE"

In October 1923, Florence Mills, one of the most famous African American performers of the decade, joined the cast of the *Greenwich Village Follies*, which was playing at the Winter Garden Theatre in New York City. Mills had previously established herself as a performer of considerable talent when she stepped into the hit musical *Shuffle Along* (1921), and her return to Broadway was met with great excitement among the standing-room-only crowd. Performing six numbers in the revue, she confirmed her reputation as one of the shining stars of the era. A. L. Jackson, a columnist for the black newspaper *Chicago Defender*, claimed that with this show Mills had earned a place in the pantheon of black performers, a growing list headlined by Bert Williams, who had broken the all-white color barrier of the *Ziegfeld Follies* thirteen years earlier. Mills was also appearing with a predominantly white company, but what sealed her celebrity status, according to Jackson, was the inclusion of another act that proved once and for all that Florence Mills had undeniably "arrived." One of the performers in the *Greenwich Village Follies* was a female impersonator who seemed to perfectly duplicate Mills's eccentric mannerisms and voice. Perhaps, as the old adage goes, imitation is the sincerest form of flattery, but in show business, impersonation is the surest sign of stardom.

Performances by female impersonators were not uncommon in the revues of the 1920s, but they did not usually include a racial component. Moreover, impersonated celebrities, including easily identifiable stars like Mae West and Gloria Swanson, tended to be white. Combining blackface and drag, the *Greenwich Village Follies* performer took impersonation to a new level in the presentation of a *white* man performing as a *black* woman. "We guarantee that you will have a hard time," wrote Jackson about the female impersonator's performance, "in making up your mind not as to 'her sex,' but as to 'what is she' after that. The wig and complexion cream used by the young gentleman throw all the experts, black and white, who profess the ability to 'tell 'em anywhere anytime' into confusion until the final scene."[1] Will the real Florence Mills please stand up?

In the 1920s and 1930s there was a fair amount of persistence in attempting to define and redefine identity categories—thus the emergence of the "New Negro" and the "Modern Woman." In fact, the most prominent members of the black intelligentsia, including Alain Locke, W. E. B. Du Bois, and Charles S. Johnson, argued that the theater was a place to resolve once and for all the kind of "confusion" in racial identity with which the *Greenwich Follies* toyed. In 1922, for example, Locke pointed to the success of the Irish theater at the turn of the century and wrote in his essay "Steps toward the Negro Theatre" that a black national drama would help banish stereotypical images from the stage and replace them with positive depictions of black life and people.[2] Du Bois held a similar belief, but unlike Locke, he advocated an overtly propagandistic form of theater. Arguing for plays written *about* African Americans, *by* African Americans, *for* African Americans, and presented *in* or *near* their communities, Du Bois stressed that theater must be for the express purpose of presenting truthful (and moral) views of the black experience.[3] Johnson, on the other hand, rejected the notion of pure propaganda and cultural separatism. He stressed the importance of removing the artistic constraints on black artists, which would in turn allow them to make meaningful contributions to the arts. "What is most important," he explained, "is that these black artists should be free, not merely to express anything they feel, but to feel the pulsations and rhythms of their own life, philosophy be hanged."[4]

As evidenced by the appearance and impersonation of Florence Mills in the *Greenwich Village Follies,* however, representations of race and gender in the theaters and nightclubs of the era were often highly ambiguous, ambivalent, and bewildering. This is the central premise of this current study. Set within the social and artistic context of the New York City of the so-called Harlem Renaissance, *Bulldaggers, Pansies, and Chocolate Babies* focuses on the ways in which depictions of blackness and whiteness, male and female, homosexual and heterosexual, highbrow and lowbrow merged and coalesced in the theater and performances of the 1920s and 1930s. While white and black political leaders, social scientists, and artists often attempted to fasten and delineate the divides between these identity qualifiers, a varying number of writers, performers, and producers of different races, economic classes, and sexual orientations were the creators of the popular entertainment of the era. Additionally, contrasted with fixed, unchanging published literary texts, performances and scripts were mutable, depending on individual artists' contributions and the desires of the demographically shifting audiences.

The performances I am drawn to are the ones that teased the limits of social decorum on New York's stages of the 1920s and 1930s, and I want to shed light on controversial artists and productions that have not yet received their due but contributed mightily to the artistic heritage of the United States. This book is not intended to provide a chronological and critical history of theater and identity formations in the Harlem Renaissance, but there is, I hope, enough contextualization of the plays, performers, and performances to convey the richness of the period for readers unfamiliar with its culture, social life, and ideological tensions. This study focuses the spotlight on plays and figures that are often relegated to footnotes or parenthetical statements. Because they carry less weight of representation and overinterpretation, these plays and performers yield valuable insight into the artistic, political, and social collaborations and fissures among Blacks/whites, bourgeoisie / working class, women/men, heterosexuals / sexual nonconformists. The usual stars and leaders of the Harlem Renaissance are, therefore, recast in secondary roles, and in some cases as walk-ons (or less). The exceptions in this book are the aforementioned Florence Mills and the world-famous Ethel Waters, who were truly theatrical superstars (to use a later-twentieth-century appellation) of the era. Coincidentally, they appear in the second-to-last chapter in the book, corresponding with the placement of the "headliner" on a vaudeville bill, but this is not to imply any kind of qualitative assessment. Mills's and Waters's influential and widely discussed personae in the 1920s haunt the study at every turn, so it seems neces-

sary to showcase them in a book about performance in the Harlem Renaissance. Another haunting presence is the fictional figure Lulu Belle, who is the title character of Edward Sheldon and Charles MacArthur's 1926 Broadway play.
While largely forgotten today, Lulu Belle became synonymous with any social-
climbing black seductress, who left a trail of oversexed, psychologically spent,
and pitiful men in her wake.

Within Harlem Renaissance studies, there is some disagreement about pe-
riodization, but for the purposes of this study, I define it as loosely beginning in
the early 1920s (from a theater perspective, *Shuffle Along* [1921] remains a
benchmark) and ending in the mid-1930s (from a social and economic perspective, the Great Depression and the Harlem Riot of 1935 drastically curtailed
black performance and idealism in Harlem). I am also aware of the problems of
labeling this era the Harlem Renaissance, which has been variously referred to
as the Negro Renaissance, the New Negro Movement, the Negro Awakening,
and the Jazz Age. As James Hatch explains, none of these titles is completely accurate, for there was nothing "new" about the Negro,[5] and the sense of a "renaissance" implies "rebirth" (from what?), and "awakening" connotes "sudden
awareness" (of what?). And certainly for the millions of blacks who were faced
with poverty, enforced segregation, and frequent threats from the Ku Klux
Klan, the notion of nonstop music and dance as suggested by the *Jazz Age* terminology would have been highly conjectural. Finally, Harlem was indeed a
cultural center, and many of the black artists at the time gravitated to this
neighborhood. Some, however, lived in other parts of New York City (e.g.,
Greenwich Village) or in outlying cities and communities (e.g., Brooklyn). In
addition, other urban centers across the country, chiefly Chicago, Baltimore,
and Washington, DC, had thriving black social and cultural communities. Yet
Harlem Renaissance is the term that is most often used in cultural studies and
social histories of the era.

Apologia aside, the setting of this book *is* New York City, and I primarily
concentrate on artists who worked at least occasionally in Harlem. There are
brief excursions to out-of-town tryouts and an examination of a West Coast
television appearance in the 1950s, but the chapters, in the main, traverse between Harlem and midtown Manhattan. Mapping the landscape of black theater and performance in this specific time and place, I examine a variety of
venues. I broadly define "theater" as both the place of performance (more often
than not in this era, it would have a proscenium stage, as one would see in
Broadway or vaudeville houses) and the showcased works (either plot-based,

character-driven dramas or the looser-structured musical revues). By "performance" I mean the dramatic interpretations and musical presentations through song and dance offered in the legitimate theaters as well as in the more intimate and interactive nightclubs, speakeasies, and semiprivate neighborhood parties. My definition of performance also takes in the postmodern idea of an "offstage" expression of identity, the most obvious example being nontheatrical drag.

In recent years, there have been a number of biographies of Harlem Renaissance performers (Paul Robeson, Josephine Baker, Bessie Smith, the Whitman Sisters, Florence Mills, among others, immediately come to mind), but there have been surprisingly few full-length considerations of the performing arts as a vital site of analysis in the history of black theater, American popular culture, and African American studies. The notable exceptions are David Krasner's *A Beautiful Pageant* (2002) and Paul Allen Anderson's *Deep River* (2001), which explore, respectively, the multiple aspects of drama and performance (including sports, parades, and pageants) and the importance of music (such as spirituals, jazz, and blues) in the negotiation of social memory within a national identity.[6] The primary voices of the discourse, however, are those from literary studies.

That said, literature and the performing arts were closely linked during the Harlem Renaissance, and many of the literary luminaries wrote plays or dabbled in the arts in some fashion. Some of these deserve mention. In 1913 W. E. B. Du Bois assembled a cast of 350 for his pageant *The Star of Ethiopia,* which was presented in several cities over the next twelve years.[7] Langston Hughes wrote several plays, including *Mulatto* (1935), which ran almost four hundred performances on Broadway; and his contentious collaboration on *Mule Bone* (1930; unproduced professionally until 1991) with Zora Neale Hurston is the stuff of theater legend. In addition, Hughes used jazz and blues themes, rhythms, and compositional structures in a number of his poems and helped legitimize these musical forms. Individually, Hurston also had strong connections to the performing arts. Two of her plays, *Color Struck* (1925) and *The First One* (1926), took first prizes in *Opportunity* play competitions, and she contributed sketch material to a Broadway musical revue called *Fast and Furious* (1931).[8] Anthea Kraut has written about Hurston's work with Bahamian dancers for a series of dance/music concerts in the early 1930s.[9] Countee Cullen, who was dubbed the "poet laureate" of the Harlem Renaissance, was working on the book of the musical *St. Louis Woman* when he died in 1946. And Broadway audiences of *Porgy* in 1927 probably did not realize that some of the supernumer-aries (or "extras") in the play's Catfish Row included the prominent writers, Richard Bruce Nugent, Wallace Thurman, and Dorothy West.

The literary criticism of the Harlem Renaissance is also very much inflected by theater and performance discourse. Houston Baker, Jr., Arnold Rampersad, and Michael North, who have offered compelling "modernist" readings of Harlem Renaissance texts, often use theatrical images and metaphors, such as "racial ventriloquism," "minstrelsy," and "mimicry," to probe the construction of an African American identity. Henry Louis Gates's use of "signifyin(g)" also offers a valuable tool in analyzing the ways in which performers mimicked and sometimes parodied racial stereotypes, potentially evacuating them of their racist meanings.[10] Scholars Hazel Carby, Cheryl Wall, Angela Y. Davis, and Hortense Spillers have provided important (re)readings of Harlem Renaissance texts through a feminist lens, and they have extended their analysis to black performers and lived black experiences of women, especially in a field that was almost entirely male-oriented until the 1980s. Even more recently, scholars such as A. B. Christa Schwarz and Thomas H. Wirth have built on the work of Eric Garber to consider sexual orientation as a fundamental element of lesbian and gay writers and public thinkers in the Harlem Renaissance. It is only fitting that the scholarship reflects the diversity of the voices of the era.

Harlem of the 1920s was itself remarkably diverse, and while its pluralism adds complexity and dynamism, it stymies any attempt to really *know* Harlem. As Wallace Thurman pointed out in 1927, casual observers tended to lump all black people together into the monolithic category "Negro." While most of the Blacks migrated from other parts of the United States, specifically the South, a good number, about 40 percent according to Thurman, were born elsewhere. Harlem attracted people from the British West Indies, Africa, and South America.[11] In addition, the class system was especially knotty because it did not cut down traditional economic lines. The black bourgeoisie, as A. B. Christa Schwarz explains, "included distinctly blue-collar workers like Pullman porters who were often educated but, due to racial discrimination, unable to enter other professions."[12] Because they were, as Sterling Brown mentioned, "only one re-move" from the black masses, the black middle class had little success influenc-ing cultural representations of African Americans.[13] As George Hutchinson de-tails, Harlem's recent manifestation as a black bastion meant that "traditional elites," defined by family wealth and political clout, did not have a stranglehold on black culture, as they did in other major urban centers across the country.

This situation made the community more tolerant, if not accepting, of "the experimental development of new forms of 'racial' expression."[14]

As social historians George Chauncey, Lillian Faderman, and Kevin Mumford have shown, the lesbian and gay communities emerging in Harlem and elsewhere in New York City were similarly diverse. The press, gossip sheets, and moralists tended to label all so-called sexual deviants as "sexual inverts" or members of the "third sex," and to them they were easily discernible. Lesbians, who were referred to as "bulldaggers" and "bulldykes" (or "bulldykers"), were associated with "manliness" and masculine clothing. Gay men, who were called "pansies," "fairies," and "fags," were identified by their "femininity" and their affinity for dresses, makeup, and wigs. Men and women who did not fall into these categories were much more able to experiment with same-sex trysts or establish lasting relationships and avoid being found out, because of "the straight world's ignorance of the existence of a hidden middle-class gay world."[15] In the last few decades, social historians and queer theorists have given us finer distinctions in discussing same-sex desire, experimentation, and cross-dressing, thereby providing more complex readings of lived experiences and literary texts of the era.

One must be cautious to avoid a similar kind of lumping of the whites who descended upon Harlem in the 1920s. The white tourists were often referred to as "Downtowners," implying that all of the people who were part of the "white invasion" lived somewhere below 110th Street. On the one hand, there were a good number of visitors from Greenwich Village and the Upper Westside, and many came from the rich and glamorous set. Carl Van Vechten, the notorious white author of *Nigger Heaven* (1926), had apartments on East Nineteenth Street and then on West Fifty-fifth Street. Cole Porter, who riffed on Van Vechten's title with his own song lyric, "Happy Heaven of Harlem," for the musical *Fifty Million Frenchmen* (1929), had an apartment in the Waldorf-Astoria. And stage and screen star Mae West was a habitual Harlem clubgoer and friend to the black artists in Harlem, and she wrote her own novelistic response to Van Vechten in *Babe Gordon* (1930), about a white prostitute in Harlem.[16] Many other white celebrities and socialites who maintained apartments in Midtown and near Central Park also frequented the scene, as evident in gossip sheets and personal diaries. In the smoky speakeasies, one might see people from Greenwich Village bohemia, the Brooklyn working class, and young gay men from Hell's Kitchen.[17] On the other hand, a sizable number of visitors were from out of town or other countries, which is made clear by the numerous newspaper reports by people who "experienced" Harlem on their visits and the report of the Committee of Fourteen, a council organized to investigate vice and corruption throughout the city, which stated that taxicab drivers often solicited male tourists, offering to take them to "some nice quiet place" in Harlem and "meet some swell girls."[18] Some claimed that Van Vechten ran a similar service. In an attempt to drum up business for his book and his pals in Harlem, Van Vechten wrote numerous articles and piloted his non–New York guests to the neighborhood to help spread the word about the neighborhood's cultural treasures.[19]

Not everyone was getting in on the act, though, and it is misleading to assume that all whites had suddenly cast off their Victorian moral restraints. In February 1927, the *New York Times* ran the ominous headline "Hint of Police Raids to Clean the Stage."[20] Through the rest of the decade, the black clergy and bourgeoisie railed against filth in the theaters and streets of Harlem, and white moral watchdogs pressured the police department, the mayor, and the governor to rein in the moral laxity apparent in New York theaters, nightclubs, and speakeasies. New York papers soothed—to a degree—the feeling among some that the city was sinking into a moral abyss with articles about "dirt plays" being censored, actors getting arrested for "indecent" performances, and speakeasies being raided for selling alcohol. In May 1927, for example, the *New York Times* reported that 381 people were arrested in a gentlemen's smoking club on 125th Street. Of those arrested, 375 were men, and the night court on 123rd Street stayed open past midnight to process all of the male prisoners and the six women performers who were taken in the raid.[21]

The mass of contradictions permeating the Harlem Renaissance—marked by the simultaneous empowerment and oppression of African Americans; titillation and disgust with sexual experimentation; and liberation and anxiety over the era—provides the backdrop for this book. The chapters, which may be viewed as expository snapshots, do not attempt to reconcile these contradictions, but they offer a particular perspective on the social and professional connections between artists, audiences, and critical observers at this crucial historical juncture. It is a truism to state that theater and performance are collaborative, but in the 1920s there were some truly interesting artistic alliances and quite a few very strange bedfellows. Ann Douglas and George Hutchinson have effectively documented and theorized the complicated cross-pollination of black-white culture, and this study extends the discourse to include the participation of lesbian, gay, bisexual, and transgender voices.

The examples and analyses presented here are a highly selective representation of the dramatic literature, musical theater, and performances of the

Harlem Renaissance within the social, political, and cultural context in which they appeared, but they offer a way of exploring performance-related "texts" and their cultural connections. Although I am not a music scholar and must leave the deeper analysis of musical compositions to experts (thereby protecting readers from my critical tone deafness with songs and dance arrangements), I use jazz and blues—which have stalwart social, literary, and theatrical associations—as a guiding motif. Each chapter title derives from a song lyric of the period. The first chapter provides both a sociohistoric and performance criticism foundation for the rest of the book. Harlem parties were often discussed in the black newspapers (on the society page, arrests section, and any page in between), and they offer a site for looking at the emergence of social communities as well as a training ground for developing musicians and performers. On the other hand, while the rent parties of the Harlem working class attracted, according to jazz musician Willie "the Lion" Smith, people from all walks of life, including "formally dressed society folks from downtown, policemen, painters, carpenters, mechanics, truckmen in their workingmen's clothes, gamblers, lesbians, and entertainers of all kinds,"[22] these affairs were not as impulsive as the press would have had people believe. These parties were carefully "staged" and could be quite profitable for the "producers." Furthermore, lesbians and gay men relied on private parties as spaces safe from potential personal and professional scandal and from prosecution, and the chapter focuses on the cultural attitudes toward sexual nonconformists.

The famous dramatization of a rent party in William Jourdan Rapp and Wallace Thurman's Broadway melodrama *Harlem* (1929) links the second chapter with the first. More importantly, the former focuses on the play as a reflection of the political struggles in defining a black identity in the 1920s. Rapp and Thurman's *Harlem* is of especial interest here because other plays of the era that treated African American subjects were authored by either white or black playwrights. *Harlem* was cowritten by a white playwright (Rapp) and a black (Thurman). The authorship arrangement embodies Locke's utopian notion of a convergent black and white modernism to "discover and release the national spirit" in a pluralist, universal art.[23] Locke's contemporary, George S. Schuyler, was even more radical in saying that there were no cultural distinctions between the races; they were both "plain American."[24] Central to an analysis of the play is sorting through the hodgepodge of theatrical conventions and racial stereotypes to see how the play reflects the fraught political and deeply engrained notions of representation and whether or not it is possible to move beyond them.

The third chapter primarily explores the alliance of the gay subculture and one of the most popular plays of the 1920s, Edward Sheldon and Charles MacArthur's *Lulu Belle* (1926). It has been credited by several Harlem Renaissance scholars as one of the cultural initiators behind the surge of white interest in Harlem, but there has been surprisingly little attention paid to it by theater historians. While I hope to rectify this slight, the chapter will also examine the critical reception of the play in light of the contemporary attitudes toward single black women (whom Lulu Belle, performed in blackface by white actress Lenore Ulric, supposedly represented). Lulu Belle's spirit pervades chapter 4, "'Hottentot Potentates': The Potent and Hot Performances of Florence Mills and Ethel Waters." These two performers were linked in the public and theatrical imaginations with Lulu Belle. This chapter considers the ways in which black women performers, who were variously referred to as "chocolate babies" (as mentioned in the "It's Getting Dark on Old Broadway" lyric), "cuties," and "chocolate drops," worked with white writers, composers, and directors, and in their collaboration they negotiated and contributed to what today would be considered stereotypical and derogatory images. At the time, however, they were considered pioneers and represented racial uplift and progress.

The fifth chapter focuses on Gladys Bentley, one of the most controversial (and underresearched) performers in the Harlem Renaissance. It offers a biographical portrait of this "blueswoman," who was a prominent figure in the Harlem Renaissance but sank into obscurity by the middle of the 1930s. The chapter also concerns the theoretical construction of identity, since Bentley's own persona was greatly influenced by the fictional character Stephen Gordon in Radclyffe Hall's classic novel *The Well of Loneliness* (1928). Customarily, Harlem Renaissance scholars debate the success or failure of the movement to produce lasting cultural traditions. This chapter concludes with an extended postscript on Bentley's reemergence in the 1950s, demonstrating the resilience, artistry, and political commitment of the performers and performances in the Harlem Renaissance. I end the book with a summary of my project, and I leave the reader with a sketch of a black performer, whose transgression of social and cultural borders of race, class, gender, and sexual orientation reflects the need to expand the discourses in Harlem Renaissance studies.

"Gimme a Pigfoot and a Bottle of Beer": Parties, Performances, and Privacy in the "Other" Harlem Renaissance(s)

Gimme a pigfoot and a bottle of beer
Send me, gate, I don't care

Check all your razors and your guns
Do the shim sham shimmy 'til the risin' sun

Gimme a reefer and a gang o' gin
Slay me, 'cause I'm in my sin
Slay me, 'cause I'm full of gin

—"GIMME A PIGFOOT" BY WESLEY WILSON*

"DO THE SHIM SHAM SHIMMY 'TIL THE RISIN' SUN"

In *The Big Sea,* Langston Hughes famously wrote, "The ordinary Negroes hadn't heard of the Negro Renaissance. And if they had, it hadn't raised their wages any."[1] Hughes referred, of course, to the "high" literary renaissance of the 1920s that included writers such as Countee Cullen, Claude McKay, and Nella Larson. As part of this "Negro Renaissance," he was also most likely referring to black performers, including Roland Hayes, Fletcher Henderson, Charles Gilpin, and Paul Robeson, who became internationally known in concert halls, opera houses, and legitimate theaters. But as Mark Helbling shows in *The Harlem Renaissance: The One and the Many,* there were several different Harlem Renaissances. Helbling primarily focuses on the intersections between the "high" and "low" Harlem Renaissance as well as on theoretical, literary "multiple selves" through the negotiation of the primitive, the folk, and the modern in key texts by Alain Locke, Zora Neale Hurston, and Jean Toomer, among others.[2] A similar reading may be applied to the performance traditions of the "ordinary" people in Harlem, which reflect the uneasy merging of social classes and same-sex activities.

Although "the ordinary Negroes," or working-class African Americans, to whom Hughes refers may not have read much of the literary outpouring of the artists in their midst and did not necessarily have the opportunity (or inclination) to see the performances of some of the music and theater world's greatest stars, I would argue that most knew they were part of a cultural movement. For good or ill—there were at least as many people opposed to Harlem's transforming social atmosphere as there were for it—they were surrounded by, if not participants in, the cultural scene. Traffic snarls, late-night revelers disturbing the peace, and increased crime rates offered palpable evidence of the neighborhood's changing landscape and provoked a community outcry. Rent parties, "buffet flats," and even private society functions received a good deal of attention in the black press, and by the mid-1920s, some Harlem residents would have regarded them as the antidote to the overpriced, exclusionary cabarets. The rent parties, in particular, included a preponderance of the working class in Harlem, and while these parties were originally staged from economic necessity for Harlem residents, they became quite marketable for entrepreneurial residents and shadowy underworld figures. Furthermore, because they were often a training ground for young musicians and performers, the raucous, sexually charged rent parties of the 1920s offer a crucial site of inquiry in analyzing the theater and entertainment of the Harlem Renaissance.

Rent parties and private social events were especially important in developing a sense of community among the Harlem residents and helping to establish cultural solidarity along socioeconomic class lines. The black newspapers covered many of the high-profile parties, and gossip about party guests, activities, and performances contributed to the neighborhood lore. Geraldine Dismond, who wrote a weekly "Social Snapshots" column for the *Inter-State Tattler,* helped assure her readers that the neighborhood had a very active and glamorous high life. In a typical column she would list the attendees of a charity benefit and ball and who was spotted where and wearing what. For individuals who might never receive an invitation to one of the legendary parties thrown by well-heeled, much-moneyed, and known homosexual Clinton Moore, for instance, Dismond would write about the celebrities in attendance gathered around a piano and singing. "At five," she once wrote, "the cocktails were still flowing, and only a few of us remembered that we had homes to which we were supposed to go."[3] Parties thrown by black millionairess and socialite A'Leilia Walker, the daughter of Madame C. J. Walker, who had made millions in the second decade of the century from her hair products for black women, were especially grist for the gossip mill. The guests at these parties were usually at the opposite end of the socioeconomic scale than those attending most Harlem rent parties, but the same sense of reckless abandon and liberation was often evident. The *Amsterdam News* and the *New York Age* frequently printed the guest lists of her parties and indicated that they were not at all the stodgy society gatherings one might expect. In December 1924, for example, the *Age* described a party at Walker's "palatial residence" as a "brilliant affair," which included music "furnished by Joshua Europe's Orchestra." As the article explains, "The guests assembled at 11 p.m. and dancing was enjoyed until early Monday morning. The house was elaborately decorated and a buffet breakfast was served."[4] Word around town, however, alleged that Walker's parties often offered much more than just music, dance, and a buffet breakfast.

Mabel Hampton, a black entertainer who performed in the choruses of shows in Coney Island, the Lafayette Theatre in Harlem, and the Cherry Lane Theatre in Greenwich Village, vividly recalled one of A'Leilia Walker's parties, which she attended upon her arrival in Harlem in the early 1920s, and confirmed the truth behind these widespread rumors. One night in 1921, Hampton arrived at Walker's mansion in Harlem's Sugar Hill section at 108–110 West 136th Street, where she was supposed to meet her female companion who had secured the invitation. She rang the bell, was greeted by one of Walker's manservants, and was escorted into a large, sumptuously decorated room. She waited ten minutes in this room before A'Leilia Walker, wearing a maroon robe and slippers, welcomed her and asked Hampton to follow her to another section of the house. As Walker pushed open the folding door to a room, Hampton was amazed at the tableau in front of her. There were some fourteen or fifteen men and women, black and white, none of whom were wearing any clothes, lounging about on oversized pillows. Soft music filled the room, gentle lights emanated from the floor, and the men and women lay in each other's arms. When she looked more closely, though, Hampton noticed something even odder: The men were lying on top of other men, and women were lying on top of other women. "Lookit here!" she thought as she surveyed the room. "O.K., as long as they don't bother me."

After a short time, Hampton relaxed into the scene, removed her own clothes, put on a robe supplied by her hostess, and took a seat on one of the pillows. As she sipped a glass of wine, she took in the ambience of the room, and as she remembered the scene: "Some man over there was kissing another one. A woman over there was kissing another one. Boy—everybody was kissing." Finally, about an hour later, her friend arrived. Her friend took off her clothes, made herself comfortable on a pillow next to Hampton, and in no time the two women were hugging and kissing as well. As Hampton summarily explained: "Seen the rest of them do it, what the hell, I'll do it too. It was fascinating."[5]

A'Leilia Walker's parties were notorious for their sexual experimentation, but even in more modest dwellings, such as Harlem rooming houses and apartment buildings, nonheterosexual coupling was not uncommon. As George Chauncey, Lillian Faderman, and Eric Garber have documented in their histories of lesbian, gay, and bisexual subcultures in New York City, private parties in Harlem provided protected spaces for lesbians, bisexuals, and gay men to meet and mingle. The parties, like the one Hampton described, may have taken place in luxurious Harlem homes, but more frequently they were held in less affluent apartments. Hampton, for example, especially remembered the nightly parties "with the girls" in her apartment building on 122nd Street. People would pay a small amount at the door, and while at the soiree, they danced, sang, and, of course, enjoyed the standard rent party culinary fare (for a small price): bootlegged liquor, pig feet, chitlins, and cold beer. But the particular parties Hampton generally attended were open to women only. According to Hampton:

> The bulldykers would come and bring their women with them. And you wasn't supposed to jive with them, you know. They danced up a breeze. They did the Charleston, they did a little bit of everything. They were all colored women. Sometimes we ran into someone who had a white woman with them. But me, I'd venture out with any of them. I just had a ball.[6]

Within a private home nestled in a very public Harlem, Mabel Hampton and her lesbian cronies could congregate socially and enjoy the sexually liberating music, dances, and attitudes that characterized the Harlem Renaissance away from the penetrating stares and disdain of curious onlookers.

Theatrically, the parties served an important function. Many of the gatherings featured entertainers, ranging from famous jazz and blues performers, including Thomas "Fats" Waller and Bessie Smith, to popular comedians, such as Jackie "Moms" Mabley, to infamous and bizarre "specialty" acts that played the uptown party circuit. High up on the list in the latter category would have to be a young black singer and pianist named "Joey," whose particular talent was removing his clothes, sitting on a lit candle, and making it disappear.[7] Whatever the individual's talent, though, the parties provided a performer an appreciative environment in which to try out a new song, comic sketch, or vaudeville routine. After further refinement, the act might find its way into a Harlem nightclub, in black vaudeville, and perhaps eventually on Broadway. In an article entitled "Where Jazz Was Born," Wallace Thurman proposes that the private Harlem parties were the birthplace of many dance crazes that were subsequently performed for, and then appropriated by, mainstream audiences.[8]

"UP IN HARLEM EVERY SATURDAY NIGHT"

Rent parties, although romanticized in the literature, music, and drama of the period, began as a creative measure in dealing with the dire economic circumstances facing many African Americans in Harlem beginning in the 1920s. Lower wages and higher rents forced black residents to develop inventive means of making ends meet. In 1923, the *New York Age* reported that "many of the ills Harlem is suffering from as a community can be traced to the evil of high rents and overcrowding, which are more acute in this section than anywhere else in the city."[9] By 1928, the New York State Department of Health announced that because of poorly constructed and overcrowded housing in Harlem, "the tuberculosis death rate among [N]egroes in New York was three and one-half times greater than that of the white population."[10] For some individuals, necessity forced them to open their homes to illegal activities, which under normal circumstances they would never have condoned. Bernice Gore, a Bermuda immigrant, for instance, once said she "thought rent parties were disgraceful" because of the "corn liquor," gambling, and sexual activity they offered. But when her husband deserted her, leaving Gore, as she stated, "with a sixty-dollar-a-month apartment on my hands, and no job, I soon learned, like everyone else, to rent my rooms out and throw these Saturday get-togethers."[11]

The particularly high rents that plagued Harlem were actually a direct result of the unparalleled arrival of migrating Blacks that began around World War I. In addition, greedy landlords played on the fears of white residents and homeowners who tried to maintain the white composition of a particular block. By threatening to rent to black people, these landlords intended to force the sale of properties at inflated prices to wealthy white owners intent on preserving the racial status quo. As late as 1925, near the pinnacle of the so-called black invasion, attempts at staving off further black encroachment were still evident in the predominantly white borders of Harlem. An article appearing in the *New York Age,* for example, recounts the efforts of Nat Levine, an owner of a private home in a "fashionable section of West End avenue, at 101st street," to sell his building at a disproportionate cost to a buyer interested in keeping black families at bay. The house was adjacent to a well-appointed apartment building where, according to the article, Supreme Court justice Aaron J. Levy (who is credited as "the author of the law which forbids discrimination in New York State in public places because of race or creed"), John C. Knapp, vice president of the Otis Elevator Co., "and several other prominent people live." Levine, who is identified in the article as a "Jewish milliner," posted a sign advertising: "Furnished Rooms for Rent for Colored Folks. Inquire Within." Although the article explains that "it is not thought that [Judge Levy] or others in the apartment [building next door] would make objection to living besides respectable colored people," the sale was apparently averted when Harlem's papers identified the ploy and urged prospective black renters to avoid being "catspaws" in such a scheme. The article also proudly claims that "the colored tenant is becoming wise to the selfish plan of certain property owners who want to get rid of holdings at a greatly inflated price, and use a threat of renting to Negroes as a means to that end."[12] Still, black people continued to pour into Harlem throughout the 1920s, creating an unprecedented housing crisis and cramped living conditions. As Herbert Gutman records, by 1925, "about half of all black households had one or more lodgers in them, and about one in five households had one or more relatives other than members of the immediate family."[13] Many residents also employed a "hot bed" system, which meant that tenants on different work shifts shared the same mattress.[14]

Social historian Gilbert Osofsky attributes the rapid deterioration of the neighborhood to the en masse migration into the rather limited geographical area. In fact, Osofsky points to the 1920s as the period in which Harlem emerged "as a slum." He writes, "Largely within the space of a single decade Harlem was transformed from a potentially ideal community to a neighborhood with manifold social and economic problems called 'deplorable,' 'unspeakable,' 'incredible.'" And quoting the chairman of a New York City housing reform committee in 1927, he adds, "The State would not allow cows to live in some of these apartments used by colored people ... in Harlem."[15] Statistically, the state of affairs was indeed distressing. In 1923, the *New York Age* reported that the average black worker earned $25 per month (or roughly $1,300 a year), and spent from one-half to two-thirds of these monthly wages on rent. The report also states that black tenants generally paid twice as much for rent as white New Yorkers. "In one case," the article explains, "on 145th street, colored tenants moved into a five-room apartment paying $80 per month although the former white tenants only paid $40 per month. There are still many white families in this house with apartments the same size and just as good who do not pay more than $40." The article cites another example, a private house on 130th Street previously rented to white tenants for $70 per month, for which the black residents paid $175.[16] And as the decade proceeded, the situation became even more bleak.

In 1924, the *New York Age* reported that a five-story apartment house on 139th Street near Lenox Avenue had set a new high for rentals in the neighborhood. The one, two, and three-room apartments in the building were going for $45, $65, and $85 per month. Although the prices were exorbitant, the apartments were anything but luxurious. The bathrooms, the article points out, were considerably smaller than those in analogous apartment buildings, because they included shower baths rather than bathtubs, and furthermore, the reporter claims, the "cheapest materials" had been used in the building's construction.[17] Yet because of the social desirability of the neighborhood and the ease with which black people could acquire apartments compared with other places in the city, overpriced apartments did rent, and the fleecing of tenants by landlords was often grudgingly tolerated.

Rarely did occupants and prospective tenants wrangle over the inequities with which they were faced, and when they did, they were confronted with extremely difficult battles. In 1925, a group of tenants from 574 St. Nicholas Avenue took their landlord to court for extortionate rentals. They argued that their rent was considerably higher than that paid by the former white tenants, who had been all but succeeded by black tenants. Additionally, the litigants alleged that when the building had been rented to whites, the landlord had employed a separate operator for the switchboard and elevator. When the apartment house had become predominantly black, however, the landlord dismissed one of the employees, making a single person responsible for both duties. When the tenants complained about the greatly reduced services, as well as the increased costs of phone calls, the landlord purportedly responded that "if they were not satisfied with the rents, to get out and into other houses with a lower scale of rents, houses that were of a class to which they were accustomed."[18] Each tenant's case was tried separately, and the outcome is unclear, but one individual involved in the suit complained that the judge "made the direct assertion that the tenants should pay the asked for rent or get out and find other quarters."[19]

Although many black residents were oppressed economically, Harlem was not remotely—contrary to Osofsky's estimation—depressed. As Lewis concedes, "Whatever its contradictions . . . the one certainty almost all who lived there shared was that Harlem was no slum. Ghetto, maybe. Slum, never."[20] This description should not be taken as merely coy semantics. Within the confined neighborhood, black people took immense pride in their community and exuberantly paraded their social liberation. In black publications such as the *Amsterdam News, New York Age, Inter-State Tattler,* and the *Messenger,* black journalists and essayists triumphantly declared the political, academic, and cultural accomplishments of Harlem residents even more boldly than they did the terrifying housing statistics, arrests, and artistic disappointments. Socialites were toasted; recent college graduates were honored; and famous and not-so-famous performers, authors, and sport stars were feted in the pages of the weekly and monthly issues. The doomsday reports published by the Committee of Fourteen, the New York State Department of Health, and the New York City Housing Department belied the attitude of racial pride held by most of the black residents north of Central Park. Much of the population that lived there may have been economically oppressed, but most surely would not have admitted that technically Harlem was indeed a "ghetto." Rather paradoxically, this seemingly willing ghettoization of Harlem was largely responsible for the generous outpouring of artistic and cultural riches from the black community.

In *The Pleasure Principle,* Michael Bronski points to the multiple functions of the ghetto. In addition to "containing" a minority group to "ensure that the minority is 'visible' and easy to detect," the ghetto provides protection for its inhabitants.[21] That is, an African American would be less likely to encounter police harassment and racially incited violence in a predominantly black neighborhood than in a white one. For the most part, in the 1920s black people could walk down the streets of Harlem and not be afraid of random acts of prejudice. As Elton Fax, a black resident once recalled, "Man we *strolled* in Harlem. This was our turf."[22] And to many black immigrants, the neighborhood seemed to be the embodiment of racial security and represented a guarded cocoon from racism. For many in the Harlem community, the rent parties of the 1920s reflected this social and political liberation.

In numerous poems as well as in his autobiography, Langston Hughes rhapsodized over the raucous, communal spirit of Harlem rent parties, which were also called "whist parties." For Hughes, throughout the 1920s they remained the one authentic black social event that was unspoiled by white tourism. As he explained in *The Big Sea:*

The Saturday night rent parties that I attended were often more amusing than any night club, in small apartments where God knows who lived—because the guests seldom did—but where the piano would often be augmented by a guitar, or an odd cornet, or somebody with a pair of drums walking in off the street. And where awful bootleg whiskey and good fried fish or steaming chitterling were sold at very low prices. And the dancing and singing and impromptu entertaining went on until dawn came in the windows.[23]

Even more importantly, he claimed that these parties offered a social outlet for the black working class, who were denied access to some of the more glamorous nightclubs and speakeasies in their own neighborhood. At the parties that he regularly frequented, Hughes recalled mingling with Harlem's laborers, including "ladies' maids and truck drivers, laundry workers and shoe shine boys, seamstresses and porters."[24] And Wallace Thurman remarked similarly that rent parties were to the working class what elaborate parties such as A'Lelia Walker's were to Harlem's elite, "as essential to 'low Harlem' as the cultured receptions and soirees held on 'strivers' row' are to 'high Harlem.'"[25] Most notably, the music and dance were far less refined than one would hear and see at one of Walker's parties, but the atmosphere was no less sexually charged. Describing the dancing at a typical rent party, he wrote:

> The "mess around" is also a body dance, and the couples are standing transfixed beneath the solitary red globe which provides the light; they bounce on the balls of their feet, while the mid-sections of their bodies go round and round. Still another couple is doing the "fish tail" dipping to the floor and slowly shimmying into an upright position then madly whirling a moment before settling into a methodical slow drag one-step.[26]

The admixture of alcohol, jazz music, and feelings of political and social liberation engendered at these parties contributed to a sense of sexual freedom as well. At the end of the week, the parties offered a social outlet for the pent-up economic difficulties that many of Harlem's residents faced.

Rent parties were not held exclusively on Saturday nights, although this was the favored day of the week. Of course, Saturdays were particularly popular because people did not have to work on Sunday, and often a party followed a payday. Everyone was welcome at a rent party, but the only provision, according to Thurman, was "that the public pay twenty-five cents admission fee and buy plentifully of the food and drinks offered for sale."[27] But as rent parties became more and more ubiquitous, as well as more profitable, competition arose among organizers, who resorted to ambitious, but surreptitious, advertising strategies. While avoiding too much publicity that might attract the attention of the police, who might, Thurman pointed out, "want to collect a license fee or else drop in and search for liquor,"[28] residents deposited brightly colored cards around Harlem, such as in subway stations, pool halls, cigar stores, and the gates of apartment buildings' elevators. These tiny advertisements, which were the size of business cards, were printed with catchy slogans and listed the name and address of the resident throwing the party. For example, blues singer Clara Smith posted the following card around town:

> Come on Boys don't be Ruff, just have a nice time,
> and Strutt Your Stuff
> ——AT——
> A SOCIAL WHIST PARTY
> GIVEN BY
> MRS. CLARA SMITH
> *at 18 WEST 130th STREET*
> Saturday Evening, June 16, 1928
> GOOD MUSIC   REFRESHMENTS[29]

Likewise, Mabel Hampton remembered going to parties quite frequently, particularly ones exclusively for women. On September 22, 1932, she met her life-long partner, Lillian Foster, while waiting for a bus. Just a few days later, Foster invited Hampton to a party that was advertised on a pale blue card with the following exhortation:

> Hard times are here, but not [to] stay
> So come, sing and dance your blues away, at
> A Sunday Matinee
> Given by
> LILLIAN
> 151 West 130th Street, Room 12
> Sunday, September 25th, 1932
> Good Music   Refreshments Served[30]

In fact, a central purpose of the parties was building and celebrating a sense of community, and a sexual energy often infused the occasions. As jazz musician

Willie "the Lion" Smith pointed out, "The parties were recommended to newly arrived single gals as the place to go to get acquainted."[31] Additionally, rent parties functioned as the gateway, for better or worse, between the margins of Harlem life and the rest of the world.

The rent parties, for the most part, provided supportive and sympathetic audiences, and they were the ideal space for artistic development. Entertaining in private homes allowed performers to try out new material away from the critical gaze of newspaper reviewers, theater-owners, and paying spectators. The venues were both public and private environments since invitations to the rent parties, even though they were confined to the neighborhood, could only be partially restrictive. The situations were perfect for developing new work because artists and audiences mingled within intimate surroundings, and feedback for the performer was immediate. And the partygoers, who were usually neighbors, were there to enjoy the social freedom denied them in many parts of the city.

The clearest indication of this function is in the meteoric success of jazz pianist and composer Thomas "Fats" Waller, who cultivated his prodigious talent in the rent party circuit. Waller, in fact, wrote one of the most famous compositions about a rent party, called "The Joint is Jumpin'," and began his professional career playing piano at one of these uptown "struts." According to Barry Singer, seventeen-year-old Waller made his rent party debut in 1921 at the Lenox Avenue Apartments on 141st Street. An "unofficial" rent party booker named "Lippy" Boyette orchestrated the engagement, and according to Singer, "Waller dazzled his co-performers, as well as the strut's assembled revelers."[32] Waller's legendary personality was particularly well suited to the party atmosphere. A man of huge talent, but with an equally great lust for enjoyment, Waller ate and drank voraciously, and exchanged his remarkable abilities for ready cash. He sold songs anonymously, made piano rolls, and played burlesque houses all for a pittance to indulge his appetites. In the early 1920s, he ventured into recording, but as David A. Jasen and Gene Jones explain, "His recordings were aimed at the urban race market (that is, Harlem), yet his target audience could hear him practically any hour of the day or night, performing without pay at rent parties and clubs as long as the free food and liquor kept coming."[33] With Waller's prodigious gifts, it was just a matter of time before (despite his self-destructive leanings) he made a name for himself outside of the ghetto as one of the greatest nightclub pianists of the 1920s, and later as a singer and Broadway show composer.

Waller's advancement from the rent party circuit to widespread appreciation is symptomatic of the black entertainment apparatus of the time. Because rent parties occurred in noncommercialized, semiprivate spaces, they were accorded a great deal of cachet, representing a point of origin for many of the musical compositions, club acts, and dance crazes that characterized the Harlem Renaissance. This presumed authenticity made the products of the rent parties especially attractive to mainstream audiences, who craved the "real thing." As J. Martin Favor has shown, the "real," or the notion of an "authentic blackness," was hotly contested (and remains so), but in the 1920s "true blackness" was associated with the masses and southern folk. The African American bourgeoisie represented "materialism and a loss of race consciousness."[34] Therefore, class and geographical origins were considered stronger marks of authenticity than phenotypes and ancestry. Rather quickly, the performances developing out of the rent parties, or versions of these performances, filtered into the wider culture through the work of savvy musicians, singers, and dancers. Ann Douglas refers to the process as "instant assimilation."[35] In the case of certain music and dance forms, the cultural attributes were subsumed as they became more popular and were adapted to different performance styles. For example in his novel *Parties,* which offers a sensational look at New York's parties from Harlem to Greenwich Village to Brooklyn, Carl Van Vechten wrote prophetically on the eve the lindy hop became a national dance craze:

> Nearly all the dancing now to be seen in our musical shows is of Negro origin, but both critics and public are so ignorant of this fact that the production of a new Negro revue is an excuse for the revival of the old hoary lament that it is a pity the Negro can't create anything for himself, that he is obliged to imitate the white man's revues. This, in brief, has been the history of the Cake-Walk, the Bunny Hug, the Turkey Trot, the Charleston, and the Black Bottom. It will probably be the history of the Lindy Hop.[36]

As Bronski reminds, while culture often develops in the ghetto and among subcultures, "it can quickly become commodified and marketed."[37]

Black performance, appropriated from the half-hidden and semiprivate enclaves of the widely visible but inscrutable ghetto, was devoured by the larger culture, which is always on the lookout for the newest vogue. The "mysteriousness" of the performances, the new mechanisms that connected popular entertainers, and the anonymity of the black "originators" guaranteed fast, sure, and undetected passageway into the mainstream. As Ann Douglas writes, the technological advances in mass media in the 1920s, including developments in radio, recordings, and film, "ensured that black performance would be transmitted to the larger culture and absorbed by it in a state both incomplete, even mutilated, and strangely, potently, intact."[38] The style of a dance like the black bottom, for instance, might become slightly more refined and genteel as it passed into public venues frequented by middle-class whites, but the madcap vitality, the liberating physical abandon reflecting the mood of the black ghetto from where the dance emerged, could not be squelched. That is, the *spirit* of the dance remained undiminished even after the choreography was co-opted by dancers who adapted the black bottom to their own style.

In 1928, Wallace Thurman described the manner in which black performance was appropriated, adapted, and assimilated by the mainstream in an article called "Where Jazz Was Born." He posits that the Harlem rent party was where everyday black people congregated, and this was the breeding ground for new dance steps and performance routines. At a typical party, he says, one is sure to see what Thurman calls a "stereotyped [N]egro vaudeville performer," or a black entertainer who feeds off and exploits Harlem's newest artistic creations. Thurman explains that this performer "makes it his business to patronise the most colourful of these parties whenever he can and once there he becomes a part of the crowd, observing their every action and following as best he can the most original and most striking of their dance steps." The following day, the performer faithfully reproduces what he learned at the party, refines it, and then teaches "the finished product" to his vaudeville partner. Next in the process, the dance team presents their act on the black vaudeville circuit, where other entertainers imitate the new dance. This continues "until finally some white performer on a big vaudeville circuit appropriates what he has seen a less well-known performer do, labels it with a catchy name and presents it as his own." The cycle completes its course when the dance infiltrates the most staid environments. Thurman explains: "In a few more months scandalised society matrons object to dashing debutantes disturbing the decorum of their fashionable dances by reproducing refined versions of the mad, stark, dance rhythms first seen in a Harlem 'house rent party.'"[39]

The process that Thurman describes demonstrates the profound influence that the veiled side of Harlem had on the dominant culture. But by the 1920s, the rent party became yet another interactive performance venue for individuals looking for new and unique forms of entertainment. While there may have indeed been spontaneous rent parties thrown to assist financially strapped residents, the staging of a rent party became big business. The rent party, while still frequented by working-class Blacks, became another element of the mythologized Harlem as an exotic, waiting-to-be-discovered new continent that was just a quick cab ride away from New York's Midtown. For the black middle class, it became yet another nuisance, socially and culturally.

In an article for the *Inter-State Tattler,* theater critic Theophilus Lewis attempted to debunk the "highly colored and idealized" view of the rent party and reveal its theatrical connections and similarities. After all, he informs readers, the rent party takes the place of nightclubs and theaters for "the poorer classes of the community." Recognizing that not all of his Harlem readership regularly attends rent parties, he provides a context: "Since there are a great number of Negroes who know less about the Harlem they live in than the white folks from downtown, it may not be amiss to explain the purpose of the rent party." Arguing that the impulsive, economically practical parties had become commercially institutionalized, Lewis writes:

> Newspaper writers have gained the impression, and are giving their readers the impression, that giving rent parties is a common domestic practice in Harlem. This is not true. It is a business conducted by specialists who are mainly members of the half world. In order for the backer of a party to stay in the black— that is, to break even or a little better—he must attract at least twenty-five guests. If the party is to be fairly profitable he must have fifty. This shows that the rent party is an institution which is backed by skilled promoters and supported by working people who pay their own rent out of their wages.

While Lewis stresses the production aspects of the party, which would also include the cost of printing and distributing the business-card advertisements, he reveals his own affinity for rent parties and his preference for them over nightclubs. He fears, nevertheless, that just as black cabaret shows had been restaged on Broadway, rent parties might face a similar fate:

> Now that the rent party has been introduced to the white world, the question is, what will the ofays do with it. They have a way of borrowing the customs of Harlem which I fear will be hard to break. They have borrowed our music, our dance and our frank way of making love. It does not require any stretch of imagination to fancy white folks adopting the rent party. Two or three years from now it may be quite the thing for racketeers out on bail or actors out of work to replenish their funds with a Rialto version of the rent party.[40]

Theater people would surely bristle at the parallel association of "racketeers out on bail" with "actors out of work," but the article points to the rent party as a potential profit maker for more than just a struggling tenant.

Harlemites themselves recognized the profits to be made from tourists to the neighborhood. Perpetuating the notion that Harlem was an inscrutable grotto with hidden mysteries around every corner, shrewd entrepreneurs capitalized on the desire to explore the furthest depths of the neighborhood. After all, with insider tips of the party circuit, or the right map of the "invisible city," or a well-informed "slumming" guide, anyone could permeate the heart of Harlem. In 1926, the *New York Age* described a service that for five dollars (not including the cost of drinks and admission to parties and nightclubs), one could see the "private" side of Harlem that outsiders rarely had a chance to see. Advertised on small cards with a picture of a glamorous black woman wearing a formal evening gown and a matching hat with a wide brim, the invitation offered:

> Here in the world's greatest city it would both amuse and also interest you to see the real inside of the New Negro Race of Harlem. You have heard it discussed, but there are few who really know. Because the New Negro will be looked upon as a novelty, I am in a position to carry you through Harlem as you would go slumming through Chinatown. My guides are honest and have been instructed to give the best of references of being both capable and honest so as to give you a night or day of pleasure. Your season is not completed with thrills until you have visited Harlem through Miss ——'s representatives.[41]

The proposal also noted that "two colored guides, one male and one female, would accompany the party."

The focus on the forbidden and the "real inside," as well as the chance to penetrate the neighborhood's private side, underscore the culminating eroticization of Harlem's geographic space. That is, Harlem was perceived and advertised as a site that tempted visitors with possibilities of both social and sexual transgressions. Tourists could enjoy the "authentic" performances of the rent parties and nightclubs, but they could also experiment themselves with the taboo. This was, to use a contemporary description, environmental theater. Harlem offered the audiences a setting to publicly enact their private fantasies. In many ways, the neighborhood was also viewed as a pornographic playground. For example, in the alluring advertisement just quoted, "Miss ——" is painted as the equivalent of a high-class madam, and her "representatives," like those in the most respected escort service, are assured of their "honesty" and "capabilities." Likewise, the language of the invitation is charged with sexual innuendo (including the seductive, "I am in a position to carry you through Harlem"), but the enticement is never sleazy. And notably, the "thrills" and "pleasure" one might receive "through these representatives" are highlighted by the presence of both a male and a female guide. On one hand, the presence of a black man might provide a sense of security for timorous tourists afraid of what might lurk around dark corners, while a black woman guide could offer warmth and matronliness. On the other hand, having guides of both genders on the tour makes it possible to accommodate a variety of sexual fantasies, with the prospect for experimental coupling.

Not everyone in Harlem was excited about the possibilities inherent in the rent party phenomenon as an entertainment and social forum. For the members of the upper classes and intelligentsia concerned with racial uplift and advancement, the rent parties propagated the worst possible images of black people. With an emphasis on riotous partying, sexualized dancing, jazz music, and liquor, the parties reinforced the stereotypes they were trying to dismantle. In this regard, black and white moralists were on common ground. Just as high-minded whites were trying to eliminate activities associated with sex, performance, and liquor, members of the black community were trying to achieve similar goals. The editor of the *New York Age* along with the Reverend Richard M. Bolden, the chief pastor of the First Emmanuel Church in Harlem, urged the police commissioner to help maintain "a high class of respectability" in the black community. A particular "evil," he asserted, was the growing rent party trend, in which "all manner of debauchery was engaged in." He recognized the difficulty in dealing with the problem "because of the question of personal liberty involved," but he encouraged intervention by the police.[42] Similarly, Edgar M. Grey, a columnist for the *Amsterdam News,* frequently bemoaned the poisonous effect that Harlem's nightlife had on the community and its residents. In his "Intimate Glimpses of Harlem," he explained that the rent party, or "Parlor Social," is especially pernicious because "it plays havoc with the morals of the participants and the rests of other residents who wish to sleep."[43] The parties were more than just corruptors of morals and murderers of sleep; they were also a legal nightmare.

In the mid-1920s, W. E. B. Du Bois owned an apartment building at 606 St. Nicholas Avenue. One of the banes of his existence was a tenant named Mrs. Turner, who frequently held rent parties. Du Bois sought legal action because of the disturbances the guests caused at these functions. He complained, "The men urinate out of the windows, and the women sit with their feet out of the front windows."[44] His entreaties received no attention, and Du Bois sold the building in 1928. Theophilus Lewis, Wallace Thurman, and Langston Hughes all romantically suggest that the success of a rent party was indicated by the appearance of the police, since this meant that the party was big, loud, and out of control. In his novel *Gentleman Jigger,* which was unpublished until 2008, Richard Bruce Nugent includes a house rent party in which the police stop in to quiet the party but end up staying for a drink, then the night, and offer to wash one of the male characters' back in the bathtub.[45] Others did not see the affairs in that romantic light, though. To them, the parties were hotbeds of crime. In many ways, they were right.

The papers were filled with reports of disorderly conduct, drunken brawls, and murders. For example, in 1925, a Harlem judge called rent parties a "menace" because "murders and crimes in Harlem for the most part have their origin at parties that are operated weekly to defray expenses for the upkeep of houses."[46] In 1926, the *New York Times* printed an article about a crap game that ended in murder "during a 'rent raising party' at the home of Mrs. William Deas, 412 Lenox Avenue."[47] Over the course of one Saturday night through Sunday morning in September 1927, the police took in 250 people in raids, 110 of those from a party on West 130th Street.[48] In 1928, the *Amsterdam News* reported that "drunken brawls" were occurring practically on a daily basis.[49] Earlier that summer, the paper reported the attempted murder of a man at a rent party. According to the paper, the victim "had gone into partnership" with his friend and rented an apartment on 144th Street for the express purpose of holding "house-rent parties." On this particular Saturday evening, "the apartment was jammed and everybody was just having a fine time until about 4am, when two friends began to argue over a girl." A fight broke out, and one of the guests pulled out a gun and shot the young man in the chest, arm, and shoulder.[50]

The rent parties provided their own form of domestic drama during the 1920s and became a major part of the cultural milieu. In 1929, Wallace Thurman and William Jourdan Rapp brought the rent party to the next level of theatricality. In their play *Harlem,* which is the central focus of the next chapter, the playwrights' *coup de théâtre* was their onstage re-creation of a Harlem rent party. Although many of the New York critics balked at the "lewdness" and "animalistic exhibitions" of the scene in the play, Thurman and Rapp publicly acknowledged that the goings-on were nothing compared with the spectacle of an actual Harlem party. As Thurman and Rapp claimed, "The party on the stage of the Apollo is a tame affair compared to the average Harlem rent party."[51] As private homes became sites of public entertainment, and torrid en-

FIG. 1. The famous rent party scene from *Harlem* (1929). © White Studio. (Billy Rose Theatre Division, The New York Public Library for the Performing Arts, Astor, Lenox and Tilden Foundations.)

tertainment and sensual dancing entered the private realm, the neighborhood's decline seemed all but imminent to many who lived there. For the working-class Blacks who frequented these parties each week, however, this was their Harlem Renaissance.

"PROVE IT ON ME BLUES"

Concurrent with the manifestation of a "low" renaissance in Harlem, as typified by the rent party phenomenon, there was also a burgeoning "queer" re-naissance, which was connected with the increased visibility of lesbian, gay, bi-sexual, and transgendered individuals. Just as house parties were an important element of fostering community among working-class Blacks, they were also an essential element of the emergence of the lesbian and gay subculture of the 1920s. But in the popular imagination, while the house rent parties represented a celebration of working-class family life, as evident in newspaper accounts and theater productions, lesbians and gay men threatened this vision of domestic fortitude. The second half of this chapter examines the merging boundaries of public/private spaces and racial/sexual identity within the shifting political and cultural geographies of New York City. Before returning to the ways in which lesbians and gay men used domestic spaces to strengthen communities, I will detail the complex attitudes toward same-sex identities as they were forged by popular entertainment, social backlashes, and exploitative journalism through the 1920s.

The "queer" renaissance was not confined to Harlem. Because it intersected racial and class boundaries, this renaissance was not ghettoized to a single neighborhood. Private and public spaces around the city became the not-so-secret meeting places for lesbians and gay men, and the press and legal establishment went to great lengths to divulge these locations. The theater was particularly susceptible to attack. Not only did it seem to offer a sanctuary for lesbians and gay men, but it also depicted scenes of this so-called degenerate lifestyle.

By the 1920s, Times Square and Greenwich Village were already recognizable enclaves for homosexual activity, but as Harlem evolved more fully as a distinctly racialized and sexualized site, it soon attracted nonheterosexual (or at least bi-curious) downtowners to its clubs, speakeasies, and dance halls. Lillian Faderman argues that lesbians and gay men gravitated to Harlem because they felt a "bond" between themselves and African Americans. She contends that "they compared their social discomfort as homosexuals in the world at large with the discomfort of black people in the white world."[52] Kevin J. Mumford echoes Faderman by arguing that "racism and then sexual repression from without helped to forge cultural bonds between subordinated groups."[53]

Additionally, African Americans were a vital part of this mix, for as George Chauncey points out, New York's institutionalized segregation established Harlem as the sole area where black lesbians and gay men "could congregate in commercial establishments," and he adds that "they were centrally involved in many of the currents of Harlem culture, from the creative literary circles that constituted the Harlem Renaissance to the blues clubs and basement speakeasies where the poorest of Harlem's residents gathered."[54] And as has been documented elsewhere, a lesbian and gay subculture thrived in Harlem in the 1920s. Indeed, it is now almost common knowledge that many of the leading literary, musical, and theatrical figures, including Countee Cullen, Alain Locke, Wallace Thurman, Richard Bruce Nugent, Alberta Hunter, Gertrude

"Ma" Rainey, Bessie Smith, and Ethel Waters at some point engaged in lesbian, gay, or bisexual relations. There is also speculation about Langston Hughes's sexual orientation, but there is no clear evidence to make a strong case that he was in fact gay.[55] In an age in which many young artists staged a backlash against Victorian morality, sexual rebellion was another component of modernism. Even Florence Mills, the most popular African American performer in the early 1920s, was rumored to have had affairs with women (but again, there is no strong support, just gossip). When asked if Florence Mills was "in the life," Mabel Hampton responded, "Yeah, all of them girls were. Every last one of them. They didn't call it 'gay'—I don't know what they called it—but all of them was one of these."[56]

Even with the numerous arrests records, newspaper articles, and literary allusions that point to an active homosexual subculture, one has to be very cautious to avoid overinterpreting this evidence. This was not a utopian vision of prevailing tolerance. Acceptance was extremely limited among both white and black communities in New York, and few individuals privately or publicly identified themselves as exclusively nonheterosexual (which most likely explains why Hampton could not recall the term people used at the time). Notably, none of the above-mentioned figures, except Richard Bruce Nugent, openly acknowledged his or her homosexuality. In this era of Prohibition and reactionary conservatism, simply because so many people were enjoying frequent or experimental same-sex activity did not make it legal or morally acceptable. Preachers in Harlem railed against the evils of homosexuality from the pulpit, antivice organizations exposed purported dens of iniquity in published reports, and newspapers sensationally dramatized New York's "perverse" underworld, listing the names, ages, and addresses of people arrested for such indiscretions. Accordingly, the performers, writers, and artists in this variable subculture often found sanctuary in the theater, in private salons, and in shared apartments. The "ordinary" people were generally not so lucky. They were the ones implicated in the police raids and moralist tirades as the city cracked down on "degeneracy" reflected in the arts. The *Amsterdam News*, for example, published the names, ages, and addresses of individuals arrested for indecency. In June 1929, a nineteen-year-old valet was arrested for "masquerading in female attire." The following week, a seventeen-year-old man was convicted of the same crime. They were both sentenced to the workhouse. In another case of "masquerading in female attire," a twenty-seven-year-old was sentenced to a staggering six months in the workhouse because "the police say he was convicted three times before for a similar offense." In September of that year, a young man was more fortunate. His charge was dismissed since he was arrested "on his way to a masquerade ball."[57]

Subway washrooms in Harlem were also sites of elicit activity, and there are numerous records of pairs of men arrested for "conducting themselves in an objectionable manner" in the 125th and 135th Street stations.[58] Lesbians in Harlem were also rooted out, with their crimes sensationally reported. In March 1929, for example, a twenty-one-year-old Harlem resident pleaded guilty to "soliciting school girls for immoral purposes." According to a police officer, such situations were not as uncommon as one would have liked to believe. "Sex conditions among school girls is alarming and disgusting. It is the practice, he said, of a group of girls of abnormal sex habits to wait outside the school and make dates with girl students. The female party would then go to the home of one of the girls whose parents or relatives were not at home and conduct their 'sex circus,' the officer explained."[59] Yet for all of the transgendered transgressions and the "sex circuses" supposedly rampant in Harlem, this aspect of the Harlem Renaissance remained, for the most part, a "culture of secretness," to employ Michael Bronski's phrase.[60] It may have been a relatively "open secret," just as the places that served bootlegged liquor were not particularly covert, but it was a "secret" just the same.

Moreover, the greater conspicuousness of lesbians and gay men on the stages and streets throughout New York aroused increased cultural anxiety about their supposed assaults on traditional morality. Gay and lesbian history has shown that intense conservative counterattacks generally accompany an evolving homosexual visibility. This counterattack in the 1920s, resulting in stigmatization and enforcement of sodomy and decency laws, propelled lesbians and gay men to develop underground social networks and institutions. Jeffrey Escoffier explains that "the social stigma and the criminalization of homosexuality—both of which reinforced the necessity of homosexuals themselves controlling information—contributed to the construction of what we now call 'the closet.'"[61] In the 1920s, lesbians and gay men secretly remapped New York's urban landscape, while reclaiming, reshaping, and refashioning public spaces as their designated meeting spaces. But establishments that catered to, or at least tolerated, a lesbian and gay clientele had to be particularly careful not to invite too much publicity that might trigger a raid or police shutdown.

Puritanism and priggishness were certainly not new to New York in the 1920s. The city had already witnessed the one-man crusade to stamp out moral corruption in the form of Anthony Comstock, who established the New York

Society for the Suppression of Vice in 1873. While working in the name of that organization, Comstock had over three thousand people arrested for inde-cency, and he eradicated nearly 160 tons of literary materials that he deemed obscene. Perhaps Comstock is most famous, though, for impelling the Depart-ment of the Interior to fire Walt Whitman and in 1905 for bringing legal pro-ceedings against George Bernard Shaw for his play *Mrs. Warren's Profession.* In response to that incident, Shaw invented the term *comstockery,* referring to strict censorship of allegedly immoral literature.[62] Most people agreed, how-ever, that Comstock went too far when he brought legal action against depart-ment store window dressers for clothing naked mannequins in front of passersby, charging that such blatant displays of nudity might corrupt the morals of the innocent. For once, his overzealousness became a source of laughter and derision. But even after his death in 1915, Comstock's legacy re-mained firmly in place.[63]

By the 1920s, Comstock's era of enforcing Victorian prudery was long past, but attempts at protecting the morals of a supposedly susceptible public were not. John S. Sumner took over as head of the New York Society for the Sup-pression of Vice after Comstock's death, and he was a driving force behind much of the censorship campaign that nearly brought Broadway to its knees in the 1920s. Such attempts at waging war against the nation's rising liberalism went against the grain of the decade's defining spirit. Social and artistic tradi-tions and prohibitions were fair game for toppling.[64] This widespread cultural revolt precipitated a conservative counteraction by Sumner and a staunch old guard, represented by newspaper publisher William Randolph Hearst, a hand-ful of prominent politicians, religious leaders, and even several people associ-ated with the theater. The result was a fierce backlash that played itself out through strict sexual censorship in the popular theater.

The development of a lesbian and gay subculture in Harlem was a conse-quence of the sexual culture wars fought in lower Manhattan, and the main battleground was Broadway. The popular theater, compared with the private, ghettoized performances of rent parties, offered a public venue for perfor-mances of race and sexuality, and it represented a main source of tension be-tween traditional patriarchal values and the decade's "new immorality." Societal "problems" such as "loose women," "fairies," and "bulldaggers," all associated with the subculture, found their way in great numbers onto the characteristi-cally upstanding Broadway stage in the 1920s. While these images of sexual out-lawry were often disparaged from the pulpit and in conservative newspaper ed-itorials, they did not become the subject of national disgust until they were portrayed (*exploited* might be a more appropriate term) in mainstream Broadway shows. It should come as no surprise, then, that the theater became the contentious center where the opposing forces of progressiveness, conservatism, and public titillation were hotly debated and censured.

Police raids and threats of theater closings were de rigueur in New York of the late 1920s, and in February 1927, *Variety* even reported the presence of a "U.S. Censorship Epidemic" that was agitated by several controversial shows playing on Broadway.[65] The climax of this epidemic occurred on February 9, 1927, when three Broadway plays, including *The Captive, Sex,* and *The Virgin Man,* were raided, and the casts were arrested on obscenity charges. Similar incidents erupted across the country, but the reverberations were felt especially acutely in Harlem. When the nation's attention focused on New York's "obscene" and "immoral" entertainment, naturally reformists also looked directly uptown. With its steamy musical revues and nightclub floor shows, Harlem seemed to be a teeming hotbed of immoral stage productions. In April 1927, for example, *Variety* noted that several of the large nightclubs, which included nude and scantily clad women in their floor shows, were threatened with a massive police crackdown. Although the club owners expected that charges would be dismissed in court, they "covered up their girls" because they "[did] not wish to antagonize the police and [would] go to any lengths to avoid a pinch." The article also speculated that political ambitions motivated the actions, explaining that "Governor [Alfred E.] Smith is planning now for the 1928 Democratic Convention in New York again and wants a spotless town."[66] In a similar incident, nine chorus girls along with the director of the "Club Kentucky Revue" at the Lafayette Theatre in Harlem were arrested April 14, 1927, for "presenting and participating in an immoral and indecent act." The defendants were released on $500 in bail; the manager of the theater responded that he was only producing "the kind of show the Harlem public wanted."[67] The concerted effort to "clean up" shows in Harlem and throughout New York continued throughout the year. As a result of this campaign, new and stronger legislation clarified what was immoral on the stage, and for the first time, there were laws that expressly forbade images and discussions of homosexuality in dramatic works.

Such legislation was clearly a reaction to the sudden emergence of several popular plays that pushed the boundaries of traditional definitions of stage decency. In 1927, there were at least nine "dirt plays," as *Variety* liked to refer to them, including *Sex, The Virgin Man, American Tragedy,* and *Lulu Belle.*[68] Two of the plays on *Variety*'s list, *The Captive* and *New York Exchange,* revolved explicitly around homosexual characters and issues, and a play by Mae West

called *The Drag,* subtitled *A Homosexual Comedy in Three Acts,* was playing out
of town in Paterson, New Jersey. *The Drag,* a play about a wealthy (and married) gay man who hosts a party for his cross-dressed friends, was heading toward Broadway, and most historians agree that this destination was the impe-
tus for the censorship campaign that hit New York in the early months of 1927.
The play prompted the Republicans in the New York State Assembly to reex-
amine the state's obscenity law, the Penal Code of 1909. In turn, the Assembly
amended this mandate to include restricting any show "depicting or dealing
with the subject of sex degeneracy, or sex perversion."[69] Furthermore, Section
1140A of this legislation declared that theaters would be padlocked for one year
should the owners refuse to close a show that a jury believed "would tend to the
corruption of youth or others."[70] This new ordinance, formally known as the
Wales Law after its originator, was widely referred to as the Wales Padlock Law,
and it remained on the books for nearly fifty years.[71] In February 1927, a meeting of seventy-six theater managers was called to devise a plan to halt *The Drag*
from opening on Broadway. In effect, the managers agreed to make the play a
sacrificial lamb to appease a vengeful censor intent on bringing "respectability"
back to Broadway. According to the scuttlebutt, many of those present at the
managers' meeting said they "feared" the consequences should Mae West's play
come to New York after its engagement in New Jersey. *Variety* reported, "If *The
Drag* is as raw as reported, the managers figured it might bring about the closing of some of the current plays. They are said to have planned to agree not to
book *The Drag* on Broadway."[72] Likewise, Actors' Equity opposed *The Drag* on
Broadway and actively campaigned against its coming to New York, and it
never opened on Broadway.[73]

The homophobia of the theater community in the 1920s is well documented. Publicly, people in the theater tended to deride homosexuality, and
they consciously disassociated themselves from gay men and lesbians. Even
show business magazines and newspapers campaigned vigorously against homosexuals. Most notably, *Broadway Brevities,* a New York monthly tabloid devoted to the theater, spent a great deal of space rooting out the names of "fags"
and "bulldikers" in the entertainment industry, as well as their meeting places
throughout the city. Blind items and rumors were the principal components of
this magazine, which often poked fun at an innocent and amusing quirk of a
popular performer: "How would you like to consume twelve pineapples each
week? Ask Charlotte Greenwood." But a typical entry might also speculate on a
person's sexuality with coded innuendo: "Why is [silent screen star] Dick
Barthelmess so fond of Childs [a well-known cafeteria where gay men often

hung out after hours] at 58th and 5th? We thought Dick liked the swell food-eries."[74] Another item might disclose the name of an eatery or theater that shamefully, in the editor's opinion, permitted homosexual activity. In a passage entitled "Lesbians Hit the Movies," the editor acknowledges a letter received that addresses the "peculiar conditions on the first balcony of the Plaza Theatre at Madison and Fifty-ninth." Apparently, the informant "recently observed four pairs of loving Lesbians—*nauseating* would be a better word, he adds—and ex-presses wonder that these inverts haven't been noticed." The women, the infor-mant also pointed out, go to the movie theater "singly, looking for prey, and are never troubled by the ushers, even after complaint is made." The editor, conflat-ing homosexuality with the lower class, admonishes: "As the Plaza has a clien-tele of 'upper class' character, and is a house of fine repute, we hope this item may reach the eyes of the proprietors thereof and a 'No Parking' sign go up promptly."[75] Such exposure, while almost surely providing useful information to lesbians and gay men, became a righteous cause for the editors of *Broadway Brevities*.

Beginning in 1924 and lasting over a year, the magazine published a monthly series called "Nights in Fairyland," which uncovered the likely places one could, on any given night, encounter lesbians and gay men throughout the city. The most popular hangouts, according to the unnamed reporters, were Paul & Joe's Italian restaurant on Nineteenth Street near Fifth Avenue; Trilby's, a small restaurant they describe as a "cellar of carnality in the Village"; Louis' on East Forty-ninth Street, where apparently, contrary to popular perception, "the fags outnumber the Lesbians two to one"; and the aforementioned Childs, where "on almost any Sunday morning at one o'clock you may—if you have an eye skilled in identifying the nance—see from one to two hundred rouged and powdered sissies petting and coquetting." The spectacle at Childs was especially abetted by the fact that it was the preferred after-show haunt for gay chorus boys, whom the reporters describe as "pasty of face and coquettish of gait." The writers explain: "The Broadway chorus fairies—and there are hundreds of them—furnish the only midnight novelty at Childs. They naturally aren't free to join their fellow-psychopaths until after the show, so you can have a close-up at Childs at twelve of the dear sweet things that pranced and curtsied earlier in the evening in the ranks of the Winter Garden, 'Vanities' and Music Box Revue."[76]

There was speculation at the time that the authors might be "in the life" themselves. To those reading the articles, such an intimate knowledge of the community seemed inconceivable for an outsider to possess. Nevertheless, the writers denied the accusation. The specific details printed in the series more than likely provided a useful Baedeker directing gay men and lesbians through the subculture's hot spots, but the articles' stated intention was to hold the community up for contempt and ridicule. Accompanied by cartoons, and an artist's conception of "Fag Types," the pieces stress the infiltration of lesbians and gay men and the ways they may be identified. By offering hints for recognition—such as the tell-tale evidence of makeup on men, as well as the "fairy cry," that is, the delighted scream that gay men make when they are with other gay men (a cry that the reporters describe as "the most terrifying, the most pitiful, of all human sounds"), and the short-cropped, pageboy haircuts and masculine dress for women—the series intended to provide the necessary tools for bringing to light homosexuals carefully hidden within the reader's own community. The reporters stress that there are subcultures within all of the major neighborhoods in the city, stating portentously:

> In the Bowery poor and shabby fags of every breed may be seen; in the Bronx, fags of Jewish descent; in Mulberry [S]treet inverts Italiano; in Chinatown the comical oriental urning. Not less may be observed in the colored neighborhood of Lenox Avenue, on that long reach from 110th Street to 160th Street, hordes of "big boys," flamboyantly arrayed, plying the oldest and most noxious of all trades. And so on throughout the city—throughout the nation—throughout the world.[77]

Ironically, the "problem" with homosexuals, it seems, was not that they "may be seen" in the city's ghettoes, rather the more crucial cause of anxiety was their ability to blend in with the urban milieu. This invisibility made homosexuals both dangerous and socially corrupting.

Beneath the general exuberance and optimism of the decade lurked a palpable uneasiness. The seeds of the grim economic situation that choked the nation in the 1930s had already been sown, and New York's growing housing crisis, first evident in Harlem and then in pockets throughout the city, offered tangible proof of this fact. In addition, the family, the central unit of American moral and economic stability, was also changing. Immigrants continued to pour into the city and competed for the same jobs as white, working-class men, forcing other family members to find employment. In 1924, efforts to reverse this trend led to the Immigration Law, which established a quota system that was biased against all groups other than northern and western Europeans. Likewise there was, according to Nathan Irvin Huggins, "a spectacular revival of racism." The New Negro evidently posed a tremendous threat to white Americans, for "the new Ku Klux Klan found white support throughout the country, and violence against [African Americans] increased."[78] On the suffragette front, many women were declaring their independence, and they began taking up formerly male-defined behaviors such as smoking, wearing masculine clothing, and voting. Some were even entering the workforce. This new economic freedom that many women enjoyed stimulated a much higher divorce rate, which rose sharply in the 1920s. Sociologist E. J. Graff cites statistics showing that "between 1867 and 1929, the population of the United States grew 300 percent, the number of marriages increased 400 percent, and the divorce rate rose 2,000 percent."[79] The only ground for divorce in New York State, however, was adultery, but as Graff explains, "Everyone knew that you could get a divorce simply by having your picture snapped lying on a hotel bed with a co-respondent-for-hire."[80]

Homosexuality, in the cultural imagination of the 1920s, presented a particularly formidable threat to the nuclear family. Not only did lesbians and gay men apparently have ruinous effects on a household, but they were also cast as notoriously deceptive and conniving. For example, in 1926 when *The Captive,* Arthur Hornblow's adaptation of Edouard Bourdet's *La Prisonnière,* opened on Broadway, audiences saw the domestic devastation wrought by an irresistible lesbian. The plot centers on a French diplomat's daughter, her upstanding husband, and a beguiling woman who secures the young woman's affections. The turn of events causes the husband to attest to the duplicity of women and the horrible reality that if one is not ever watchful, a woman "can poison and pillage everything before a man whose home she destroys is even aware what's happening to him."[81] Reviewing the play in the *American Mercury,* theater critic George Jean Nathan called it "the most subjective, corruptive, and potentially evil-fraught play ever shown in the American theatre," and he added that it was "nothing more or less than a documentary in favor of sex degeneracy."[82] Other New York critics were much more appreciative of the show, including Brooks Atkinson, who found it "written with taste," and "acted with style and reticence."[83] Nevertheless, after the show had proven to be a huge commercial success, and after it had played 160 performances without incident, the Empire Theatre was raided. Accompanied by a deluge of photographers and scandal mongers, the entire company and management were arrested. But rather than face a lengthy trial, the producer opted to close the show instead.[84] Atkinson later wrote, "As usual, the district attorney could not tell the difference between literature and hokum."[85]

Just as despicable as the lesbian in the cultural imagination was the gay man who married a woman and "played on her innocence" so that he could fit into heterosexual society. In *The Drag,* for instance, when the central character makes a pass at his friend who happens to have designs on the young man's wife, the friend scolds: "Why, I think it's the most contemptible thing you could do—marry a woman and use her as a cloak to cover up what you are."[86] This secrecy, which magazines like *Broadway Brevities* hoped to expose, contributed to the perceived treachery of homosexuals. They could, judging by widely held beliefs of the time, be anywhere and anyone. The most terrifying aspect of homosexuality in the 1920s was that it was everywhere, but it was often concealed behind images of respectability and domesticity. Mae West indicated this belief in an interview in *Parade* magazine (September 1929), when she described the casting of *The Drag.* She explained: "Five thousand perverts applied for fifty parts when we were casting for *Drag.* One vice-president of a large bank begged me to let him act secretly in *Drag* because there only could he do what he was starving for—act like a woman and wear expensive, beautiful gowns."[87]

Unlike other groups, which were identified by their racial or ethnic origin, the homosexual subculture lacked a designated ghetto in New York that would contain, separate, and put its adherents on display. According to reports of the day, pockets of homosexuality were evident throughout the city, making the gay and lesbian presence seemingly uncontainable and uncontrollable. Therefore, it was not the fact that lesbians and gay men had gone *public* with their affections and culture, but it was their relative *invisibility* that was particularly frightful. As the reporters of the "Nights in Fairyland" in *Broadway Brevities* righteously and dramatically sermonized:

> Verily, in this year of our Lord, 1924, the question is—as a brilliant psychiatrist remarked to us the other day—not of "who is" but of "who isn't." Into the very warp and woof of our modern social fabric has eaten devastatingly this cancer of sexual inversion, wiping out manhood and womanhood, making a mockery of natural love, of normal behavior, wrecking homes and lives untold. The sickening stench of homosexuality is in the nostrils of all of us, and for all of us its menace is stupendous. It is, indeed, the pestilence that stalks alike at noonday and night, enfeebling and degrading our civilization, making a by-word of all that is clean and sweet and of good repute. If, in these articles, BREVITIES has been able to abate by one jot this epidemic of shameless lechery, then we feel that our efforts have not been in vain. And to such noble purpose are dedicated the still more relentless exposures to come![88]

During the 1920s homosexuality became much more publicly visible, but so did a more concerted effort—as evidenced by the *Broadway Brevities* articles—to quash acceptance of this lifestyle.

More so than other New York neighborhoods (except perhaps Greenwich Village), Harlem provided a degree of tolerance for lesbians and gay men. There remained throughout the decade the threat of arrest (particularly in election years), but in general, there was more leeway from exposure and censorship. Drag balls, speakeasies catering to the drag subculture, and acts featuring "pansies" and "bulldaggers" were not altogether uncommon. Female impersonators were regularly featured in nightclub acts throughout Harlem, from small speakeasies, like the Pullman Café on Lenox Avenue near 126th Street,[89] to the majestic Harlem Opera House, where Ella Fitzgerald was discovered in a 1934 amateur night performance. In the same year Fitzgerald received her break, an African American performer, the self-proclaimed "Darling of Female Impersonators," capitalized on the gay iconographic status of Mae West to appear on a bill with the legendary Fletcher Henderson at the Harlem Opera House. Sepia Mae West, as the performer was promoted, did not fare well with the critics. A reviewer of the *New York Age* raved about "Fletch" and his band but was appalled by the drag performer. "There is only one spot on the program which might really be classed as 'putrid,'" he wrote, "and that is the demonstration of just how freakish humans can become as offered by something which is styled as the 'Sepia Mae West.' The less said about it, the better."[90] The critic said nothing else about the act.

At the same time that lesbians and gay men felt a sense of affinity with African Americans, Harlem residents were often bewildered by their presence. Claude McKay captured the essence of this confusion with a snippet from an untitled blues song overheard in a Harlem speakeasy. A character in *Home to Harlem* sings, "There is two things in Harlem I don't understan' / It is a bull-dycking woman and a faggotty man."[91] Similarly, a character in Carl Van Vechten's *Nigger Heaven* refuses to go to a particular club because he feels there are "too many pink-chasers," or black people who like associating with whites, as well as "bulldikers."[92]

In an era when there were no antihomophobic organizations such as the Mattachine Society, Daughters of Bilitis, or ACT UP, negative attitudes toward homosexual visibility accomplished exactly what conservatives and commentators feared: Many homosexuals were forced underground, and they hid behind veils of respectability and within the ghettos of large urban centers. Removed from the threatening public spotlight and severed from the fetishistic gaze of Harlem tourists who were aroused by their otherness, lesbians and gay men could monitor the hatred and fascination they inspired from the private fortresses they constructed. This relative safety within the confines of the ghetto validates David Savran's argument that the closet "is both a means of concealment and a privileged perspective on both the dominant culture and what it seeks to police and contain."[93] Escaping from public view, many lesbians and gay men developed elaborate social systems to avoid detection. In Harlem, for instance, private homes became exclusive places of homosexual congregation and performance for a night.

From tenement buildings to upscale apartment buildings, private parties in Harlem became the safest way for lesbians and gay men to meet, sing, dance, and drink plenty of bootlegged alcohol. Because of the dire concern for periodic moral crackdowns by the city and police, the Harlem homosexual subculture—particularly a burgeoning lesbian community—developed a flourishing social network operating out of private spaces. Mabel Hampton remarked that lesbians often took rooms next to one another, and the "girls," as she referred to them, had "parties every other night."[94] And as Lillian Faderman explains, it may not have surprised many residents of the era to know that there was "a whole boardinghouse full of lesbians who [were] allowed to live in Harlem undisturbed."[95] A scene in Wallace Thurman's *The Blacker the Berry . . .* bears this supposition out. While searching for a room in Harlem, Emma Lou, the novel's central character, meets an insistently unmarried landlady named *Miss* Carrington (emphasis in the original). The woman becomes surprisingly and—to the young heroine—"unexpectedly" intimate, by setting "her hand on Emma Lou's knee," and "put[ting] her arm around her waist." *Miss* Carrington assures Emma Lou that she would be quite welcome in this apartment house, which she refers to as the "Old Maid's Home," claiming, "there are lots of nice girls living here." As an added incentive she says, "We have parties among ourselves, and just have a grand time. Talk about fun! I know you'd be happy here." Uncomfortable and apprehensive, Emma Lou makes a hasty retreat and continues her search.[96]

Because of the intended secretiveness of parties staged exclusively for lesbians, there are few written accounts about them. These soirees received much less publicity than the heterosexual-organized equivalent parties in Harlem, which were often, as indicated earlier, announced by blind leafletting throughout the neighborhood. Invitations to a lesbian bash tended to be verbal and much more discreet, explaining why Faderman presumes that lesbians only "*sometimes* attended rent parties," and adding that "those gatherings were generally predominantly heterosexual."[97] But evidence now suggests that lesbians created their own circuit of parties. And to ensure that they remained relatively private, such parties often "traveled" within the neighborhood, and individuals would take turns hosting. The mobility of the parties made the get-togethers more elusive, and neighbors might be less likely to complain if the parties did not become regular events. Only if the police were called in to break up a party would the event receive undue publicity.

This is exactly what happened in November 1926. The *New York Age*, Harlem's most respected newspaper, reported the circumstances of a particular rent party that got out of hand and ended with a murder. Although the article does not specify directly, one may presume the participants in the tragedy are black. It seems that the rent party's hostess, Reba Stobtoff, "crazed with gin and a wild and unnatural infatuation for another woman," seized "a keenedged bread knife and with one fell swoop, severed the jugular vein in the throat of Louise Wright," who was also attending the party. According to witnesses, Stobtoff had accused Wright of paying too much attention to a woman named Clara, who was known in this "underworld" as "Big Ben" because of her "unusual size and from her inclination to ape the masculine in dress and manner, and particularly in her attention to other women." The article points out that Big Ben was not present at the affair, but witnesses overheard Stobtoff warn Wright "to stay away from the 'man' woman." When the fight broke out, Wright tried to escape, but Stobtoff "grabbed [her] by the hair, jerked her head back, and swept the knife across her bent throat, cutting the head almost off." The reporter adds, "Death was practically instantaneous." The police arrived shortly after and stated that "only women were present, and it is said that no men had attended the affair."[98]

Two weeks later the *Age* editorialized on the event using it as an opportunity to note the rise of rent parties in Harlem and the economic necessity behind them. Of the particular incident in question, the editor compares the situation to the plot of *The Captive*. Notably, the editor remarks that the similarities between the two indicate that homosexuality is not limited to Harlem. The editor writes: "That the story of *The Captive* should have found its parallel in this locality is a revelation of the fact that the frailties of human nature are much alike, whether in Paris or New York, regardless of complexions." The piece concludes with the following moral: "In the meantime the combination of bad gin, jealous women, a carving knife and a rent party is dangerous to the health of all concerned."[99]

The account reflects the oftentimes violent and tragic interplay between the private and public realms of Harlem. Music, dance, and comedy routines that developed in tenement houses and apartment buildings frequently made their way to the stages of Broadway and into the popular imagination, and dramas based on supposed "scenes from Harlem life" found their way into the mainstream theater. Yet responses to the "Rent Party Tragedy" demonstrate that the process worked in reverse as well. The popularity of *The Captive* on Broadway influenced the way in which lesbians in the 1920s were recognized and identified. Sensationalism, melodrama, and moral lessons were the narrative tools used to represent them in the press, and the story confirmed images that had already been implanted in the cultural consciousness. Finally, the editor's description of universal "human frailties" from Paris to New York recapitulates the popular notion that homosexuals could not conceal themselves within the ghetto. There would always be some indication that would expose their true identities. Like the racial performances of Harlem's private parties, traces of a homosexual existence continued to leak out into the mainstream. Such exposure was inevitably met with simultaneous fascination and abject disgust. And true to 1920s form, Harlem's ghetto could not suppress the private world of the lesbian and gay subculture. Instead, it became one of its grandest and most eagerly awaited annual spectacles in the New York social scene. While lesbians and gay men forged new communities in private houses and apartments, they celebrated their identities publicly in Harlem's Hamilton Lodge drag balls, which are explored in depth in the third chapter.

CHAPTER 2

"Harlem on My Mind": New York's Black Belt on the Great White Way

Harlem . . . Harlem
Black, black Harlem
Niggers, Jigs an' shiney spades
Highbrowns, yallers, fagingy fagades
". . . Oh say it, brother,
Say it . . ."
Pullman porters, shipping clerks an' monkey chasers
Actors, lawyers, Black Jews an' fairies
Ofays, pimps, lowdowns an' dicties
Cabarets, gin an' number tickets
All mixed in
With gangs o' churches
Sugar foot misters an' sun dodgin' sisters
Don't get up
Till other folks long in bed . . .

   —"HARLEM" BY FRANK HORNE*

"OFAYS, PIMPS, LOWDOWNS AN' DICTIES"

In March 1926, Anita Handy edited a new magazine called *A Guide to Harlem and Its Amusements*, in which she planned to provide tips for touring Harlem's most popular attractions. When her inspiration was denounced in the black press for focusing only on the neighborhood's lurid side, she responded that she only intended to satisfy the curiosity of those who had recently seen David Belasco's Broadway production of *Lulu Belle* and read Carl Van Vechten's controversial novel *Nigger Heaven*. She claimed that these two works had "caused a great number of people, especially white people, to visit Harlem," but regrettably, in her opinion, these crowds did not know "how to see the community intelligently."[1]

The highlight of Handy's tour would include a trip to the epicenter of this thriving nightlife, a stretch known as "Jungle Alley," which was located between Lenox and Seventh avenues on 133rd Street. Many of the nightclubs, such as Barron's Exclusive Club, one of Harlem's oldest (having opened in 1915), Connor's, and the Clam House, were found on this block. In her publicity, she also promised that she would not show just the "night side life," but also "the better side of Harlem," including its churches, schools, and modest homes. Admittedly, she indicated, "The night life side is the only side the white tourists care to see, as it is the only side they have heard about."[2] For those wishing to experience the "real thing," Handy's guide presumably offered an invaluable service to visitors who only knew Harlem from what they saw on the stage and read in popular fiction.

As this account indicates, white fascination with Harlem was fueled in large part by its representations in the popular literature and entertainment of the 1920s. Plays, novels, and songs depicted an idealized, exotic, and rather risqué view of life among New York's black denizens above 125th Street, and the images lured white people to encounter the authentic milieu on their own. New nightclubs and speakeasies could not open fast enough to oblige the hordes of white tourists. Writers, entertainers, and producers capitalized on the newest vogue and aroused further interest in Harlem's seamier side by continuing to simulate it on stage and in fiction. Practically over night, these simulations of Harlem became the basis for how the "real" Harlem would be seen and experienced by white visitors. Concurrently, however, black community leaders attempted to counter these representations by publicizing the high moral standards of the residents and arguing that the decadence was a result of "the hundreds of downtown white people" who go to Harlem for a "moral vacation."[3]

In the 1920s, Harlem was a contested space for representation, and this chapter examines that contestation through the distorted margins separating private and public, natural and staged, and authentic and manufactured. While the previous chapter explored this phenomenon via the semiprivate rent party institution in Harlem and the lesbian and gay demimonde throughout New York City, here I will focus on how the commercial theater of the 1920s complicated the struggle for a representative view of black life and how competing forces attempted to define the "real" Harlem. The pithily titled *Harlem* (1929) serves as one of the clearest enactments of this struggle.

Harlem is a Broadway melodrama by Wallace Thurman and William Jourdan

Rapp, and the production is historically significant because it was the first commercially successful Broadway play written by an African American—Thurman (although it was cowritten by Rapp, a white playwright). In *Harlem,* Thurman and Rapp consciously recycled many of the conventions of popular Broadway melodrama, which they profitably combined with the white attraction for Harlem's nightlife. The final product is a fascinating hybrid that also includes elements of black folk drama, musical comedy, and social realism. The drama, which was billed as a "Thrilling Play of the Black Belt," demonstrates what George Hutchinson calls "the cobbling together of traditions out of heterogeneous elements and a babel of tongues."[4] This "hybridity," which paralleled the contemporaneous divisive public debate inside and outside the black community, reveals that "real life" 1920s Harlem was a fragmented site of identification, and demonstrates the impossibility of determining an "authentic" African American identity for that era. Even more notably, through the collaboration of the black and white playwrights, depictions of the "old" and "new" Negro, and the attempt to re-create Harlem in Times Square, there is a genuine attempt to blur the boundaries between the races and create a work of art that transcends racial categorization.

If this sounds particularly grandiose for a play that was subtitled *A Melodrama of Negro Life in Harlem,* the *Harlem* playwrights called their work an "educational drama," and they deliberately intended to assail the stereotypes traditionally associated with Blacks on stage, such as the mammy figure, the slow-witted, superstitious "darkie," and the cunning but malapropism-spouting trickster. Indeed, Thurman and Rapp strove to "present the [N]egro as he is" in a veritable, starkly naturalistic environment, and they even included a "Glossary of Harlemisms" in the playbill for deciphering the hip, jazz-inflected, colloquial dialogue spoken on stage. The drama contains a cross-section of a black community, which in the world of this play includes licentious, unrestrained young women, barbaric, sexually out-of-control partygoers, gun-shooting, handsome gangsters, as well as displaced, pious, southern folk, and idealistic, male social climbers. The conflicting images within Thurman and Rapp's play fly in the face of black bourgeois critics, who insisted on images that put Blacks in a positive light and assisted in the task of racial uplift. While simultaneously hoping to educate their audiences, the playwrights were required by their producers to construct a play that would also appeal to the tastes of their mainstream Broadway audience, who craved larger-than-life characters, thrilling drama, and, as one contemporary producer instructed, a "wow" in the third act.

"SO LIKE VAN VECHTEN, START INSPECTIN'"

Broadway audiences were conditioned to a particular view of Harlem that had permeated the popular culture by 1929. To appreciate the pressure on Rapp and Thurman to embody this vision, one need look only at the controversy surrounding the publication of Carl Van Vechten's *Nigger Heaven,* which helped initiate the Harlem vogue.[5] Before examining Rapp and Thurman's depiction of Harlem, this section will provide a context for the literary and theatrical representation of an "insider's view" of Harlem as it was stimulated by that novel.

In August 1926, *Nigger Heaven,* by white novelist and socialite Carl Van Vechten, appeared in bookstores across the country.[6] The novel was an instant best seller, and within just a few months, it went through nine printings. In addition, the novel's subsequent international success helped make Harlem an obligatory stop for tourists visiting New York City. Although the book was never adapted for the stage or film, its relationship to popular entertainment is not at all tangential. Its depiction of black life in Harlem had a tremendous impact on the way in which images of race were presented, perceived, and discussed in the era. As a result, nearly all of the African American performers on Broadway and in the nightclubs of the 1920s were influenced, arguably both positively and adversely, by this novel. More importantly, the arguments it raised about cultural difference laid the groundwork for public discussions over African American representations performed in a variety of venues.

A great deal has been written about Van Vechten's novel and the firestorm it provoked among literary and political leaders in the era, but because of its connections to the New York theater and nightclub worlds, it is worth discussing in this context. In brief, the melodramatic plot concerns the tempestuous romance of two young African Americans, Byron Kason and Mary Love. Naive, beautiful Mary is a librarian and Byron a struggling writer, and the two develop a wholesome, deep love for one another. Byron, however, grows increasingly caustic from a lack of success selling his stories, and as his failure becomes more and more debilitating, he considers Mary's love smothering and patronizing. Soon after, he falls for the impetuous and exotic Lasca Sartoris, who was based on Nora Douglas Holt, a wealthy socialite of the 1920s and good friend of Van Vechten's. In the novel Lasca shows Byron the pleasures of the flesh and material wealth (as well as introducing him to Harlem's raucous night life). Eventually Lasca tires of Byron and dismisses him for Harlem's numbers king (who now would be known as a "bookie"), Randolph Pettijohn. When Pettijohn is killed in a nightclub by a Harlem "sheik," who is also angry at his taking Lasca away from him, Byron is circumstantially linked to the murder. Seeing no way out of this turn of events, Byron unloads his own pistol into the corpse of Pettijohn and succumbs to the law and his own fate. Thus ends the story of an idealistic young black man who comes to the Big City and is destroyed by its callous indifference.

The responses to the book culminated in perhaps one of the most contentious debates over black representation in American history and demonstrated the deep divisions within the community and among the cultural leaders. Alain Locke, Rudolph Fisher, James Weldon Johnson, and Charles S. Johnson gave the book high praise. Wallace Thurman, who offered faint acclaim for the book as a work of literature, spoke out against the damnation heaped upon the novel. In "Fire Burns," an editorial printed in the first and only edition of the literary magazine *FIRE!!*, Thurman wrote:

> Group criticism of current writings, morals, life, politics, or religion is always ridiculous, but what could be more ridiculous than the wholesale condemnation of a book which only one-tenth of the condemnators have or will read. And even if the book was as vile, as degrading, and as defamatory to the character of the Harlem Negro as the Harlem Negro now declares, his criticisms would not be considered valid by an intelligent person as long as the critic had had no reading contact with the book.[7]

A large vocal black contingent, however, was incensed by the book's publication even though many, as Thurman and others indicated, never got past the title page. This outcry did not, however, stop people from reading the novel, and more likely added to its success. Robert F. Worth surmises that the novel sold more copies "than all the books by black writers of the Harlem Renaissance combined."[8] Many Harlemites, though, believed their community had been betrayed and exploited by Van Vechten, whom they had treated with the greatest hospitality or at least quiet tolerance as he did his "research."[9] Andy Razaf poked fun at Van Vechten's methodological explorations in his song, "Go Harlem." The lyric includes the line: "So, like Van Vechten, / Start inspectin', / Go, Harlem, go Harlem, go."[10] Many in the community scorned Van Vechten's sensationalized portrait of their community, and unsuccessfully tried to ban him from visiting Harlem.

The title was especially offensive to some, but Van Vechten vociferously claimed that his use of the term was not intended to offend—perhaps he wished for it to shock—but he used the term *nigger heaven* ironically, both as a theatrical allusion and as a metaphor for Harlem. On a literal level, it refers to the second balcony in downtown theaters, where black audiences were relegated when they attended a Broadway show. The packing of black people into the gallery, requiring them to use separate doors and unadorned stairways, which contrasted with the ornate passageways leading to the orchestra and mezzanine sections of Broadway theaters, was a powerful social reminder of their status. (Incidentally, these characteristics are still evident in the existing Broadway theaters built around the turn of the century.) Even when the whites in the orchestra and mezzanine below were joyously applauding an all-black show like *Shuffle Along*, the theatrical spaces dictated, or better yet, "disciplined" in Foucauldian parlance, the great racial divide.[11]

Metaphorically, Van Vechten's title refers to Harlem itself, pointing to the neighborhood as a segregated section for Blacks, situated geographically at the top of Manhattan Island. Although the title suggests a paradise-like quality of this community and its separation, in Van Vechten's intended usage, the novel ironically presents Harlem as an overcrowded enclave for its black residents. The central character of the novel, Byron, articulates this view in an oft-quoted passage:

> We sit in our places in the gallery of this New York theatre and watch the white world sitting down below in the good seats in the orchestra. Occasionally they turn their faces up towards us, their hard, cruel faces, to laugh or sneer, but they never beckon. It doesn't seem to occur to them that Nigger Heaven is crowded, that there isn't another seat, that something has to be done.[12]

Unfortunately, Van Vechten's social commentary is lost within the melodramatic proceedings of the book. Overpowered by the exciting and vibrant nightclub scenes, which include the exploits of black gangsters, loose women, and dedicated revelers, Byron's rant seems more like sour grapes than a social indictment.

In his defense, Van Vechten never intended to exploit or insult his black hosts; in fact he had envisioned "taking up the Chinese and the Jews" in future fictional exposés (he never did).[13] He championed black causes in his *Vanity Fair* columns and was a patron to several black artists, including Langston Hughes. He was a tremendous supporter of many black artists and entertainers, and his renowned parties included numerous African American guests at a time when New York's high society was strictly segregated.

In an era when black identity was being forged, and positive images were at a premium, Van Vechten seemed to be more interested in rebelling against white middle-class ideals and intent on sending a cultural shockwave through New York's elite.

Van Vechten's book had an even more profound effect, and it touched a nerve among African Americans when racial tensions were especially high across the nation. In 1926, news of lynchings from the South continued to seep into Harlem, and there was still not a Senate-passed antilynching bill that would at the very least reflect a modicum of white concern. In a highly theatrical protest in December 1926, two political organizations, the National Negro Development Union and the National Negro Centre Political Party, gathered in Harlem in response to the lynching of Bertha Lowman and her two brothers in Aiken, South Carolina. Demanding that President Coolidge take action to halt the activity of the Ku Klux Klan, S. R. Williams, a Wilberforce College professor, used Van Vechten's novel as evidence of white culpability. After denouncing *Nigger Heaven* and reading excerpts from the novel, he tore two pages from the book and asked the energized crowd what should be done with the pages "to show proper resentment of their contents." As the crowd responded "Burn 'em up!" Williams lit the pages on fire and held them over his head until they were completely incinerated. There might be another ceremony, Williams told the crowd, to burn the rest of the book.[14]

In addition to showing *inter*racial divisions in the 1920s, the controversy surrounding *Nigger Heaven* reflects *intra*racial splits and fragmentation. While critics and reporters of the era attempted to depict Harlem as a community united by racial commonalities, the response to *Nigger Heaven* attested to the depth of the fissures with which it was bisected. Class divisions, varying national origins, political affinities, and religion were just some of the ways in which the community was divided, and Van Vechten created a call to arms. Apart from the occasional political protest, the battle over *Nigger Heaven* was mostly academic, and the theater of operations was the black mainstream and scholarly press, the black intelligentsia and religious figures its main warriors.

James Weldon Johnson, a good friend of Van Vechten's, championed the novel in the black journal *Opportunity,* and he pointed to the multifaceted presentation of Harlem in the novel. In his review, he applauds Van Vechten as the first white novelist to portray Harlem life not as a single experience, and he says the author presents "the components of that life from the dregs to the froth." Johnson sees the book as a truthful, nonmanipulative narrative and a genuine documentary of Harlem, but at the same time, one that is literary and artful.

Commenting on Van Vechten's treatment of Harlem's less wholesome elements, Johnson focuses on the universalism of the love story at the novel's heart:

> The scenes of gay life, of night life, the glimpses of the underworld, with all their tinsel, their licentiousness, their depravity serve actually to set off in sharper relief the decent, cultured, intellectual life of Negro Harlem. But all these phases of life, good and bad, are merely the background for the story, and the story is the love life of Byron Kasson and Mary Love.[15]

Johnson maintains that the book is surely going to be "widely read," and will undoubtedly "arouse much discussion." Understanding that some people will have difficulty getting beyond the title and try to talk knowingly about the book anyway, he concludes: "This reviewer would suggest reading the book before discussing it."[16]

In his scathing review in *The Crisis* (also a black journal) several months after the novel's publication, Du Bois never mentions James Weldon Johnson by name, but he responds to Johnson's appraisal point by point. He refers to the book as "a blow in the face" to the black community. Although he objects to the title, he says that that is the least of the novel's offenses, asserting, "after all, a title is only a title." In particular, Du Bois condemns the book for being an unflattering and false representation of Harlem. Assuming the opposite of Johnson's position, he calls the work's portrait of black life a "caricature," which, he explains, "is worse than untruths because it is a mass of half-truths." He writes: "Probably some time and somewhere in Harlem every incident of the book has happened; and yet the resultant picture built out of these parts is ludicrously out of focus and undeniably misleading."[17] He defiantly refutes any allegation that the depiction of Harlem is fair and balanced, and he posits a critique of the white, one-sided perception of Harlem, which focuses only on its scandalous images. He writes:

> [Van Vechten] is an authority on dives and cabarets. But he masses this knowledge without rule or reason and seeks to express all of Harlem life in its cabarets. To him the black cabaret is Harlem; around it all his characters gravitate. . . . Such a theory of Harlem is nonsense. The overwhelming majority of black folk never go to cabarets. The average colored man in Harlem is an everyday laborer, attending church, lodge and movie and as conservative and as conventional as ordinary working folk everywhere.[18]

In a conclusion that seems to answer Johnson's appeal for people to read the book, Du Bois says: "I read *Nigger Heaven* and read it through because I had to. But I advise others who are impelled by a sense of duty or curiosity to drop the book gently in the grate and to try the *Police Gazette*."[19]

Du Bois's argument that the title was not a metaphor for Harlem, as Van Vechten posited, but rather a synecdochical archetype, was reiterated by community and religious leaders, who mourned the adverse effect it had on the neighborhood. They viewed such works as *Lulu Belle* and *Nigger Heaven* and their depiction of Harlem as a "paradise for cheap sport" with dismay. This was a small element of Harlem life, they argued, and the more dominant "good" and "decent" side of their neighborhoods was ignored. Reverend William Lloyd Imes, a pastor of St. James' Church, asked:

> Would white folk like to be judged by their cheapest and vilest products of society? Do they feel flattered by the sordid, degrading life brought out in our courts? Those who really know Negro Harlem find its good, decent homes, its schools, its churches, its beginning of business enterprises, artists, musicians, poets, and scholars, influential civic organizations, modern newspapers and magazines published and controlled by the race, all of which is a veritable romance in itself.[20]

And in a tongue-in-cheek, ironic piece for the *Messenger,* George S. Schuyler wrote that Harlem had very recently earned a degree of respect for its growing number of intellectuals, writers, and poets. But he claims that these achievements have been nearly forgotten due to the interest in the vulgar nightlife. Facetiously, he states that Carl Van Vechten and Broadway impresario David Belasco would soon be participating in a public debate to determine who is "most entitled to be known as the Santa Claus of Black Harlem, a community described as the Mecca of the New Negro but lately called 'Nigger Heaven.'" Poking fun at Belasco and Van Vechten's capitalization on black life and their self-serving "support" of black literary and cultural life, he concludes, "Both contestants are well known for their contributions to the Fund for the Relief of Starving Negro Intelligentsia and for their frequent explorations of the underground life north of 125th Street."[21]

Within a year, *Nigger Heaven* became an integral part of the popular culture and was synonymous with Harlem entertainment. Its representations of black cabaret performers, singers, and dancers were replicated in the nightclubs, musical shows, and plays in New York and other cities across the United States. A blunt example of the circulation of the title and its images can be found in George S. Oppenheimer and Alfred Nathan, Jr.'s song "Nigger Heaven Blues," which appeared in *The Manhatters,* a musical revue that first appeared in Greenwich Village in the late spring of 1927 and moved to the Selwyn Theatre in August of the same year. The song was set in a cabaret scene and performed by whites in blackface, and the lyric attempts to capture the rag-tag, sexual spirit of the novel and includes the verse, "High yaller girls, choc'late and buff, / Doing their stuff, doing it rough / Oh boy, I got the Nigger Heaven Blues."[22] As critics warned, the original socially and politically ironic intentions of the title were consumed by the depictions of salacious dancing and unending jazz music.

Even more than being a cultural marker, the novel became a travelogue, a tourist's guidebook for visiting Harlem. The book was deemed a work of fiction, but people wanted an unmediated experience of the scenes from the novel because they seemed so "real" and "authentic." An article from 1929 printed in the *Jamaican Mail,* a Kingston, Jamaica, newspaper, reflects this desire to experience the real, untainted Harlem. The author of the piece, Viscountess Weymouth, writes that since reading *Nigger Heaven,* she has wanted to experience Harlem, "this colourful Mecca of jazz, high spirits and drama." Fortuitously, she met Carl Van Vechten at her first party in New York, and he "promised that he himself would unlock the ebony gates of Nigger Heaven" to her and her unidentified traveling companions. Their first stop was Connie's Inn, where she saw a not very satisfying musical revue. Her disillusionment with Connie's arose from the fact that except for the waiters and entertainers (she was quite impressed in particular by "a beautiful negress" who performed "an exotically barbaric dance"), there were nearly no "coloured people in the room." She states sadly: "I was disappointed; the whole atmosphere was so obviously faked to lure the tourist." The club lacked the authentic environment that typified her reading of the novel. Her spirits rose, however, with their arrival at the Sugar Cane, which figures prominently as the model for Van Vechten's fictional "Black Venus" speakeasy in *Nigger Heaven.* Upon entering, she thought the place empty, but then "realized that black faces were beginning to extricate themselves from the dark background." She recounts the scene with a cinematic detachment, almost as an ethnographer recording her observations on the behavior of her black subjects: "All of them dance beautifully, but violently, keeping quite still about the shoulders and swaying from the hips. When the band stopped they again faded quietly into darkness."[23] All in all, she was more than satisfied by her trip to this club because the speakeasy lived up to the expectations established by Van Vechten's novel.

Her evening concluded at an unnamed, carefully secluded pub. At first she was anxious and afraid as she entered the dimly lit club. She notes, "It was crowded with dusky faces; ours were conspicuous as the only white ones. I do not think we should have been admitted had Mr. Van Vechten not been there." Her initial fright at the sense of impending danger and overall sense of foreboding recalls the Black Mass scene from *Nigger Heaven*. And like that unnamed space, she regarded this club as so covert and genuine, she was careful not to disclose its name or exact location. Publicizing it in her account would destroy the ineffable dark secrets she had learned. The sense of excitement and lawlessness of the scene was heightened by the "well-stocked bar" that greeted her upon entering, for as she reminded her readers, the United States at this time was "the land of prohibition." Her fear finally dissipated and her sense of security returned later in the nighttime when a white policeman strolled in, "had a drink," and left "happy."

To Weymouth, this club was the most educational and pleasing of all her stops, as she could also watch black people interacting in an environment untainted by white intrusion (except for Van Vechten's guided party, of course). She recalled listening to "St. Louis Blues" "wailing" around her, and she described the music as "the broken, melancholy chant of a race of slaves, alive with a throbbing rhythm running through it, and breaking free at the close, dominant and virile."[24] Her tour concluded with a breakfast of waffles and fried chicken at the speakeasy, and she and her small party of whites left the club after dawn. Cynical observers, as well as a significant segment of the black community, referred to this particular version of Harlem as "Van Vechtenland," one that was created and strengthened in the white imagination. Thurman and Rapp's *Harlem* was originally intended as an antidote to this vision with a more accurate delineation.

"CITY OF REFUGE, CITY OF REFUSE"

When *Harlem* opened on Broadway, Whitney Bolton, a critic for the *New York Telegraph,* called the play "the most unretouched and, therefore, the most accurate of the photographs made at Seventh avenue and 132d street." To Bolton, the photographic accuracy of the play extended to the treatment of its socially realistic characters: "The dark man of Manhattan Island and his girl of tantalizin' tan receive here the consideration and study that no play which touched them has had before this work of William Jourdan Rapp and Wallace Thurman was written."[25] Other New York critics also praised the production's veracity within its dramatic framework. One critic found the muddled melodramatic plot rather contrived, but said that "it is the many bits of authentic [N]egro life and Harlem color that make it humanly novel and interesting." Similarly Alison Smith pointed out that even when the "feeble and disjointed" plot lagged in spots, "There [was] always the sense of an authentic picture" of black life. And Brooks Atkinson of the *New York Times* wrote, "As [N]egro melodrama, *Harlem* has a ring of authenticity that comes from the [N]egro influence in its authorship."[26] The generally mixed reviews of the play notwithstanding, most of the responses in the press pointed to the impressive skill with which the neophyte, white director Chester Erskin and the playwrights, one black and one white, recreated Harlem life on the Apollo stage on 43rd Street (which is not to be confused with Harlem's Apollo Theatre on 125th Street, which opened in 1934).

Although it was not the phenomenal success that *Lulu Belle* had been in 1926, *Harlem* managed to turn a small profit during its brief run on Broadway. Produced by Edward A. Blatt (who, several decades later, was the company manager of the Broadway play *The Great White Hope*, starring James Earl Jones), *Harlem* opened on Broadway on February 20, 1929, and played 93 performances (just shy of the 100-performance mark deemed necessary to be considered an unqualified hit within the industry). A few months later, a national tour of the play opened in Chicago, and while some members of the African American community petitioned to close the show, proclaiming that it offered a distorted view of black life, the production did quite well.[27] In June of that year, the Broadway version closed rather abruptly after some financial rancor— the cast demanded they be paid the equivalent rates of other Broadway performers. The press reported that Erskin publicly called the actors "a bunch of crafty niggers" and that he vowed to shut down the show "not withstanding crowded houses."[28] Thurman spoke out against the reports and asserted Erskin's innocence. After reassembling the cast, which included just five members of the original Broadway company along with most of the actors from the touring cast, the producers transferred the show to the Eltinge Theatre on Forty-second Street on October 21, 1929. The timing could not have been worse. The stock market crashed exactly one week later, and the reopened *Harlem* closed after sixteen performances.

The play was the brainchild of Thurman, a major literary voice in the Harlem Renaissance and best known today for his novels *The Blacker the Berry* ... (1929) and *Infants of the Spring* (1932), both of which also depict Harlem life. Iconoclastic and caustic, Thurman riled the old guard of the Harlem Renaissance with his "lukewarm interest in promoting African American identity."[29]

Contemporary accounts by people who knew him, including Langston Hughes, Richard Bruce Nugent, and Dorothy West, describe him as self-loathing, morose, and extremely bitter. These qualities, Thurman's early critics claimed, were evident in his writing. In his review of *The Blacker the Berry,* W. E. B. Du Bois said that Thurman appeared to "deride blackness."[30] Recent scholarship, especially by Eleonore Van Notten, David R. Jarraway, Amritjit Singh, and Daniel M. Scott III, paints a different picture. Thurman's characters are far more varied than earlier thought. Rather than focusing on images of racial uplift or forwarding propaganda, Thurman created much more complex views of black life. He eschewed racial and sexual boundaries, and his work reflects this orientation. For example, in his novels he presents black characters who successfully pass for white (*Berry*) and ones who engage in both hetero-sexual and homosexual affairs (*Infants*). Thurman was intent on breaking down the barriers between the races, an effort best articulated by Raymond Taylor, the protagonist of *Infants of the Spring:* "Anything that will make white people and colored people come to the conclusion that after all they are all hu-man . . . the sooner amalgamation can take place and the Negro problem will cease to be a blot on American civilization."[31]

It is probably safe to surmise that this "amalgamation" was what Thurman had in mind when he enlisted the help of writer and friend William Jourdan Rapp to write a three-act play about the experiences of a representative black family in Harlem. Rapp, a former feature writer for the *New York Times* and ed-itor for *True Story Magazine,* had written the scripts for numerous radio soap operas and was a burgeoning playwright in his own right. By the time Rapp died in 1942 at age forty-seven, he had coauthored three other Broadway plays, including *Whirlpool* (1929), *Substitute for Murder* (1935), and *The Holmeses of Baker Street* (1936). None of these was as successful as *Harlem.* Rapp and Thur-man collaborated on two other plays, *Jeremiah the Magnificent* (1929),[32] which received just one performance in 1933, and *Black Cinderella* (1929), which was apparently never completed.

The basis for *Harlem* is Thurman's short story "Cordelia the Crude," which he wrote for the 1926 black literary magazine *Fire!!,* and which focuses on a young woman's descent into prostitution after the sexually reticent narrator gives her two dollars after their first tryst. The climax of the story takes place at a Harlem rent party and offers a sensationalized view of Harlem after dark. This depiction of Harlem became the raison d'être for the play and the backdrop for Rapp and Thurman's collaboration. Their partnership was, by all accounts, a felicitous one, and they established a strong, lasting friendship. Thurman's correspondence with Rapp from 1929, the year *Harlem* opened, to 1934, the year of Thurman's death, shows a strong professional and personal bond between the two men.[33] Thurman entrusted Rapp in managing his financial affairs during his divorce from Louise Thompson and asked that Rapp be the first to be notified of Thurman's death by the officials of the tuberculosis sanitarium where he died. In addition, Thurman confided in Rapp about the basis of the divorce suit, a sexual incident that occurred in the bathroom of 135th Street subway station. In a narrative that has a great deal in common with "Cordelia the Crude," twenty-three-year-old Wallace Thurman was broke, hungry, and without prospects, and he accepted two dollars from a man in exchange for sexual favors. When Thurman accepted, two plainclothes police officers emerged from the mop closet and took them both to jail. Thurman gave a phony name and address, spent two days in jail, and scrounged up $25 for the fine. The other man, a repeat offender, received a six-month sentence.[34]

The level of trust between Thurman and Rapp is also evident in the numerous articles they wrote in conjunction with the play's opening. In an essay unpublished in his lifetime, "My Collaborator," Thurman offers a glimpse of their working relationship:

> I have often wished for a movietone camera during our play writing sessions. Posterity should not be deprived of the picture of Bill Rapp, excited over the possibilities or difficulties of a scene, leaping from his chair, pacing the floor, frantically gesturing the while he shouts Negro dialect with decided East Side overtone.[35]

The essays also suggest why the final version of the playscript seems to be a jumble of different artistic perspectives. The play attempts to integrate Thurman's expertise in recording realistic scenes from Harlem nightlife with Rapp's experience writing radio soap opera. Even the onstage rent party, the high point of the show, seems tacked on. Most likely this impression has to do with the fact that it was a rather late addition to the play, the "wow" that producers claimed the script lacked in its earliest incarnation. In "Detouring *Harlem* to Times Square," Rapp and Thurman said that there were several versions of the play as they tried to "wow" the third act. They finally did, and Chester Erskin and Edward A. Blatt came aboard.[36]

When *Harlem* was finally produced, the problems with the script did not go unnoticed by the critics. The physical production received generally very favorable reviews, but the script was faulted for its disjointed craftsmanship. Many critics remarked that it was serviceable, but its tone and style were inconsistent and seemed to go in several different directions at once. Indeed, as indicated by the snippets from the reviews already quoted, *Harlem* is a "cobbling together" of familiar dramatic genres, including melodrama, social realism, and black folk play. As evidenced by the reactions in the popular press, however, in between the structural junctures of these dramaturgical forms there were flashes—or ephemeral snapshots—of presumably "natural" black behavior, "authentic" Harlem sights and sounds, and "real" black Harlemites (as opposed to actors) at work and play. The effects of this *re*construction reaffirmed the "truth" of those images for Broadway theatergoers, but at the same time, they also pointed to the constructedness of those images in the "real" Harlem.

In brief, the plot of *Harlem* centers around the Williamses, a poor and struggling black family in Harlem, and the tumultuous events that arise from a raucous rent party in their home one Saturday in late November. The play also includes a hard-boiled, young black woman who will stop at nothing in her quest for wealth and fame, gun-shooting gangsters, the murder of an oily gambler, the subsequent frame-up of a hardworking, young black man, and proper justice as generated by a shrewd white detective.[37] But at the core of the melodramatic maelstrom and musical mayhem is a modest black family trying to eke out a life in this strange new neighborhood. The audience learns within the first few minutes of the play that the family is new to Harlem, having only recently come north. The idealistic oldest son, Jasper, had recognized the numerous job opportunities that New York's industrial center promised, moved there with his own wife and children, and shortly afterward summoned his extended family to this "City of Refuge" from their economic and racial oppression in the Deep South. However, the promises of a better life have been unfulfilled, as articulated by the family's matriarch, referred to only as "Mother Williams," who calls Harlem a "City of Refuse." She proclaims:

> City of Refuge! Dat's what you wrote an' told us. Harlem is de City of Refuge. Is yo' shure you don' mean City of Refuse? Dat's all dere is heah. De people! Dese dark houses made out of de devil's brick, piled up high an' crowdin' one another an' smellin' worse dan our pig pen did back home in summer. City of Refuge! You—I—God, have mercy on our souls.[38]

From the outset, this ambivalence toward Harlem is at the heart of the play and recalls the situation in the real-life neighborhood. But the tension between the "actual" conditions and the presumed conditions, or those associated with images of Harlem from popular culture, is defused onstage for theatergoers as it was for tourists visiting the district after dark. On the one hand, the economic and social situation of the family is rather miserable, but on the other, the sensational and riotous atmosphere belies the play's ameliorative attitude toward their poverty.

In its various drafts prior to opening on Broadway, the play was called *Black Mecca, City of Refuge,* and *Black Belt,* but in all cases, *Harlem* intended to present an authentic view of the neighborhood from an insider's perspective. As responses in the black press confirmed, however, this "view" catered to that of its mostly white spectators. According to a report in the *New York Age,* an African American publication, the play's press representative said that no advance publicity or opening night tickets were sent to the black press because the "show was primarily for 'white consumption.'"[39] It was presumably intended to give whites a privileged view of Harlem that black people would not need to see since they lived it. The black press did attend, however, and the criticism surrounding the play echoed that which greeted *Nigger Heaven* three years before. Reactions to *Harlem* in the black press once again stimulated the debate over visibility-at-all-costs versus the propagation of positive black images. For example, Theophilus Lewis remarked on the equality of the play's black representations, presented within a dramatic form typically reserved for whites. That is, the play presents melodramatic black characters the same way in which white characters would be presented in a similar kind of play. Rather than addressing an essential black difference in the drama, which plays about "exotic" black life tended to do, Lewis believed that the playwrights fashioned a play around "ordinary" individuals. He wrote, "Its characters are not abnormal people presented in an appealing light but everyday people exaggerated and pointed up for the purpose of melodrama." Salem Tutt Whitney of the *Chicago Defender,* on the other hand, argued that the exaggerated images were particularly harmful to developing racial attitudes. In an argument similar to Du Bois's about Van Vechten's novel, he said:

> There is no denying the fact that "Harlem" possesses dramatic value. It moves swiftly. Events take place in rapid succession that sometimes thrill and always entertain. But it is impossible for us to like the story. It is the Race situation that furnishes the ground for my objection. Most of the white people who see "Harlem" say, and are anxious to say, that it is a true portrayal of Race life. They do not say one phase of our Race life. To me it is not realism, it is exaggeration. And thereby we are condemned as a race.[40]

Yet as these reviews depict, the most fascinating aspect of the play is the way in which it combines both "exaggerated" and "realistic" images of black life. The play's varied dramaturgical approaches reflect the constantly transforming terrain of Harlem and the futility of defining an "authentic" blackness. Thurman's utopian vision of an "amalgamation" of the races is only occasionally successful in the final product, and it more strongly points to the fragmentation and hybridity of a black identity shifting and buckling under the weight of excessive conflicting representations. The pressure of accommodating the demands of a popular theater apparatus—intent on confirming racial stereotypes—all but makes the work of two artists trying to transcend racial categorization burst at its seams. If we employ Homi Bhabha's terminology, examining the "in-between spaces" of the extremes of "realism" and "exaggeration" shows the impossibility of claiming a "truth" for a particular race of people, and this in itself is a form of transcending racial categorization.[41]

"GO, HARLEM, GO HARLEM, GO"

Framed by a rather hackneyed melodramatic structure, the underlying motive for the play is undoubtedly its presumed presentation of naturalness and unfettered scenes from black life. To this end, the play celebrated pluralism, but one could argue that it also reaffirmed attitudes of white superiority. This was accomplished in a few subtle ways. Most obviously, it recapitulated the exoticizing white gaze. Unlike those attending an actual Harlem nightclub or rent party, white theatergoers could sit in their orchestra seats and study the customs and behavior of the Blacks onstage, whom the publicists went to great length to say came directly from Harlem. The play allowed audiences an opportunity to penetrate black life, in a manner similar to Viscountess Weymouth's Van Vechten–escorted excursion, while maintaining a comfortable social distance, which is not guaranteed in an integrated club or party.

The segregated theater conditions contributed to the separation of the races. The irony of this is evident in a letter that Wallace Thurman wrote to his *Harlem* collaborator William Jourdan Rapp: "Five different times I have bought seats for myself to see *Harlem*—including opening night—and tho I asked for center aisle seats (as much as a week in advance) not yet have I succeeded in not being put on the side in a little section where any other Negro who happened to buy an orchestra seat was also placed."[42] Audiences could gawk at the black actors on stage, but they were not compelled to come into contact with them from their unobstructed and comfortable positions in the socially hierarchical

Broadway theaters. Under these circumstances, *Harlem* on Broadway offered a view of Harlem that few audience members would have had the opportunity to see in real life.

Most of the play occurs in the Williamses' household, a five-room, 132nd Street railroad flat, which the family shares with several tenants. The setting's careful attention to physical and atmospheric detail, as described in the stage descriptions, pictures from the production, and critical responses, demonstrates the way in which the production strove for photographic realism of a Harlem flat. Reconstructed in a highly naturalistic manner, the apartment is in need of repair, "feebly lit," and constantly assaulted by outside noises such as the screeches of clothes line pulleys, screaming and cursing neighbors, and the "salacious moans of a deep toned blues singer" emanating from a nearby Victrola. The audience is constantly reminded that the Williamses' home is cramped and the rest of the neighborhood is closing in on it, invoking the crowded living conditions of the community.

The careful attention to details of the environment (within the confines of the Williamses' home as well as its relationship to the "real" Harlem) is indicative of the play's claim to naturalism. The description of the set, for example, seems to be a direct imitation of Strindberg's "backdrop-at-an-angle" design that enhanced the naturalistic effect of *Miss Julie*. In the stage descriptions, the playwrights say that the living room of the Williamses' home is to be constructed "on a slant in relation to the footlights, so that the end of the rear wall on the right is nearer the front wall on the left."[43] Because this gives the sense that the walls are literally closing in on the characters (from the audience's standpoint anyway), the design would reduce the playing space, causing the flat to appear crowded and too small for the family and the several lodgers. More importantly, however, is the sense that the play offered a wholly different view of Harlem. The effect of this slanted depiction of the Harlem home would be what Strindberg called "an unfamiliar perspective" for the audience.[44] The play's naturalistic setting offered a perspective of Harlem seldom seen by tourists—the private, domestic lives of Harlem residents.

Through this heightened realism and overt claims of "authenticity," Thurman and Rapp wanted to galvanize new images of African Americans and the neighborhood. Previously, works using the neighborhood as their setting tended to depict Harlem's public spaces, such as the streets, nightclubs, and speakeasies. But *Harlem* not only offered an after-hours view of the neighborhood, it also depicted a domestic side of the community. As Una Chaudhuri says in her discussion of stage naturalism, this manner of disclosure of the private within a public sphere allows for a theater of "total visibility," or one that promises to "deliver the whole truth" of the world it unmasks.[45] Even though the play's exposure of a private realm pointed to the dire economic and social situation of the neighborhood's residents, its emphasis on crime, jazz, and sultry dancing also revealed the depths of the presumed mysterious, exotic world of lower-class black people. The realistic scenic design and staging exposed the peripheries of the primitive, unrestrained behavior of black people in their natural setting.

The play's heightened realism and presumed authenticity also stemmed from the careful attention applied to the dialogue. According to press reports, the playwrights attempted to capture the speech patterns and singular phrases of the neighborhood and to further portray the foreignness of Harlem. To this end, they liberally peppered the script with "genuine" bits of dialogue supposedly spoken by native Harlemites. The "Glossary of Harlemisms" (an authenticating device Carl Van Vechten also employed in *Nigger Heaven*) listed in the playbill included twenty-four terms, defined so white audiences would not feel alienated by the language. A few examples include:

Sweetback. A colored gigolo, or man who lives off women.
Dicty. Highbrow.
Monkey-hip-eater. A derisive name applied to a Barbados Negro; supposed to have originated with the myth that Barbados Negroes are passionately fond of monkey meat, particularly "monkey hips with dumplings."
Chippy. A tart; a fly, undiscriminating young wench.
Mess-around. A whirling dance; a part of the Charleston.
38 and 2. That's fine.
Forty. Okay.[46]

The use of these terms and the printed translation may have provided local color and a level of verity to the play, but there is also a potential parodic element in their inclusion.

In the play language is used in a manner similar to the black folklore recorded by Zora Neale Hurston. In the introduction to *Mules and Men* (1935), Hurston describes rural black folk's use of language as a method of resistance. That is, they will speak only in "pleasantries" and superficialities and not divulge what they truly think and feel to meddlesome whites. According to Hurston, Blacks' language to strangers is evasive, and while white strangers may think they understand black speech, they really don't: "He can read my writing but he sho' can't read my mind. I'll put this play toy in his hand, and he will seize it and go away. Then I'll say my say and sing my song."[47] While white Broadway audiences assumed that the glossary was provided as a tool for cracking the code created by idiomatic expressions and regional dialect, this may have been Thurman's elaborate play toy for the audiences.

Parodic or not, Thurman and Rapp took great pains in the press to argue that the value of *Harlem* was not simply as a form of entertainment. In an article written together called "Few Know Harlem, the City of Surprises," they state that the play highlights the differences between black and white people, which boils down to class distinctions. They point out, for example, that there is a steadily increasing black middle class, who similar to their white counterparts "go for vacations in Europe, Atlantic City, the Maine woods and Southern California." But on the other hand, they state, "There are some phenomena peculiar to Harlem alone, phenomena which are inherently expressions of the Negro character before it was conditioned by the white world that now surrounds him." These main differences include the numbers game, which they call "Harlem's most popular indoor sport and the outlet for the Negro's craving for gambling," and the house rent parties. They report, "Some people have found rent parties so profitable that they have become professional givers of house rent parties, getting their whole income from them." Although the playwrights insist that the community is marked by its economic and ethnic diversity, it is the last two "institutions peculiar to Harlem" and not the hobbies of the "Americanized" black middle class that are given life in their play.[48]

The comments reinforce the notion that class, as Martin Favor explains, is "a primary marker of racial difference."[49] Du Bois indicated as much when he invited *Crisis* readers to respond to a questionnaire about appropriate representations of black people in art and literature. Among other questions associated with class differences, he asked: "Can publishers be criticized for refusing to handle novels that portray Negroes of education and accomplishment, on the grounds that these characters are no different from white folk and therefore not interesting?"[50] The question itself points to the conflation of middle-classness with whiteness (and bland normalcy). "Authentic blackness," then, is not determined by the color of one's skin but primarily by the (lower) class status of the black individual.

Within this conceptual framework, Thurman and Rapp attempted to present a more complex portrayal of familiar character types. In another joint essay, for instance, they claim that their play earns the right to be called "educational theatre" because *Harlem* "presents the [N]egro as he is," rather than reasserting the age-old images of the "stage Negroes," or as they bluntly call them, "white folks' niggers." The latter images, according to the authors, consist of "the old servant or mammy type known derisively among Harlemites as 'Uncle Toms' and 'handkerchiefs,' the lazy slowfoot type typified by such vaudevillians as Bert Williams and [the *Shuffle Along* creators] Miller and Lyles, and the superstitious, praying type who is always thrown into abject fear by darkness, lightning and thunder." In the same article, they quote an unnamed black critic who praises the play for making black people "understandable" to white audiences and for "educating the theater-going public." The critic writes: "The [white] man in the orchestra seat may not sympathize with [the black characters'] motives, but he can readily understand them. And understanding these characters helps him to better comprehend the concrete Negroes he has seen in the subway or reads about in the crime columns of the newspapers."[51] Of course, as the critic implies, these two nonsegregated arenas would have been the most common places for whites to encounter black people directly.

To Thurman and Rapp, *Harlem* would offer a different version of the incomprehensible, scandal-driven image propagated in the press and in literature. Therefore, in order to make the "inhabitants" of Harlem's Black Belt understandable, they presented a cross-section of "concrete Negroes," reflecting the multiple, often conflicting, and sometimes derogatory representations of Blacks in Harlem. The play and its Broadway production, however, were constantly at odds with this objective. The goal of redefining Blacks on the Broadway stage was a noble one, but nevertheless it often perpetuated "exotic" and "primitive" images of African Americans. For example, a publicity handbill hailed the play for those very images: "Harlem! The City that Never Sleeps! A Strange, Exotic Island in the Heart of New York! Rent Parties! Number Runners! Chippies! Jazz Love! Primitive Passion!"[52] The "educational" intentions of Thurman and Rapp were pitted against the desires of Broadway theatergoers, who expected to see a version of the "real" as perpetuated by *Nigger Heaven* or *Lulu Belle*.

The public relations campaign helped to ensure that these expectations would be met, and it often reconfirmed the worst possible stereotypes of black people in its effort to demonstrate the "naturalness" of the performances on stage. One of the most egregious examples of this appears in a *New York Times* profile of the twenty-five-year-old director Chester Erskin two weeks after the show opened. Erskin, according to the article, understood "that good [N]egro dramatic players are rare," so he "visited dives, speakeasies, rent parties, restaurants, cabarets and private homes" to find suitable, authentic "personalities" for

EDWARD A. BLATT *presents*

"HARLEM"

THE THRILLING PLAY OF NEW YORK'S BLACK BELT

By William Jourdan Rapp and Wallace Thurman   *Staged by* Chester Erskin

Harlem! . . . The City that Never Sleeps! . . . A
Strange, Exotic Island in the Heart of New York! . . .
Rent Parties! . . . Sweetbacks! . . . Hincty Wenches!
Number runners! . . . Chippies! . . . Jazz Love! . . .
Primitive Passion! . . . Voodeo! . . . Hot-stuff
Men! . . . Uproarious Comedy! . . . Powerful Drama!

MAJESTIC THEATRE
CHICAGO

Commencing Sunday Night, APRIL 28th

FIG. 2. *Harlem* program cover for the touring production at the Majestic Theatre in
Chicago circa 1930. Artist unknown. (Billy Rose Theatre Division, The New York Public
Library for the Performing Arts, Astor, Lenox and Tilden Foundations.)

his production. The young director accumulated his cast in this manner, and with the patience that "could give Job a tussle," Erskin "instructed" his cast on the fine points of acting. Reconfirming a stereotypical notion that black people are naturally inferior to whites, the article explains the procedure in which Erskin staged the play:

> [Erskin's] first direction was to make his players repeat the lines after him, word for word, until they could recite them from memory. Then he permitted a few gestures and later he taught them the art of entrances and exits and how to ignore the audience. When they proved a bit slow in grasping things, their great lament was: "You know, Misto' Erskin, we'se colored people. We cain't think as fast as white folks." When the play actually opened and they were praised for their individual performances they replied, "Misto' Erskin done it."

While Thurman and Rapp took great pains in their attempts to banish the "Uncle Tom" and "the lazy slowfoot" types from their play, as well as the white cultural imagination, the publicity reinserted it. The article concludes with another instance of the childlike image associated with African Americans in a tribute to Erskin's paternal patience and kindness: "[The black actors] at first insisted that he sit in the front row and watch them during every performance and often he still does. Whenever they are applauded they look in his direction for his approval."[53] The playwrights were evidently powerless to halt the Broadway publicity machinery that relied on such tactics to make a "black play" sell to its mostly white audiences. Yet the conflicting images, which combined those based on elements left over from minstrelsy with more progressive representations, enacted the struggle to form a fully integrated black identity. In this regard, the play *Harlem* mirrored the racial complexities that characterized the neighborhood.

"THE DOOMED CHILDREN OF HAM"

The characters of the play are from the poor working class, and the neighborhood is certainly taking its toll, especially on the older characters. They are being gradually subsumed by the effects of modernization. On one level, the exposure of the social and economic conditions of the characters was not unlike other Broadway plays of the era that theatrically realized the lives of the urban poor. Although contemporary descriptions of the play highlighted the racy rent party dancing and the melodramatic hijinks of the gangsters and detectives who appear prominently in the play, *Harlem* also evokes the social realism of such plays as DuBose and Dorothy Heyward's *Porgy* (1927) and Elmer Rice's *Street Scene* (1929). The genre was a familiar one on Broadway in the 1920s, and the plays within the category tended to address the distressing results of "an oppressive urban environment."[54] As with these plays, *Harlem* stresses the tragic dehumanization of its characters as a result of city living, and points to the personal and familial rifts that the corrupting environment causes. In Thurman and Rapp's play, for instance, several of the characters pine for a simpler (though far from idyllic) southern lifestyle, which they have recently left, and they repudiate the northern urban environment, which now consumes them.

One of the most caustic and darkly comic expressions of this urban discontent is Father's response to another character's complaint about the crowded subway conditions. He answers, "Dey may lynch you down home, but dey shure don't squeeze you to death on no subway."[55] Whereas the South has its share of random misery, the North's modern conditions are much more stifling and suffocating (both physically and socially). According to Father, there is, ironically, far less freedom for black people in this new environment than there had been in the South. It is certainly not the "City of Refuge" black migrants had been promised. For Broadway audiences, however, *Harlem*'s constricting backdrop seems little more than a mere gripe for party poopers like Mother and Father who complain nonstop about the living conditions and who refuse to enjoy the raucous rent party.

In addition to the Broadway realism of the play, there are characteristics of other genres that were also prevalent in the 1920s. These variant dramaturgical components, as several critics pointed out, do not always successfully meld in *Harlem*. Brooks Atkinson, for instance, called the play "a rag-bag drama and high pressure blow-out all in one," and Richard Lockridge described it as "a play which at its least is sudden melodrama, broken by pistol shots, and at its best a colorful, changing picture of the dark civilization within our lighter one."[56] Arthur Ruhl saw a dramatic structural divide based on the supposed logical outcome of its racially divergent authors. He writes that the play "was composed of two different strains, and one of these what might be described as the white or Broadway element overlaid the black."[57] Judging from the critics' reactions, one can see that the familiar conceits of the melodrama and social realism (forms associated with white playwrights) did not integrate well with the "authentic" pictures of black life (identified with Thurman's contribution).

The opening of the play, for example, juxtaposes the expectations of the urban social realism drama, and its tawdry, tragic implications, with a kinder, gentler form. Aside from the laments about the ill effects of urbanization,

Harlem later gives the impression that it is closer in form to a folk drama, which tended to employ provincial settings. For instance, the first act begins in the Williams household as the family prepares for the rent party, and the act concludes with the party itself. Little else happens between. The characters clean, discuss burned bread, and debate whether or not they are better off in Harlem than they were down South. *New York World* critic Alison Smith praised this slice-of-life aspect of the play, stating, "It has the deep, half unconscious thrill of compassion which the Negro actors give to a study of nostalgia, the bewildered, inarticulate homesickness of a little family, lured from their North Carolina cabin into the smouldering jungle of Harlem."[58] The domestic setting and the leisurely unfolding of the action bear the hallmarks of black folk drama form, especially in its presentation of a family faced with adversity. This form, incidentally, would not have been a completely unfamiliar one to many in the audience at Harlem.

The black folk drama was primarily a staple of church groups and playwriting competitions in black journals, and the plays occasionally appeared in commercial theaters. In fact, the first nonmusical play written by an African American to appear on Broadway, Willis Richardson's *The Chip Woman's Fortune* (1923), fit this genre. Historically, the folk drama form, to which Richardson subscribed, was consciously modeled after the Irish folk plays of writers such as J. M. Synge and Lady Gregory—a comparison echoed by Heywood Broun's remarks. Just as Thurman and Rapp intended to banish the "white folks' niggers" from their play, the Irish authors intended to banish the stereotypically sentimental, drunk, and pugnacious "stage Irishman" and instead depict honestly the provincial Irish.[59] Similarly, the African American folk playwrights attempted to capture, in James Hatch and Leo Hamalian's description, "the everyday life of ordinary black people during hard times."[60] The hand wringing, destitute Mother of *Harlem*, for instance, who continually prays for the souls of her family, seems to be the direct descendant of the keening Maurya in Synge's *Riders to the Sea* (1904). An indication of this background occurs midway through the first act, when Mother, overwhelmed by the family's misfortunes and their propensities for rent parties, "buries her head in her hands and sways the upper part of her body," beseeching: "Father in heaven! Father in heaven! Forgive dis sinful household. Lawd, fo'give dem. Save my poor wicked children. Watch over dem. Show dem de light. Guide dem, Father. Shield dem from de devil and cleanse der bodies with de Holy Spirit. Amen! Father! Amen!"[61] Yet pitted against the urban realities of this play, the folk characteristics come off as quaint, nostalgic, and outdated.

The two oldest family members, Mother and Father, for instance, are par-

ticularly denotative of the folk drama form. They represent bucolic domesticity, but they are subsumed by urban industry. The stage directions, for example,
describe Mother as a "typical southern woman, ready to moan and pray at the
slightest provocation,"[62] but she has no control over her children. About Father,
a large, gruff man, the stage directions say, "The North has rendered him help-
less. He is just a big hulk being pushed around by economic necessity."[63] Displaced and discontent, Mother and Father represent what Alain Locke in 1925
called the "Old Negro." That is, as opposed to the "New Negro," who is "inevitably moving forward under the control largely of his own objectives,"
Mother and Father represent the previous generation of Blacks who lack autonomy, consciousness, and self-respect. These characters are bereft of proper
names in the play perhaps because, as Locke also explains, the Old Negro "was
more of a formula than a human being—a something to be argued about, condemned or defended, to be 'kept down,' or 'in his place,' or patronized, a social
bogey or a social burden."[64] Even more significantly, the parents lack control
over their family as well as the rent party in their home. The parental roles actually belong to Jasper, who brought the family to Harlem, and his sister
Cordelia, who runs the household.

Mother and Father have succumbed to what Cornel West describes as the
"white world's view" of themselves and their condition.[65] They have little or no
agency and do not foresee that black people will improve their conditions; in
short, they have accepted the circumstances of white supremacy. Mother places
all of her hope for progress in religion, and Father has simply lost hope that
black people will endure in a white world. As Father despairingly explains, "Dey
ain't nothin' for a nigger nowhere. We's de doomed children of Ham."[66] Their
"devaluation" and "degradation" have essentially made them void of effective-
ness in the environment in which they are placed. As West argues in relation to
Ellison's *The Invisible Man* (1952), when total submission or hopelessness satu-
rates a black individual, the situation renders him or her invisible and without
humanity, hence "nameless."[67] Mother's and Father's own namelessness corre-
sponds with their lack of connection to a community, and as West also writes,
the "theme of black rootlessness and homelessness is inseparable from black
namelessness."[68] For Father, the sense of eternal displacement, no matter where
he is placed, has turned in on itself to become a racial hatred, which is evident
in an exchange with Jasper:

> FATHER: You know what's wrong wid' Harlem? Dey's too many niggers! Dat's
> it—too many niggers.
> JASPER: You said the same thing 'bout down home.[69]

The exchange also shows the suffocating effects of segregation. The lack of diversity in a ghetto produces frustration and dissatisfaction among the clustered masses.

Whereas Mother and Father appear antiquated and ineffectual in this environment, and the hope of a new homeland for industrious African Americans and a place where they may establish roots is unrealized, the promise of social betterment is rendered through their oldest son, twenty-eight-year-old Jasper. He represents the epitome of Locke's definition of the "New Negro" and is the model of racial uplift that Du Bois and others advocated in the black arts. Unlike his parents, Jasper is forward thinking, hardworking, and optimistic about improved social conditions for Blacks. More importantly, rather than being subsumed by Harlem, he is empowered by it. He says about his environment, "Why, Harlem is the greatest place in the world for Negroes. You can be a man here. You can ride in the subway and go anywhere your money an' sense can carry you."[70] In direct contrast to his father's *un*manly inability to lead the family, hold a job, or secure self-respect, Jasper is autonomous, driven, and self-reliant. He also represents the powerful synthesizing of the black split subjectivity as articulated in W. E. B. Du Bois's definition of "double consciousness." In Du Bois's system of black empowerment, Jasper represents the fulfillment of the desire to integrate the fractionated black (male) subject, which Du Bois describes as the "longing to attain self-conscious manhood, to merge the double self into a better and truer self" and ultimately "make it possible for a man to be both a Negro and an American, without being cursed and spit upon by his fellows, without having the doors of Opportunity closed roughly in his face."[71] In the first act of the play, the Williams home becomes a battleground for the opposing forces of the Old and New Negro, and Locke's ideas are given dramatic immediacy.

These dialectical representations personify the transformational black cultural identity of the 1920s. As Stuart Hall articulates, "Cultural identities come from somewhere, have histories. But, like everything that is historical, they undergo constant transformation. Far from being eternally fixed in some essentialized past, they are subject to the continuous 'play' of history, culture and power."[72] The Williams home symbolizes the nexus of black culture. Past and present collide here, and black cultural identity is (to reiterate Bhabha) "in the process of being formed." But this process is certainly not without resistance. If Mother and Father represent what Blacks used to be, and Jasper represents what Blacks are "becoming" according to Alain Locke's specifications, then thrown into this atmosphere is the menace to that cultural identity, Cordelia Williams, Harlem's Pandora, Lulu Belle, and Lasca Sartoris all rolled into one.

"SUGAR FOOT MISTERS AN' SUN DODGIN' SISTERS"

Cordelia, the oldest Williams daughter, is the central character of the play and the cause of the sensational events that occur. Her madcap machinations threaten to bring down the entire house and throw the dramaturgical structure off-kilter. In fact, by the beginning of the rent party, it is clear that the quaint black folk drama form combined with the urban social realism cannot repress the divisive, unrestrained, and explosive energy that Cordelia has unleashed on this vision of the Harlem neighborhood. Near the end of act 1, the play has veered off from the picturesque realism and into full-blown melodrama, reminiscent of the white-concocted *Lulu Belle*. Similar to the title character of that play, and also like Lasca Sartoris in *Nigger Heaven* (comparisons several critics invoked), Cordelia is a brazen, hard-hearted, young black woman. Walter Winchell referred to her in his review as a "chippie off the old block,"[73] and throughout *Harlem,* she is variously referred to as a "chippie" (or a loose woman), a "hincty [or "snooty"] wench," and a "good-for-nothin' strumpet." While Mother, Father, and Jasper evoke issues of race associated with class, Cordelia is defined by her alluring, but dangerous, sexuality. From her initial appearance, the stage directions make this perfectly clear:

> [Cordelia] is about eighteen years old and has dark brown skin and bobbed hair. She is an overmatured, southern girl, selfish, lazy, and sullen. She is inspired by activity or joy only when some erotic adventure confronts her or a good time is in view. She has no feeling for her parents or for her brothers and sisters. Considering herself a woman of the world, she holds their opinions and advice in contempt. She is extremely sensual and has an abundance of sex appeal. Her body is softly rounded and graceful. Her every movement and gesture is calculated to arouse a man's eroticism.[74]

Cordelia's uninhibited sexuality and uncontrollable need for excitement explode the conventions of the outmoded folk drama form, and she sets the melodramatic apparatus into play. The backdrop for this modern morality play is the sexually charged onstage rent party (or as the playbill's glossary defines it, "A Saturday night orgy staged to raise money to pay the landlord"), which Cordelia commandeers.

By the end of the first act, the guests and musicians have all arrived, and the party is in full swing. Robert Littell referred to this scene as "a queer, sordid, good-natured orgy, with fifteen or more couples hugging each other in the most extraordinary dances."[75] The scene was particularly significant in that it re-created the Harlem that audiences wanted to see: A Harlem infused with sultry jazz music and torrid dancing. According to the responses in the press, the dancing in this scene was "sensual," "barbaric," and "anything but lovely" (one critic described it as "grizzly bear dancing"). The stage directions confirm that its blatant allusion to sexual activity was the intended result. The playwrights describe the staging in the following manner:

> Body calls to body. They cement themselves together with limbs lewdly intertwined. Another couple is dipping to the floor and slowly shimmying belly to belly as they come back to an upright position. A slender, dark girl with wild eyes and wilder hair stands in the center of the room supported by the strong lithe arms of a longshoreman. Her eyes are closed. Her teeth bite into her lower lip. Her trunk is bent backward until her head hangs below her waist, and all the while the lower portion of her body is quivering like so much agitated Jell-O.[76]

As evidenced by the critical responses, the erotic, "quivering" black bodies on display in this scene delivered the third act "wow" that the playwrights so desperately sought.

For some critics, the scene underscored the supposed cultural and instinctual differences between black people and white people. Richard Lockridge, for example, referred to the black dancers as "unself-conscious and barbaric," and in the rent party scene "the members of the cast seem to forget they are acting and . . . give themselves over to rhythms which the [N]egro has brought to the white man and which the white man, however he may try, is always a little too self-conscious to accept."[77] The seemingly "natural" and spontaneous dancing on view in the rent party scene reiterated the entrenched view of an undeniable black primitivism. For Broadway audiences accustomed to seeing the energetic, precisely choreographed dances of musical comedies and revues, the undulating, groping black dancers offered a physicality that seemed unrehearsed, unrestrained, and unconscious. That is, the scene authenticated the romantic and popular notion that black people are *naturally* "exotic" and "primitive." Lockridge, for example, went even further in his review to argue that the overtly sexual dancing actually made the melodramatic murders in the play's plot frighteningly believable. The glimpses of "actual" black behavior provided a backdrop for the formulaic aspects of the play, which gave the production a layer of truth and authenticity. He states that the actors "dance lustily, swayingly, shamelessly and reveal the simplicity and deep earthiness of their race's hold on life. And the melodrama of murder is made the more real and plausi-ble by the revelation which the dancing gives of their uncerebral directness. Men and women who dance like that have the strength for violence."[78] To this particular critic, the primal movement of the black dancers, framed within the proscenium at the Apollo Theatre on Broadway, pointed to a presumed histor-ical and biological primitiveness and barbarism associated with black bodies.

Similarly, Whitney Bolton wrote that he was "not at all sure that many of the players didn't forget they were on a stage and believed themselves actually participants in a rent party." Therefore, the enactment of the rent party poten-tially granted what Barbara Kirshenblatt-Gimblett describes as an "unmediated encounter" for the Broadway audiences, or one in which the "performances . . . create the illusion that the activities one watches are being *done* rather than *rep-resented,* a practice that creates the illusion of authenticity, or realness."[79] Sepa-rate from the contrivances of the play's plotting, the rent party scene offered not just an image of the "real," but an interaction with it and moments of com-plicity in the illusion. As Robert Littell wrote about this sensation, "Stage par-ties are as a rule pretty terrible, but the [N]egro rent-paying guests throw them-selves into it with such spontaneous go and enthusiasm that one feels as if one was there."[80]

The unrestrained sexual behavior that characterized this appreciation for Harlem, however, was not completely at home on the notoriously conservative Broadway. Activities tolerated and applauded in Harlem were cause for arrest on Broadway as a result of the Wales Padlock Law established in 1927. As Brooks Atkinson explains in his 1970 book *Broadway,* this law "empowered the police to arrest the producers, authors, and actors of plays that the police disapproved of, and to padlock the theater for a year if the courts brought in a verdict of guilty."[81] About *Harlem* and its salacious rent party scene, Burns Mantle of the *Daily News* cautioned that some theatergoers might be offended by the erotic "animalistic exhibitions" of the " 'Harlem' realists" because "unfortunately there are likely to be those in the audience who are a bit sensitive about learning the facts of life in mixed company."[82] Some of the other critics feared as well that the overly suggestive dancing by the fifty-or-so supernumeraries might cause the police to halt the show and close it down. Atkinson predicted in the *Times* review that the show would have a good run, "Or will if the police censors, who were in the audience last evening do not clang down Forty-second Street with their patrol wagons."[83] Like Atkinson, Bide Dudley of the *Evening World* im-plied that the censor might forcefully tone down the "exaggerated dancing" a bit, but Whitney Bolton said that "such dancing is on view in any [N]egro cabaret and if the police interfere with this, they ought, in fairness, to interfere uptown."[84] There were, however, no raids upon *Harlem.*

Although chiefly a gimmick to attract audiences who craved the exuberant and sensational side of Harlem, the rent party also figured rather importantly in the plot. Cordelia, who represents this image of the devil-may-care Harlemite, uses the party as an opportunity to seduce one of the guests, the "shy and slippery" Roy, a "numbers runner,"[85] and impetuously, she agrees to move in with him without the benefit of marriage. And just as Lulu Belle tormented the upstanding and faithful George and led him to ruin with her own wily ways, and Lasca Sartoris brought about the destruction of Byron Kason in *Nigger Heaven*, Cordelia leads the young man who thought he could domesticate her, the love-struck Basil, to the brink of a murder he is later accused of committing. As the curtain descends on the first act, and as the dancing at the rent party becomes more intense, Basil vows to "slit" Roy's "dirty guts" while Cordelia exits with "loud mocking laughter."[86] The slice-of-life portrait of Harlem all but dissipates, and the high-speed melodramatic antics precipitated at the end of act 1 continue into act 2. The second act takes place in Roy's apartment, where he and Cordelia have begun to make a home for themselves (in time sequence, it takes place almost immediately after the first act). Whereas the previous act takes its time in building the momentum that culminates in the rent party, in this, the shortest of the acts, the events unfurl at a breathless pace. First we meet Kid Vamp, Roy's dashing but insidious "banker." When Cordelia goes out for cigarettes, the "Kid" kills Roy for withholding money from him and hides the body behind an arras. By the end of the act, and after several dramatic twists and turns, Cordelia, not knowing that the "Kid" is a murderer, promises to move in with him. In addition, Basil, who has followed Cordelia to Roy's apartment, gets into a fight with the Kid. (Cordelia has exited again and does not witness it.) Basil is knocked out in the tussle, and the Kid seizes the opportunity to place the gun in Basil's hand, framing him for Roy's murder. And in nail-biting melodramatic fashion, Basil resumes consciousness as the police are banging on the door, and he flees out the bathroom window to safety.

By the third act, Cordelia has returned home where the rent party continues, and she has implicated her entire family in the swirl of disorder she initiated. It will take an outside (white) presence to sort things out. In this act, the various theatrical genres crash together and create an atmosphere of combustible energy. Once again, returning to the Williamses' home, the play reverts to its previous social realism and folk drama forms. For example, there are two rather lengthy bits in which Dr. Voodeo, a dealer of spiritual powders and herbs, and the Hot-Stuff Man, a dealer in stolen clothing, ply their wares. Neither character advances the plot, but they provide local color and offer a glimpse into particular aspects of black life. The Hot-Stuff Man explains, for instance, that he does such strong business in Harlem because black people cannot appear to be poor if they are to be accepted by white society. He says: "Folks in Harlem has to dress. They gotta' look as good or betta than white folks and they don' have as much money to spend. It takes fellows like me to fix 'em up—see?"[87] The scenes with these characters give way to the obligatory unraveling of the melodramatic crime, which is the central feature of the act. The tension builds increasingly, and the act includes a shoot-out, the death of the villain (Kid Vamp), and the vindication of the hero (Basil).

The troubles wrought upon the house by Cordelia are sorted out by Detective Sergeant Palmer (named Donohue in the original script)—the sole white character in the play. His presence, even in this predominantly black neighborhood, serves as a palpable reminder of the social hierarchy of the 1920s and affirms what many race theorists argue: Race as a legal construct cannot be denied.[88] In this hot pot of lawlessness and social unrest, the white patriarchal figure is on the scene almost immediately to solve the problems among the black residents and restore order to this very public domestic space. The hope for an autonomous, independent black (male) leader, as embodied by Jasper, is dashed. It turns out Jasper is powerless to control his sister, and a white deus ex machina is necessary to settle the chaos. As Daniel Gerould explains, this reinscription of the social status quo is typical of melodrama, and according to C. W. E. Bigsby, early-twentieth-century realism is characterized by "a faith in social and metaphysical order which remained curiously untroubled."[89] The play ends as Cordelia, rebellious as ever, exits the Harlem flat with one of the party's musicians, Ippy (for those who are keeping count, he is her fourth lover in the play), vowing to be a star on the stage. Mother, on the other hand, is overwhelmed by the events of the evening, and defeatingly cries, "Lawd! Lawd! Tell me! Tell me! Dis ain't de City of Refuge?"[90]

The plaintive sigh of Mother is overshadowed by the sensational exit of Cordelia and the possibilities that lie ahead for her. As Ippy explains,

She don' have to stay in Harlem. Look at Josephine Baker—makin' all Paris stand on its head! Look what Florence Mills did! Look at Ethel Waters! Why Delia got more than all of them—more voice, more shape, more pep to her dancing! Given a chance and someone to coach her, she'd set the world on fire.[91]

FIG. 3. Isabel Washington, star of Rapp and Thurman's *Harlem* and future wife of Adam Clayton Powell, Jr. Washington is shown here in a publicity pose for *Singin' the Blues* (1931) in which she appeared with her sister Fredi Washington. © De Barron Studios. (Billy Rose Theatre Division, The New York Public Library for the Performing Arts, Astor, Lenox and Tilden Foundations.)

According to the reviews in the popular press, this assessment was not too much of an exaggeration. Isabel Washington apparently played the role to the hilt in the original New York production and received mostly raves. Alison Smith described her performance as "almost fatally realistic." Robert Garland referred to her as "Vivid, cheap as cheap can be, you believe in her and her tawdry affairs." Robert Littell wrote, "The wild, raucous, hard-boiled, sensuous abandon of Isabel Washington is worth going a long way to see," and "Miss Washington's inexhaustible natural pep, and a gorgeous hoarse voice, which blows out of her like a factory whistle when she is angry, makes this character something quite new and fascinating." On the other hand, Whitney Bolton found her performance offensive in its unrestrained physical exhibition of sexuality, and in his review said that the producer, Edward A. Blatt, should "urge Miss Washington to curb her dislocations in the interest of peace and prosperity." Likewise, Bide Dudley of the *Evening World* suggested that she "pipe down a bit" and rein in her unseemly lewdness.[92]

Paradoxically, the excessiveness of Washington's performance was hailed, or disparaged in a few cases, because of its remarkable "naturalness." The reactions to the performance recall similar points that Alisa Solomon makes in her discussion of Nora in Ibsen's *A Doll's House*. Just as actresses playing Nora created a stir in their offensive portrayals of "inappropriate behavior" for upstanding women, Washington's performance as Cordelia registers as "naturalistic" precisely because it is "unbecoming."[93] This "unladylike," predatory manner was indeed not strictly a "new and fascinating" creation, as Littel writes. To a large extent, expectations of black femininity had already been conditioned by what people had read about or seen in other Broadway shows and in the nightclubs uptown. Lasca Sartoris from *Nigger Heaven* and Lulu Belle from Sheldon and MacArthur's play, for example, were well-known representations of the trope of the female, black, sexual snare. Isabel Washington, however, supplied an additional layer of authenticity to her performance that may qualify it as "new and fascinating": Unlike the stage incarnations of the aforementioned black characters, Washington was actually an African American. The few times that *Nigger Heaven* had been represented in musical reviews the performers were in blackface, and Lenore Ulric, a white actress, likewise played Lulu Belle in blackface. Therefore, the representation was certainly not new, but the chippie of Rapp and Thurman's *Harlem* was at least played by a black woman.

The fate of Cordelia in the play represents an even more transgressive dramaturgical act. Rapp and Thurman may have given the Broadway backers the third act "wow" they demanded, but the playwrights did not budge on the fate of Cordelia. In typical melodramatic structure, decadent and dangerous Cordelia, along with the gangsters and murderers, should have been punished (or destroyed) in the end. Accordingly, good must will out in the moralistic framework of the well-made play. In fact, Rapp and Thurman were advised to rewrite the ending of *Harlem* to make it more palatable for Broadway audiences and the New York censor. Ben Hecht and Charles MacArthur, the playwrights of the smash hit *The Front Page* (1928), and the latter the cowriter of *Lulu Belle*, offered a detailed scenario for the recommended revision. According to Rapp and Thurman, Hecht and MacArthur suggested "the play should show Cordelia Williams going on and on along her sinful career and finally ending up disastrously, say, in Paris."[94] This is exactly the way, perhaps not surprisingly, that *Lulu Belle* ends, and Rapp and Thurman politely declined the advice.

Wallace Thurman's tendency to avoid literary moralizing is evident in much of his work (and incensed many of his contemporary critics), and perhaps this is why he and Rapp left Cordelia's future uncertain. She is the portrait of a true individual, not bound by gender, race, or sexuality, and in her final renunciation, she claims that she is "gonna' be livin' high, standin' in de lights above deir heads, makin' de whole world look up at me."[95] She is the embodiment of youthful dreams and creative expression, a utopian view of the black artist. It is also tempting to read a little of Ibsen's Nora into Rapp and Thurman's Cordelia. Both characters are defiant in the end, leaving their confining domestic spheres for journeys of self-discovery. *A Doll's House* ends with a distraught Torvald, all alone, questioning his own moral beliefs. Similarly, Rapp and Thurman's play concludes with a keening Mother Williams reconsidering Harlem as a place where African Americans can live freely and morally. Her entreaty is drowned out, however, by the throbbing sounds of partying and jazz music.

Throughout *Harlem,* there are moments when the play threatens to collapse under the weight of the musical underscoring, metatheatricality, and overlaid dramatic forms. The strain caused by these different aspects of the play is a result of the dramaturgical "hybridity," to apply Homi Bhabha's term, and its uneasy mixture of several dramatic genres.[96] Between the gaps of the melodramatic and naturalistic forms, critics believed they detected the "bits of authentic [N]egro life," or photographic glimpses of a "real" Harlem. Within these rifts, such as during the first-act rent party scene, they argued, genuine black behavior could be observed, for as Solomon poetically explains in relation to *A Doll's House*, "realism trembles to life in the tension between melodrama and metaphor."[97] The play's moments of presumed "naturalness" were therefore the ironic result of the very visible seams of the theatrical forms. The dramaturgical forms and character representations shift and turn back on themselves in *Harlem* and make the "real" purely conjectural. Plumbing the depths of the play for a putative black authenticity reveals not a fixed cultural identity but one that is constantly transforming. The merging of the distinct forms, and the presumptions surrounding the combination of black and white elements, reflect the neighborhood's own manufactured authenticity. Harlem in the 1920s was a mass of contradictions: Determining its essential character is a foolhardy venture, for as one character says in Thurman and Rapp's play, "Harlem is sho' one funny place."[98] Yet examining the neighborhood as a contested space of racial images, weighing the varying notions of a unified definition of "African American," and sifting through the differing claims of a "real" Harlem, one exposes the fluid nature of an identity, presumed to be fixed, that is nonetheless elusive, deceptive, and fantastically mutable.

"That's the Kind of Gal I Am": Drag Balls, "Sexual Perversion," and David Belasco's *Lulu Belle*

Flaming youth, tiger tooth,
That's the kind of gal I am;
But when I'm in love with someone,
I can be a soft, sweet lamb—
When I'm through, "Toodle-oo"—
That's the kind of gal I am:

Wilder than a wild, wild rose
And smoother than the Jordan flows,
I'm just a mad-cap baby, called Lulu Belle;
Everyone in dark-town knows
I'm fickle as the wind that blows,
But how they crave this baby, called Lulu Belle.

—"SONG OF LULU BELLE"*

"WILDER THAN A WILD, WILD ROSE"

In March 1928, *Variety* reported a rather shocking situation: New York's established homosexual community was getting so large that it could no longer accept any new members. Those refused entry into this "queer elite" naturally retaliated and waged out-and-out insurrection. The article, entitled "Battle On Among Broadway Elite of the 'Third Sex,'" begins: "New York's sex abnormal males have developed caste and it threatens to break up this, the biggest colony of its kind, in the world. It is because of its increasing numbers that the trouble has arisen, the old guard refusing to recognize newcomers, with the new arrivals subsequently causing trouble by supplying information to the police, false as often as not."[1] It seems the brouhaha first erupted when the organizers of a drag ball at Harlem's Rockland Palace were forced to limit the number of tickets to participants and spectators because the annual event had recently filled the hall to dangerous capacities. The battle lines between the opposing camps were drawn over a Harlem tradition, but the reverberations were felt throughout New York City.

As intimated in the article, the Rockland "drag" was one of Harlem's grandest occasions and had all the flourish of a genteel society affair. Typically the men frequenting one of these balls, whom the author identifies as "from all walks of life," spent several weeks planning and sewing the most extravagant and fashionable gowns, which were intended to elicit cheers and rapturous gasps from the several thousand in attendance. Likewise conspicuously on view at the Rockland Palace were "certain also of their own queer class" wearing the latest in stylish men's clothing. Apparently, for a novitiate to the gay and lesbian subculture of 1920s New York, exclusion from the Rockland drag was the equivalent of social homicide.

It should come as no surprise, then, that the events surrounding the Rockland debacle caused a fiery debate within particular circles when the sponsors limited the number of "eligibles," and announced that the "newcomers to the ranks must go it on their own if they cared to." The article explains: "It has left the homo-sexuals in a panic, with discussions nightly over the matter in a Fifth avenue restaurant near the park. Sometimes one of them even faints in excitement." The edict provoked the anger of those who were refused admission, and they promptly informed the police of the soiree. Police barred the entrance to men wearing "feminine costume," thereby destroying the event, because, as the reporter points out, "a drag isn't a drag without skirts."[2]

As evident by this sensational account, in addition to the covert gatherings of gay men and lesbians at private parties and in small cafeterias and restaurants throughout New York City, large public spaces such as dance halls and ballrooms temporarily hosted lavish get-togethers for a thriving drag subculture. The *Variety* article also reflects the ambivalent tolerance, both in the press and in public, gay men and lesbians received in the late 1920s, as well as the fascination for performances that challenged white, middle-class decorum. As countless newspaper articles from the period indicate, white fascination with Harlem was motivated in large part by a controversial, lurid Broadway play called *Lulu Belle*, which wasn't precisely about the "third sex," but soon became identified with it. In the public criticism surrounding the play, reactions in the press often conflated same-sex erotic desire within images of race, class, and gender. Previously, little has been written about the play and the controversy it aroused, but the circulation of *Lulu Belle* within Harlem's gay community is significant in American theater history and merits serious attention. The discourse stimulated by the play echoed prevailing attitudes toward same-sex desire in the Harlem Renaissance, and to the drag subculture, the "flaming youth, tiger tooth" title character became a symbol of defiance against the repressive middle-class ideals of the 1920s.

On February 9, 1926, two years before the tumultuous ball described in the *Variety* article, Charles MacArthur and Edward Sheldon's controversial *Lulu Belle,* a play about Harlem life, opened at the Belasco Theatre. David Belasco's production, one of Broadway's biggest hits of the 1920s, packed audiences into the theater for over two seasons, and it had tremendous success on the road as well. The play, which was written, produced, and staged by white men and starred white actors in blackface and black actors in supporting roles, is particularly notable in that it sent whites scurrying in droves to experience "authentic" Harlem nightclubs and to witness events like the Rockland ball firsthand. And although the play does not contain any visible homosexual characters—it is more concerned with representations of race and class—the gay male community in Harlem adopted the title character as its representative and named a speakeasy after her. At Lulu Belle's, a drag club, black and white gay men and lesbians congregated nightly, and, similar to the Rockland drag ball, they parodied formal upper-class society functions.

Reactions to *Lulu Belle* in the press help explain why the play struck a chord among the disenfranchised. In general, the white press disparaged the melodrama for its immorality, and the black press, while pleased that the production used so many black actors, regarded the sexually out-of-control title character (played by white actress Lenore Ulric) as a reminder to black women to remain pure for the sake of the race. Similar to the *Variety* description of the Rockland ball participants (who are referred to as "caste," the "queer elite," and the "old guard"), the hypersexual Lulu Belle is controversial not for her erotic desire, but for her representations of class and race. As responses to the play and drag balls lay bare, the visible homosexual (that is, the cross-dressed man or woman) and the sexually unrestrained black woman, both associated with the working class, were particularly contentious figures to the African American communities in the Harlem Renaissance. They each posed a perilous threat to the advancement of the race because of their "low-class" morality, and mocked the ideals of the middle-class family toward which the communities strove.[3]

"EVERYONE IN DARK-TOWN KNOWS"

There is a direct link between the drag ball phenomenon and the world of Belasco's play. Act 3 of *Lulu Belle* takes place in the Elite Grotto, a fictional "black-and-tan" nightclub (reportedly based on one of the pioneering nightclubs, Barron Wilkins's cabaret at 133rd Street and 7th Avenue) where Lulu Belle performs. As he was known to do, producer-director David Belasco went to incredible extremes to capture the minute details of the environment in his stage design. Writing in *Liberty* magazine, he states that with his star and production staff he "made journey after journey into the night life of the Harlem Negro section" in order to replicate the milieu precisely.[4] The lengthy set description reflects Belasco's careful attention to detail, and he made every effort to replicate a basement speakeasy with its characteristic "evil and exotic charm."[5] Several tables line a small, circular dance floor; there is a small bandstand with a piano and several chairs for the small orchestra; and an old pool table is upstage left. Covering the wall are pictures of Lulu Belle, who was the main attraction at this club, and signs that warn, "No Improper Dancing or Actions Will Be Tolerated," "No Shimmie," and "Profane Language Not Permitted." As one would expect (and hope), all of these rules are violated in the course of the act. Harlem's appeal for whites was its promise that all regulations of polite society would indeed be broken.

Also on the wall of the set is a prominently displayed advertisement. Audience members familiar with the lesbian and gay subculture would immediately recognize its significance and the allusion to the Manhattan Casino balls. The sign announces: "Sheiks, Flappers and Dapper Dans! The pleasure of your company is requested at 14 Karet Boys Masquerade Ball and Dance at the Harlem Casino, January 26. Admission 75 cents. Boxes $3."[6] The reference to "14 Karet Boys" is no doubt code for the young gay men in their expensive and glittering creations.

The drag ball phenomena began in Harlem as early as 1923, in which the annual Hamilton Lodge Ball, established in 1869, evolved from a "Masquerade and Civic Ball" into what was commonly referred to as "The Fairies Ball."[7] And as John L. Fell and Terkild Vinding explain, the annual divertissement was variously referred to as "The Dance of the Fairies" and the "Faggots Ball."[8] These events were advertised in Harlem's papers, but they were discreetly promoted as "masquerades." For instance, in February 1926, the *New York Age* advertised the Odd Fellows' "Original Celebrated Old-Fashioned MASQUERADE AND CIVIC BALL." The notice also announces the breakdown of the prizes:

$30 IN GOLD CASH PRIZES GIVEN AWAY as follows: First Prize $15 in Gold; Second Prize $10 in Gold; Third Prize $5 in Gold Will be given to the persons wearing the most artistic Masquerade Costumes. The Judges will be well-known disinterested persons.[9]

There is little in this advertisement to indicate that this "old-fashioned" masquerade would offer anything diverging far from the standard garden-variety civic ball. Regardless of their appellation, the Odd Fellows, who sponsored the event, were not unlike several other auxiliaries of the Hamilton Lodge organization that presented huge dances in Harlem. In fact, the Odd Fellows were comprised of reputable, black middle-class men, and they were the rough equivalent to the Elks or Kiwanis. Moreover, there was nothing unusual about John C. Smith's Modern Dance Orchestra playing the event either. This group was a customary fixture at spring dances, charity balls, and socials. Nevertheless, this ball was quite different from most others to take place at the Renaissance Casino at 138th Street and Seventh Avenue.

According to a report in the *New York Age* a week after the masquerade and civic ball, 1,500 people packed the Renaissance Casino. Although the event was presented by a black organization, at least 50 percent in attendance were white, bohemians from Greenwich Village, and, as stated in the article, "of the class generally known as 'fairies.'"[10] The reporter points out that the male contestants "in their gorgeous evening gowns, wigs and powdered faces were hard to distinguish from many of the women." In addition, thousands of spectators filled the hall's upper boxes to view the colorful extravaganza from above, and members of the upper classes included them on their social calendars. Black socialite Geraldine Dismond gushed in her "Social Snapshots" column in the *Inter-State Tattler,* "Of course, a costume ball can be a very tame thing, but when all the exquisitely gowned women on the floor are men and a number of the smartest men are women, ah then, we have something over which to thrill and grow round-eyed."[11] Tickets for the event were always in great demand, and choice box seats were not always easy to come by. Complimentary tickets were especially scarce, as indicated by *Amsterdam News* theater columnist Romeo L. Dougherty. "For weeks before this Hamilton Lodge affair I am besieged by a number of people who consider themselves the last word in sepia society for tickets, my friends believing that because of my position I am recognized to the extent of having a number of free duckets placed at my disposal."[12]

Not all of the responses to the drag balls were enthusiastic, though. In 1929, the *Amsterdam News* admitted that the event attracted "Harlem's best known people, including prominent lawyers, doctors and business men, who were there with their wives and friends," but the reporter derisively pointed to the "girlish antics" of the participants, "whose acts certainly class them as subnormal, or, in the language of the street, 'fairies.'"[13] The article also claimed that several of "those who seized the opportunity of a masquerade to get off some of their abnormality in public were some of the most notoriously degenerate white men in the city."[14] In the following year, a similar attitude was evident at the ball itself. The *Amsterdam News* reported a strange interloper, possibly protesting the proceedings:

> A slight damper was put on the revels of the dancers by the appearance of a woman dressed in flowing robes of white carrying a Bible held in an attitude of warning and prophecy. Whether this was part of the masquerade or a sincere effort to warn "sinners," the audience was not quite sure, and soon the white-robed figure was swallowed up in the vast crowd and as quickly forgotten.[15]

This prophet of doom may have momentarily given the crowd pause, but the parade and competition went on without a hitch.

By the early 1930s, the annual "Fairies Ball" was one of Harlem's most highly anticipated events even if the critics complained that the effects of the Depression were evident in the finery, which was "not as glamorous and expensive" as in the balls of the 1920s.[16] At the February 24, 1933, masquerade, attendance at the Rockland Palace reached nearly six thousand people. In fact, by one o'clock in the morning the crowd grew so large and unmanageable that the police and fire officials were forced to close the doors, refusing admittance to anyone else. On that occasion, two people were arrested, the first charged with "knocking" a woman to the floor, and the second for opening a door to let people "sneak into the hall." And for a few tense minutes, it seemed that the huge number of spectators would destroy the raison d'être of any drag ball: the judging and presentation of the awards. As the *Age* reported:

> Special police had a time keeping the crowd back while the grand march was in progress and the officials of the lodge were judging as to whom to award the prizes. For a time it looked as though some of the contestants would take mat-

ters into their own hands but stern action on the part of judges and the special police broke up any demonstration over the awarding of the prizes.

Again, the crowd represented a diversity of race and class. The article states that in addition to the black Hamilton Lodge members, "Thousands of white spectators from Park Avenue to Greenwich Village came up and took part in the spectacle and mingled with the members of the third sex of both races."[17]

For an excellent description of a typical drag ball one need only look in Blair Niles's 1931 novel, *Strange Brother,* which offers a historically accurate picture of gay men in Harlem of the late 1920s. In chapter 11, Niles sends one of the protagonists, June, a white woman journalist (most likely modeled after the author herself), to a drag ball; the other protagonist, Mark, a self-loathing gay white man, declines the invitation because of the exploitive nature of the event. With the thousands of onlookers gawking over the men from the "shadow world," Mark feels it would be too "painful . . . to see his kind thus on exhibition, like animals in the Zoo, like freaks in the side-show of a circus."[18] To Mark, if gay men are ever to earn the respect and acceptance of society at large, they must conform to the expectations of respectable masculine behavior of that society. This respectability would include the masculine dress, values, and employment of "normal," middle-class men.[19]

Similarly, in another novel of the period, *The Young and the Evil* (1933) by Charles Henri Ford and Parker Tyler, the gay narrator surrealistically describes a drag ball he attended thus: "The dancefloor was a scene whose celestial flavor and cerulean coloring no angelic painter or nectarish poet has ever conceived."[20] To the narrator of *Strange Brother,* the dance floor below the boxes was a mass of feathers and sparkling bangles, and the costumes represented every period and style of women's formal dress. Some of the participants wore immense powdered wigs with the regal habiliment à la Marie Antoinette, and others wore bobbed wigs with modish straight-cut evening gowns of the 1920s. Still others exhibited plumed headdresses and revealing show costumes that were either created specifically for the occasion or borrowed for the night. In fact, Ethel Waters once wrote that gay men often borrowed some of her "best gowns" to wear at Harlem's drags. In her autobiography, *His Eye Is on the Sparrow,* she recounts, "One night I lent my black velvet dress, trimmed with ermine, to one of these he-she-and-what-is-it-types. But he got to fighting with his 'husband' at the affair and was locked up in a cell."[21] To her humiliation, her dress smelled like carbolic acid, "the Chanel No. 5 of the cell blocks," and she says she was unable to wear it for a month.

The exhibition of the alluring, the stylish, and the outrageous was a principal purpose (and attraction) of the affair, and the highlight of the evening was the "parade of the pansies," which preceded the competition. According to one report, "The 'beauty' pageant started at 1:45 am. Bowing, throwing kisses, snake-hipping or Lindy-hopping as the mood struck them, nearly 100 of the more expensively costumed impersonators strode across an elevated platform and courted the favor of the crowd and judges. From this group a score of semifinalists were chosen."[22] The semifinalists then walked the platform again so the judges and crowd could determine the most unique, glamorous, and graceful of the "fairies" to cross the stage. The announcement of the winner was generally met with great fanfare, and the "Queen" of the ball, in addition to receiving a monetary prize (anywhere from fifteen to fifty dollars as the balls became larger and more lucrative) was accorded tremendous acclaim. When Mickey Dell, the winner of the 1934 ball, was announced, there was, according to the *Amsterdam News*, "a roar of approbation, which rose on the fringe of the vast mob, grew in crescendo, inundated the loges and the balcony and swept to the topmost shadowed rafters." This response "was rivaled only by the reception accorded to Peaches Loraine Williams, the outgoing queen, who was not so much pretty as popular."[23] While Peaches did not take home any awards that year, she did receive "honorable mention."

The drag balls were noted for the aggregation of people of different social classes and sexual orientations, but at a time when Harlem's most popular nightclubs, including the Cotton Club and Connie's Inn, denied entrance for black patrons, these dances offered an occasion for the social commingling of Blacks and whites. Commenting on the array of people at the ball, the *Amsterdam News* described a typical scene: "Ofays in drag and in dress mingled freely with Harlem's dressed and undressed."[24] In 1932 the *Atlanta World* described the drag ball scene: "White and colored alike rubbed shoulders with the charming (?) perverts."[25] This was not, however, a utopian vision of integration, and racial distinction did not recede to the background. In fact, there remained, at least among the press corps, a rivalry between the black and white contestants. The press was quick to point out the differences between white and black drag presentation, and in 1932 the *Amsterdam News* stated that the "white masqueraders far excelled their darker competitors in the matter of makeup and costumes."[26] The article explains that the gowns of the white participants "were more carefully selected and patterned, and they did not go in for the hideous shades of color and paint exhibited by the Negro female impersonators."[27] The criticism highlights the sense of shame that some African Americans felt when seeing certain proclivities embodied by their own race. There were certain areas in which they would just as soon their race not excel.

On the other hand, three-time ball winner Bonnie Clark, a female impersonator in black vaudeville and later an actor with the Federal Theatre Project,[28] thought that race should not be a factor in determining the success of one's drag. Clark went so far as to claim racial bias among the judges of the drag balls. The committee of judges, which often included Harlem notorieties such as Carl Van Vechten, Ethel Waters, and prize fighter Jack Johnson in various years, were responsible for selecting the finalists in several categories from the often hundreds of competitors and were, as promoted in the 1926 advertisement, "disinterested persons." The judges usually made their selections based on audience response and were not generally tinged by racial favoritism, but according to Clark, this was not always the case. "You may quote Bonnie Clark as saying that there ain't no justice," Clark told the *Amsterdam News.* "And no decency either."[29] He called the judges "mean old roughnecks," who were unable to distinguish between a genuine "artistic creation" and a pedestrian "organdie dress." Clark did, however, indicate that the Harlem drag balls, unlike others he competed in during the year, included a racial diversity of judges. He said, "There is a conspiracy afoot. I participated in seven of these masquerades last year and except for the one here [in Harlem], they always arranged for the white girls to win. They never had no Negro judges."[30] In 1933 Clark came in third place and was bested by two white contestants, who both wore organdie. Three years later, the *Amsterdam News* claimed that the battle between the races officially came to an end when Jean LaMarr, "a decided brownskin with almond eyes, flashing teeth, a nifty foot and notoriously effeminate manner and carriage," won the highest honor. "Sixty-eight years of rivalry between the ofay and Mose chicks terminated when a Negro," the paper reported, "won first prize with an 'original creation' of white chiffon, created by Dan Hazel, a Broadway designer."[31] Thus, even as the press printed articles that barely concealed an attitude of flippancy and, in some cases, outright disdain for the balls, there was obvious racial pride for African American winners.

In addition to race, sexual orientation—or more crucially, expression of that orientation—was a controversial element of the drag balls. Although the focus of the drag balls was on the competition, and while the annual event had became one of Harlem's grandest social functions, the balls also offered a safe space for the physical expression of same-sex attraction. This would have been a central reason why gay men and lesbians came from great distances to attend,

Pansies Cavort in Most Delovely Manner At That Annual Hamilton Lodge "Bawl"

Lads Turn Lassies for
Evening With Silk
Gowns 'n' Frills

By ST CLAIR BOURNE.

Take it from me, Jack, them
"dolls" solidly laid it at the
Hamilton Lodge affair down at
the St. Nicholas Palace, on Six-
teenth street, last Friday
night. It was positively too
grand.

There were more than 8,000 people
who crammed the place and when that
the man into a "jam session" the
spectators tried on and started rug-
cutting in fine fashion.

Most of the "boys" fell out in evening togs and some of the creations
would put any "dutch" to
shame. Fact is, you know, is what the
more so for the real women.

Chairel Slays 'Em.

By two a.m. they put up
the parade and con-
the "gala" started pos-
so much. One of the con-
testants used to give his—no, her—
I don't know. Guess you got the
idea and stepped right out of
character, but that did not out of character, but
didn't give a tumble.

When the smoke cleared, Jean La-
Marr in a gorgeous white gown with
a train or something was up
for taking first prize. This is
third consecutive year he was
and the boys have decided to
count her Titania. In case that
doesn't you, consult Shakespeare's
"Midsummer Night's Dream."

Bebe Martin, an oفay who some of
the "gals" still insist is a girl, and a
mean elk at that, got second prize
and then went to a "pretty" whose
name was too fierce along with the unusual telephone number.

Out-of-Towners Fall In.

As usual, a gang of the "fealis" left
from out of town. During the evening they discovered a pair of twins
from Philadelphia. They're not real
ones. They only dressed and acted
it.

One of them, daintily pushing back
his gossamerlike crepe silk
and cape which covered out didn't
fit a bo-to costume. Don't get
me wrong, boys, I got this description. As a woman, declared that
the atmosphere was "instipid."—That
was the part of the general public,
too. Belle Primo was the name
given by the wearer of what was just
the most glittering costume, a
period affair with a large sweeping
coiffure like a drunk's view of a full
moon elf with antlers gilded. La
Primo, who is 6 feet 4 inches tall, confided that Nyack was her to his
hometown. Don't know what Nyack
has to say about it though.

"Ekswizite" prizewinners, with No. 1, Jean La Marr, in center. Upper sketch depicts a genuine cutie razzing a phoney.

FIG. 4. Every March for over a decade, the *Amsterdam News* reported on the winners, losers, and attendees at the annual Hamilton Lodge drag ball in Harlem. Photographer and artist unknown. (From the *Amsterdam News:* "Pansies Cavort in Most Delovely Manner at that Annual Hamilton Lodge 'Bawl,'" March 6, 1937. Image published with permission of ProQuest LLC. ©2009, ProQuest LLC; all rights reserved. Further reproduction is prohibited without permission.)

as indicated by poet Langston Hughes, who called the drags "spectacles in color" and stated that participants arrived from up and down the eastern sea coast.[32] Floyd G. Snelson, the theatrical editor for the *Pittsburgh Courier,* had a more expansive estimate. "Queer people flock[ed] from far and near," he wrote in 1932, and at least twenty-five states were represented that year.[33] The press reported that gay men and lesbians saved up all year so that they might attend, and, according to accounts, it was not just for the chance to wear the clothes of the other sex. These events afforded lesbians and gay men social and sexual opportunities as well. The *Amsterdam News* reported, "Men danced with men, women danced with women. An occasional heated love affair was observed in the corners and crevices of Rockland Palace."[34] And even if he thought the "dances should be stopped before they become the usual thing and our youth is effected [*sic*] with the virus of the perverted," Snelson offered a similarly voyeuristic view. He noted, "In the dark corners of the balcony of the ballroom several couples were seen making love in a most amorous way." "Love flared hot and quick," he observed, and "men openly kissed and caressed one another, and women likewise."[35] To the lesbian and gay attendees, the drag balls clearly offered more than just a colorful parade of pansies: They were annual rites of winter that were police-sanctioned, publicly visible celebrations of queer life.

The character of Lulu Belle, as created by MacArthur and Sheldon and as embodied by Lenore Ulric, was arguably a more befitting symbol for masquerade, transformation, and unbridled sexuality than anything else in the 1920s, and she became a mascot for the gay community. This controversial, mutable, and insatiable character, who described herself in song as "fickle as the wind that blows," willfully challenged middle-class ideals and morals. Like a Hamilton Lodge drag ball contestant, she was never quite what she seemed to be. In fact, by herself she was a spectacle in color. As performed by Ulric in blackface, Lulu Belle was a white woman passing for black who had a voracious sexual appetite not bound to any race. To many spectators, she was despicable, representing a perversion of race and sexuality. Black theater critic Theophilus Lewis described her as "a diabolical automaton which the mere humans she comes in contact with are impotent to resist."[36] Not unlike the cross-dressed Harlem "fairy," she seemed to mock the principles of polite society, and she symbolized a threat to African American advancement. But when the play that could barely contain her opened on Broadway in 1926, Lulu Belle unleashed a host of racial and sexual desires and let loose a maelstrom of anxieties revolving around black womanhood.

"A MAD-CAP BABY, CALLED LULU BELLE"

The title character's iconic status notwithstanding, in theater history *Lulu Belle* is especially important for its use of a racially integrated cast, which was a rarity on Broadway in the 1920s. The production boasted a cast of 115, of whom 100 were black. While white actors played the major parts in blackface (there are also a few minor white characters), African Americans took on the supporting and supernumerary roles. Both white and black critics singled out the white actors for their ability to pass for black. Arthur Hornblow in *Theatre Magazine* wrote, "Lenore Ulric outdid herself as the dusky wanton," and according to black author, lyricist, and statesman James Weldon Johnson, "The role of George Randall, the principal Negro male character, was finely played by Henry Hull, a white actor, whose make-up and dialect were beyond detection."[37] While many of the black critics objected to the base depiction of Harlem life, they applauded its efforts to provide greater theatrical prospects for Blacks in the theater. For instance, Hubert H. Harrison wrote in the Urban League's journal, *Opportunity,* that the production "makes it easier for the next step—an all Negro cast in a serious presentation of some other and more significant slice of Negro life."[38]

As Arthur Dorlag and John Irvine, the editors of Charles MacArthur's plays, point out, *Lulu Belle* stands very little chance being revived today.[39] Besides its often offensive references to Blacks ("real nigger style," "ascetic negresses," "young bucks," "darkies," and other derogatory expressions), in performance it runs over three hours, the melodramatic plot is confusing and meandering, and the characters exhibit little development in the course of the four acts. When it opened on Broadway in 1926, the production did have going for it, in addition to an exciting performance by Ulric, a striking visual design that one came to expect from Belasco. Brooks Atkinson reviewing the play in the *Times* wrote that Ulric "vibrates like a taut wire," and he paid tribute to the "precise and accurate photography" of the scenography. Atkinson contrasted the extreme attempts at reality of Belasco's mise-en-scène to the highly stylized "New Stagecraft" then in vogue. Whereas Belasco sought to recreate the visual minutiae of a play in his design, practitioners of the New Stagecraft, including Robert Edmond Jones, Lee Simonson, and Norman Bel Geddes, attempted to capture a text's "spirit" by using iconic objects, such as masks and imposing geometric shapes, as well as atmospheric lighting. Atkinson wrote:

> Not for [Belasco] the esthetic spurs to the imagination now practiced by our newer scenic designers and directors. Not for him the bewildering symbolism of masks and ominous shadows. To Mr. Belasco, "seeing is believing"; he leaves nothing out. At any rate, nothing except plot and story. These two elements of drama, the property of Mr. Sheldon and Mr. MacArthur, are quite lost in the jumble of exact detail.[40]

In brief, the play's plot, which owes a great deal to Wedekind's *Lulu* plays (originally produced as *Earth Spirit* [1895] and *Pandora's Box* [1904]), involves a scheming black woman who betrays the affection of her devoted lover and moves from Harlem to Paris to become a wealthy (white) count's mistress, manipulating and discarding lovers along the way. Several years later, her rejected beau, now released from prison after a fight over Lulu Belle, tracks her down, confronts her, and strangles her. Just as Wedekind's Lulu strikes a blow against conventional attitudes toward sexuality and hypocritical morality,[41] Lulu Belle can neither be domesticated nor controlled by societal laws and values.

The play opens in a black neighborhood on West Fifty-ninth Street in New York's "San Juan Hill" neighborhood. As the stage directions inform, "Everything is gay and lively and black." Flickering bar signs, "dingy tenements," fire escapes, a high-class, "pretentious" apartment building, and a movie theater currently showing—what else?—Glory Champagne in *A Lovely Sinner* set the scene; and crap-games, singing drunks, and arguments about a prizefight create the mood. As the play opens, final preparations for a "society" wedding are under way, and the hero of the play, dashing George Randall (the best man in the wedding), is visiting from White Plains, New York, with his wife and two children. An evangelist, Brother Staley, accompanied by Sister Sally and Sister Blossom, emerges from the crowd and begins leading the gathered families in prayer and song. Enter into this admixture of wealth, squalor, and religious fervor Lulu Belle.

From her initial appearance, Lulu Belle stands outside of traditional morality and middle-class values, and it is fairly obvious why the drag subculture would take up the play. As the evangelist leads the crowd in "The Old Time Religion," she makes her first entrance through the processional:

LULU BELLE: 'Lo, boys! Whoopie! Le's all git religion.
MRS. FRISBIE: Good Lawd, ef that ain't that low down Lulu Belle!

And as the stage directions state: "Lulu Belle is young and beautiful and bad. Her hair is bobbed, her clothes are the last word in negro elegance. At her side to [the] left of her is a little black hunchbacked creature, shabbily dressed, who looks up at her like an adoring dog."[42] When the preacher scolds her for her sinful dancing and tells her she is going to go to hell, she mockingly replies:

Yo' bet I'm goin' t' hell, brothah . . . goin' t' hell in a bandwagon! An' when I git theah, I'm gonna walk right up t' dat ole debbil, jes like I'm doin' now . . . (She approaches the minister.) . . . an' I'm gonna jiggle mah hippies *dat* way.[43]

Lulu Belle then publicly humiliates him by exposing his hypocrisy. She announces that Brother Staley himself is no stranger to Harlem's nightlife, having encountered Lulu Belle at the Elite Grotto, where she is a hostess and dancer: "Membah de night yo' come in plaste'ed an' you rolled dem loving eyes at me."[44]

Later in the act, immediately before she seduces George Randall, causing him to leave his respectable life as husband, father, and barber in White Plains, Lulu Belle proves that the law poses no threat to her either. When a white police officer breaks up a fight Lulu Belle has started, she taunts him too:

POLICEMAN: (with conviction) Yer a wise-cracker, aincha?

LULU BELLE: (virtuously) I'm a li'l widow mothah, dass whut I am, as anybody but a slewfoot h'ness bull could see by lookin' at me . . . (Glancing at her wrist watch) My, my, time to go home an' nurse th' baby! How time flies talkin' wid a charmin' unifo'm man! S'pose yo' could walk a piece wid me an' finish th' convusation as we go along?

POLICEMAN: (suddenly) Let's see yer hands. (He seizes them.)

LULU BELLE: Quit ticklin' my wrist!

POLICEMAN: (Still holding one) Soft as dough . . . *you* don't work!

LULU BELLE: Suttinly I wu'k!

POLICEMAN: Where?

LULU BELLE: In de Brownskin Bakin' Comp'ny.

POLICEMAN: (sourly) Whadda y' bake?

LULU BELLE: (Triumphantly) *Jelly rolls!* (She executes a shimmy. A window full of darkies and the ones at the back howl at this.)[45]

Because the officer does not want to have to go to court the next day, his day off, he lets her go with a stern warning (not to mention exposing his own hypocrisy): "If I find ya hangin' 'round here again I'll throw ya in th' hoosegow, day off or not! (He enters the bar.)"[46]

From a feminist standpoint, the exchanges between Lulu Belle and the evangelist and police officer enact a familiar narrative of the degenerate urban black woman in the 1920s. In "Policing the Black Woman's Body in an Urban Context," Hazel V. Carby traces this developing perception prevalent not only among whites, but also among the black intelligentsia and the black middle class.[47] Beginning at the turn of the century, northern cities saw a huge rise in migration of African Americans from the South. The anxieties associated with "social displacement and dislocation" produced a host of "moral panics," which

FIG. 5. Lulu Belle vamps a police officer. Edward Nannery and Lenore Ulric in David Belasco's production of *Lulu Belle* (1926). © White Studio. (Billy Rose Theatre Division,
The New York Public Library for the Performing Arts, Astor, Lenox and Tilden Foundations.)

were then transposed onto black women's bodies. These moral panics, as Carby documents with essays and autobiographies from the turn of the century through the 1920s, was traced to single, jobless black women who turned to vice and depravity because of "increasing inefficiency and desire to avoid hard work."[48] The difficulties Blacks faced in the cities were presumably rooted in the unpoliced, undisciplined, and unemployed bodies of single black women, which endangered "the success of the emergent black middle class." Black women were often viewed, argues Carby, "as signs of various possible threats to the emergence of the wholesome black masculinity necessary for the establishment of an acceptable black male citizenship in the American social order."[49]

By the mid-1920s, the image of the easily corrupted and impure young black woman had been forcefully ingrained in the public imagination, and the "problem" was addressed in numerous articles and essays. In 1925, for example, black writer Elise Johnson McDougald responded to the moral indictment directly in Alain Locke's collection of essays, *The New Negro,* and she demonstrated how widespread this characterization of black women as sexual deviants and prostitutes had become. McDougald does not refute the charges against black women's morality in her essay "The Task of Negro Womanhood," but she argues that the result was not essentially a symptom of the young women's race. Their inclinations were instead related to their class. She writes that a poor black woman's tendency to have sex without the benefit of marriage is a reaction to the enormous economic pressures "exerted upon her, both from without and within her group." McDougald vehemently rejects the implication that black women are more prone to prostitution than other ethnic or racial groups faced with the same "overpowering conditions":

> The Negro woman does not maintain any moral standard which may be assigned chiefly to qualities of race, any more than a white woman does. Yet she has been singled out and advertised as having lower sex standards. Superficial critics who have had contact only with the lower grades of Negro women, claim that they are more immoral than other groups of women. This I deny. This is the sort of criticism which predicates of one race, to its detriment, that which is common to all races. Sex irregularities are not a matter of race, but of socioeconomic conditions.[50]

She further explains that studies show African tribes have rigid sexual standards, which implies that there is no intrinsic fault in black women. The problem derives, therefore, from the unfortunate social conditions that are assigned to black women by processes that produce racial and sexual inequality. Because of their limited economic options, many black women had little choice but to turn to prostitution to support themselves.

In this context, Lulu Belle's "soft as dough" hands are particularly significant. Because she works in a nightclub and not (ironically) in a subordinate menial position, her body betrays her as not belonging to the "respectable" middle class. Even worse, she lewdly displays her effrontery to middle-class values—represented in her confrontations with a preacher and policeman in terms of motherhood and respect for the church and law. That is, to show her contempt at efforts to rein her in, Lulu Belle demonstrates the extent of her *un*disciplined body ("jiggl[ing] [her] hippies" and "executing a shimmy"). To black middle-class communities of the 1920s, Lulu Belle personified the tremendous barriers Blacks faced in cultural advancement and securing approbation from white society.

It is important to remember the central irony of Lulu Belle as representative of a problem to her race: The play was written by two white men and performed by a white woman in blackface. In addition, the audiences attending the Belasco Theatre would have been predominantly white. Generally working-class Blacks did not frequent Broadway theaters, but they would have read about *Lulu Belle* in black newspapers such as the *New York Age* and *Amsterdam News*. Indeed, "dirt" plays like *Lulu Belle,* which depicted the sexual exploits of loose women, were not particularly uncommon on Broadway in the 1920s. In 1922, for instance, *Rain,* John Colton and Clemence Randolph's adaptation of Somerset Maugham's short story and starring Jeanne Eagles, caused a sensation in its portrayal of the prostitute Sadie Thompson. *White Cargo* (1924), starring Annette Margulies as the South Pacific enchantress Tondalayo, Roland Oliver's *Night Hawk* (1926), about a self-sacrificing prostitute, and *Shanghai Gesture* (1926), featuring Florence Reed as the ruthless Chinese madam, Mother Goddam, all dealt with similar themes. *Lulu Belle,* however, struck a nerve in the black community. The black press was quick to respond to the danger that women like Lulu Belle posed to the race and viewed the play as a morality tale. In March 1926, a month after the show opened on Broadway, the *Amsterdam News* printed an article by Ruth Dennis called "Lulu Belles—All?" An editorial statement frames the article and registers full support for the issues Dennis raises: "We have never aimed to assume a position of moralist or to preach morality, but there are certain truths which we, as a race, must recognize if we hope to attain those heights which we so blatantly tell the world we are aiming for." And he adds, "Not since William Hannibal Thomas wrote 'The American

Negro' have we ran [*sic*] across an individual with enough bravery to come forth with the unvarnished truth as Miss Dennis."[51]

Ruth Dennis's exposé of the "unvarnished truth" poses the question: "Is 'Lulu Belle' based on the life of the average Negro girl?" She believes that it is. The crux of the problem, as she defines it, is that single, black, working-class women spend all of their time concentrating on their appearance when they should be out working. Their preoccupation with fashion causes a "passionate discontent" with their economic caste, and they can focus only on how they can acquire "social recognition." In order to obtain fashionable finery, they often resort to "all sorts of reprehensible follies," or "even crime." She writes, "The majority of Negro women are evading honest toil to live in licentious ease. 'Clothes, clothes, more clothes' is their one ambition."

This obsession with dress, "which [Negro women] parade with shameless audacity . . . before their envious and less successful friends," connects the women in question with the Rockland Palace ball (male) participants. The balls were competitive in spirit, as the main purpose for gathering was to show off the contestants' exquisite creations, and prizes were awarded for the most stunning. In the *Variety* article, the reporter claims that "the well-to-do votaries of the 'drags,' or the one who is being supported by a man of means will plan weeks in advance on a gown to wear, and will spend hundreds of dollars on the creation."[52] Like the Lulu Belles that Dennis describes, the men in drag display all the visible signs of belonging to the upper class, but they have not earned the distinction through honest labor. The central characteristic of the "male abnormals" is not their sexual attraction to other men but their obsession with drags and dresses. In both the *Variety* article and Dennis's, images of class subsume the representations of a deviant or rampant sexuality. The immorality or the "perversion" of the individuals is marked more by transgressing one's class (without having to work in the conventional sense) than by sexual exploits. As with the Lulu Belles that Dennis describes, the participants' parade of tremendous wealth also belies the fact they do not work. The most successful drag participants, the article mentions, are unemployed, but they are backed by rich men. Lulu Belle's relationship with her French count embodies this goal.

According to Dennis, middle-class decorum and respect for motherhood have also been assaulted by the working-class "Lulu Belles" in the black community. Proper, feminine behavior has been replaced by a passion for gambling, drinking, and dancing, and other activities motivated by "questionable novels and rotten theatricals."[53] She prophesies that if the Lulu Belles in the community are not rooted out and reformed, the race will perish. She explains: "So great a responsibility rests upon Negro womanhood that it is imperative that serious consideration be given the condition of things as they stand in reference to her. The moral status of a race is fixed by the character of its women. If 'Lulu Belle' is typical, then the Negro is doomed." The future of the race, therefore, is dependent upon the unceasing and righteous work of the "anti–Lulu Belles," or those black women who have not yet succumbed to the temptations of vice and folly. In an earnest plea to cherish the few upstanding black women in the community, Dennis writes:

> These heroines [the anti–Lulu Belles] must realize that between good and evil conduct there is a great gulf. They must be God fearing teachers of truth and righteousness. They shall lead the Lulu Belles into chaste living and the race will forever call them "blessed."

The "chaste living" here refers to preserving black women's roles as wives and mothers. She claims it is the principal duty of black women to serve as the "custodians of the souls as well as the bodies of their children."[54]

The greatest crime Lulu Belle commits in the play is breaking up George Randall's family. In one of the more excessively melodramatic moments of the play, the extent of this destruction is evident. While sitting in a Harlem nightclub, George realizes he cannot go back home to his wife even after he has been told that his son Walter has died. The young boy, in an effort to support his mother and sister by selling newspapers in the rain, caught and succumbed to pneumonia. A letter from George's wife imploring him to go home, along with her apology for not being a "better wife," cannot persuade him. And he cannot even be impelled to return after he hears his daughter's heartbreaking postscript to the letter: "Dear Daddy: Please come home." Lulu Belle has long since tired of George and commands him to go back (she tells him, "Ev'ry daddy has his day an' yo've had six months!"), but he cannot leave her. Inexplicably, George cannot escape Lulu Belle's charms; it turns out that he loves her more than he does his whole family "put t'gethah."[55] Like the "little black hunchbacked creature," Skeeter, who follows Lulu Belle everywhere, fetching her cigarettes and taking her insults, George's manhood has deteriorated. By act 3, Lulu Belle has destroyed a man and his entire family.

Within conservative circles, visible homosexuals and the lascivious black women such as Lulu Belle were often linked because of their "moral depravity," and the criticism hurled at the fictional character echoed similar arguments that lesbians and gay men encountered regularly. Just as heterosexual, single black women would inevitably bring about the downfall of the race, homosexual men and women threatened the stability of Harlem's two strongest institutions: The church and the family. As Steven Watson argues, on the one hand Harlem provided a measure of tolerance for lesbians and gay men, but on the other, the powerful Harlem church was "strictly anti-homosexual."[56] George Chauncey charts a religious campaign in the 1920s, which was directed at homosexuals, focusing on the threat they posed to black communities. The crusade was fought primarily in the black press and led by Harlem's most renowned minister, Adam Clayton Powell. On November 16, 1929, the *New York Age* printed the following headline: "Dr. A.C. Powell Scores Pulpit Evils: Abyssinian Pastor Fires a Broadside into Ranks of Fellow Ministers, Churches ... Denounces Sex Degeneracy and Sex Perverts." In a well-publicized sermon, Powell railed against the evils infiltrating society as a result of the activities in which many young people were engaging in Harlem's nightclubs and dance halls. Continuing the trend to lay the predicament of the race on women, he said he was particularly troubled by the rise in "sex perversion" among females, claiming it "has grown into one of the most horrible, debasing, alarming and damning vices of present day civilization, and is . . . prevalent to an unbelievable degree."[57] In a sermon the following week, he stated that the Negro family was particularly vulnerable to sex perverts because they induce "men to leave their wives for other men, wives to leave their husbands for other women, and girls to mate with girls instead of marrying."[58] Homosexuality was not just a moral problem; it signaled an end to the propagation of the race.

Although this public attack on "sex perversion" occurred three years after *Lulu Belle* opened, the church's antihomosexual position was not new to lesbians and gay men. In 1926, Edward Bourdet's play about lesbianism, *The Captive*, opened on Broadway, and it was met with fiery protest from the press and church for its immorality.[59] Certainly, when the black minister tells Lulu Belle she will go to hell if she does not alter her lifestyle, lesbians and gay men could identify with this vilification. Further, Lulu Belle's subversive impudence in the face of the minister must have registered a vicarious joy for those who saw or heard about the moment in the play. She does not cower when he criticizes her lifestyle; instead, she remains defiant and continues her quest for greater wealth and more fabulous clothes. Her attitude toward the law undoubtedly had the same effect on the subculture.

As indicated in the *Variety* article about the Rockland drag ball, the relationships among the homosexual community, the press, and the law was tenuous at best. On one hand, permits for such occasions could be obtained, but on the other, gay men and lesbians knew that the police might turn on them at any moment. A police report for the same ball described in *Variety* reflects the careful watch the police maintained:

> About 12:30 A.M. we visited [the Rockland drag ball] and found approximately 5,000 people, colored and white, men attired in women's clothes, and vice versa. The affair, we were informed, was a "Fag (fairy) Masquerade Ball." This is an annual affair where the white and colored fairies assemble together with their friends, this being attended also by a certain respectable element who go here to see the sights.[60]

The report mentions that because of the large number of officers inside and outside the club, uniformed and plainclothes, the three men filing the report stayed only a short time. They witnessed a number of intoxicated guests, but saw no reason to make any arrests. They conclude: "Prior to leaving [officers] B and 5 questioned some casuals in the place as to where women could be met, but could learn nothing."[61] The "women" here refers to prostitutes (one would assume that their prospects for making any money at an event populated mostly by gay men would be slim), and the report points to the cultural connection between whores and "fairies." Ethically and legally, prostitutes and homosexuals stood outside the boundaries of respectability. To middle-class Blacks, both groups were regarded as "low class" in morality and social standing.[62]

Just as Lulu Belle's impertinence toward the evangelist probably aroused satisfaction from the gay and lesbian community, so too would her coy taunting of the white police officer and her ability to avoid arrest. An impudent young black woman or defiant, cross-dressed black man on the streets of New York in the 1920s would not have been so fortunate. In an event that may or may have not been directly inspired by Lulu Belle's actions—the similarities are tantalizing—Gene Mosely, a twenty-six-year-old vaudeville entertainer and "female impersonator" of 337 West Fifty-ninth Street (coincidentally, the same street as the setting for the first scene in *Lulu Belle*), was arrested for disorderly conduct. Like Lulu Belle, Mosely apparently infuriated the police officer with his inappropriate sexual advances. *Variety* reports:

> Policeman George Meyers, West 17th Street Station, said he was passing in front
> of the 59th street address early one morning when Mosely stepped up to him,
> threw his arms around his neck and tried to kiss him. Meyers said he pushed
> him aside and then recognized him as a man who had been arrested last De-
> cember for a similar act.[63]

Mosely rejected the accusation, but when he could not provide "a satisfactory
answer" to explain why he was on the street at that time, the judge found him
guilty. Mosely's punishment further demonstrates the perceived conjunction
between charges of immoral behavior and indolence: He was sentenced to sixty
days in the workhouse.

The most profound and well-documented effect Belasco's production had
in the 1920s was its onstage presentation of "authentic" Harlem atmosphere,
which was characterized by a raucous nightlife. At the same time *Lulu Belle*
opened on Broadway, Carl Van Vechten's *Nigger Heaven* was a national best-
seller. Van Vechten's novel, like *Lulu Belle*, depicted an exotic, thrilling world of
jazz and bootlegged liquor and opportunities that were infinitely more exciting
than the ones available below 125th Street. The two works created an insatiable
desire among whites to experience the "real thing," and they traveled en masse
to Harlem, where they could take a vacation from their everyday middle-class
morality. Press coverage of the goings-on in Harlem perpetuated the appeal
and often credited *Lulu Belle* and *Nigger Heaven* with initiating the vogue.

In the comfort of the Belasco Theatre on Forty-fourth Street and Broadway,
the spectators were afforded a view of the after-hours activity above 125th Street
as seen by David Belasco. And with the legendary impresario as their guide, the
audiences vicariously "slummed" amid the Harlemites. Percy Hammond of the
Herald Tribune articulated this aspect of theatergoers' experience in his review
of the play:

> Piloted by Mr. Belasco, the playgoers last night did some slumming in the black
> belt. It was a rowdy evening among the wicked colored folk, with frequent ex-
> hibitions of their more scandalous depravities. We saw them committing nearly
> all the popular intemperances from murder to the Charleston, and doing so in
> the ardent fashion common to the Afro-American temperament.[64]

Later in the review, Hammond cautions that those who object to the company
of "tawny courtesans" and find the salacious behavior of certain women dis-

tasteful should not go see the production: "[I]n case you are weary of gender, whether saffron or ivory, and the cultural processes of a topaz harlot irk you, 'Lulu Belle' is a good show to stay away from."[65] Nevertheless, he claims that the play allows the more inquisitive theatergoers the chance to witness "the Negro New Yorker in his more animal aspects." To this critic, Belasco's production offered a photographic and cinematic portrait of black life in Harlem.

The third act in particular offers audiences the chance to vicariously experience a Harlem nightclub. Jazz music, sultry singing, and wild, pulsating dancing punctuate the act. At one point the waiters break into a routine during which they balance their trays above their heads and "undulate" with the music, which was performed by a small onstage band. A few moments later the entire cast breaks into a feverish dance, trying to outdo each other with impressive new dance steps. In between Lulu Belle's arguments with George, there are fistfights, games of craps, and more songs, including "Miami" and "Remember." But the high point of the act is Lulu Belle's Charleston, which she uses to entice the Vicomte. The excitement of the dance and the enthusiasm with which it is greeted is evident in the script:

> (The music quickens, Lulu Belle starts to dance, holding her dress above her knees. She goes faster and faster, ending in a furioso of clatter and applause.)
> HAPPY: Dass th' gal!
> HERMAN: Shake it up!
> MILTON: Do yo' stuff!
> HERMAN: Shake that thing!
> BUTCH: Burn my clothes—Lemme die *now*!
> BRYANT: Zowie!
> CORBIN: Bing![66]

The onstage crowd begs her to do an encore, and she obliges.

The effect that *Lulu Belle* had on white pleasure-seekers was almost immediate. Playwright and novelist Wallace Thurman satirized the craze the play *Lulu Belle* inspired in his 1929 novel, *The Blacker the Berry*. Midway through the novel, Emma Lou, the dark-skinned heroine, becomes a maid for a white actress named Arline Strange. Arline is appearing as a "mulatto Carmen" in *Cabaret Gal*, "an alleged melodrama of Negro life in Harlem." Like Belasco's production of *Lulu Belle*, the play within Thurman's novel centers on a reckless young black woman who eventually becomes the mistress to a "wealthy European." Emma Lou, who lives in Harlem, watches *Cabaret Gal* frequently from the wings, and the narrator explains:

> [Emma Lou] never tired of watching the so-called dramatic antics on the stage. She wondered if there were any Negroes of the type portrayed by Arline and her fellow performers. Perhaps there were, since there were any number of minor parts being played by real Negroes who acted much different from any Negroes she had ever known or seen. It all seemed to her like a mad caricature.[67]

At one point, the actress's brother comes to New York for a visit, and insists on going to Harlem to test the veracity of his sister's performance. Privately, Arline asks Emma Lou to go with them to several cabarets because her brother would "enjoy himself more" with Emma Lou, an authentic Harlemite, as their leader. When Emma Lou tells Arline that she has never been to a cabaret, the actress is shocked: "What? You in Harlem and never been to a cabaret? Why I thought all colored people went?"[68] Arline then promises that Emma Lou will receive a "big tip" if she pretends that she is a regular at the clubs. That night at Small's Paradise, an actual nightclub and famous jazz locale that was patronized almost solely by whites, Emma Lou notes the "artificiality" of the environment. The customers revel with an exaggerated lack of restraint that strikes her as false, which parallels the feeling she had while watching the actors onstage in *Cabaret Gal.* In a form of double mimesis, the actors and the club patrons duplicate the popular (stage) version of Harlem nightlife. As Emma Lou indicates, the atmosphere at Small's is highly theatrical: "only the proscenium arch had been obliterated," and "the audience and the actors were as one."[69] In the theatricalized environment of Small's Paradise, the white customers reenacted the uninhibited behavior of the actors in *Cabaret Gal.*

David Belasco did not see it this way, though. He publicly stated that his presentation of African Americans and Harlem was not based on theatrical exaggeration and artistic sensationalism. His portrait was, he argued, based on anthropological study, which he expounded upon in an article he wrote for the August 7, 1926, edition of *Liberty* magazine. In Margaret Mead–like manner, the producer-director details his experiences of observing, noting, and eventually interacting with "the black folk in their hours of play." He begins the article with a lengthy narrative of "the Negro in his native environment," an African veldt, preparing for battle with an unnamed, approaching enemy. The pounding drumbeats, gyrating bodies, and appeals to the "war god" recapitulate the popular image of the African primitive. Belasco offers a homoerotic description of the nearly naked black men as he imagines their body parts in close-up. For example, prior to the war dance, he says that "muscles tense and flex," and he calls attention to the chief's "massive chest" and the "supple black forms" of the warriors with their "huge-muscled hands." As he sets the scene: "Flickering firelights mark off silhouettes of massive torsos, rippling shoulder muscles, flash of glittering teeth and rolling eyes."[70] Belasco uses this ethnological depiction to explain that the physical reaction to pounding drumbeats with the attendant wild, mimetic war dances is psychologically innate to African Americans, and that this "emotion-expression" will find its outlet in the American theater. He is qualified to forward this theory because, as he states, "Fate has decreed that I should know the Negro of our modern days; that I should know him and his psychology intimately." And this knowledge forces him to prophesize that the "Negro, from today onward, will compel recognition through the sheer power of his instinctive mime talent."

> I will go further and declare that no race, even the sorrow-swept Jew, can surpass the Negro for instinctive stage ability. The same receptivity that drove their African ancestors to battle frenzy at the sound of war drums, has been translated by generations of contact with civilization into terms of emotion-expression, delicate and sensitive in the extreme.[71]

Belasco's insight, he claims, is a result of having worked with over one hundred black people on *Lulu Belle*.

The article goes on to show how the producer-director with his star, Lenore Ulric, and members of the production team "made journey after journey" into Harlem nightclubs so they could accurately represent the neighborhood and its inhabitants on the Broadway stage. Through his investigations, he found that Blacks, who are "emotion chameleons," were particularly "susceptible" to music, which alternately made them docile or combative, depending on the type of music played. He also concluded that they were instinctive actors, and he instantly knew that his production would be more successful if he used African Americans in the supporting roles rather than whites in burnt cork. But he would have to re-create their milieu precisely, so that the black actors would be more inclined to act naturally. This came to him when Ulric questioned their ability to play characters:

"But will an audience frighten them into stiffness? Will they forget their roles?" she asked.

"Are they less natural because we are here?" I retorted. "What we must do is to make each one so visualize and actually live his part that distractions will be impossible."[72]

The rehearsal process for Belasco was particularly gratifying, and he illustrates how much he learned from his cast. He remarks on the "sing-along" he led on the first day of rehearsal to "cement the community of interest" and their "rough-and-tumble" eating habits when lunch arrived. When one of the cast members says, "Boss-man, us craves to exercise our bones," Belasco mistakenly thinks that he means they need to go outside for a few minutes to stretch. The joke is on him when he discovers that the fellow didn't intend for the company to leave the rehearsal room at all. He meant only that they take a brief gambling break and shoot dice ("Bones gets dey exercise right here!").[73]

As evidenced by the hard work of the black cast during the rehearsal process, Belasco praised their ambition, their spirituality, and above all, their "childish devotion." Even the original "Miss Doubter," Lenore Ulric, had to admit she was impressed. When Belasco asked her how she felt about working with black people, she remarked: "They give me something indefinable out of their enthusiasm and their devotion to us all—a something which makes my work truly easy. Such loyalty and devotion as they lavish on you! I respect them greatly—and I always will."[74]

While the show had its detractors in the black community, it also had a number of supporters. Hubert H. Harrison in *Opportunity* magazine called it "a slice of Negro life, given without malice and without sentimentality."[75] Evelyn Mason, responding to the favorable coverage in the *Amsterdam News* theater page, wrote that after seeing a recent matinee of the production she "gave thanks to God for the artistic and sincere performance each person gave, which was certainly a triumph for them as well as for Mr. Belasco."[76] Even more importantly, the show provided more than one hundred black actors with work. W. E. B. Du Bois, who months before submitted his scathing review of *Nigger Heaven*, stated in *The Crisis*, "For the first time on the American stage the Negro has emerged as a human being who is not a caricature and not a comedian, and who reacts to the same impulses and emotions as other folk."[77] Actually, Du Bois's reaction is quite consistent with his moralist views of theater and literature. Although he advocated racial advancement and uplift, Du Bois was not prudish regarding base portrayals of real life, such as prostitution. In fact, he

FIG. 6. Lulu Belle double-crosses George. Henry Hull, John Harrington, and Lenore Ulric in David Belasco's production of *Lulu Belle* (1926). © White Studio. (Billy Rose Theatre Division, The New York Public Library for the Performing Arts, Astor, Lenox and Tilden Foundations.)

praised the early poetry of Langston Hughes that dealt with this topic. Du Bois insisted, however, that art serve a propagandistic function and present a clear sense of morality, or what he considered truth and beauty. While both *Nigger Heaven* and *Lulu Belle* present racist images, the former is despicable because it does not adhere to the conventions of melodramatic morality in the way that *Lulu Belle* does. In Van Vechten's novel, Byron Kason, the hero, meets with destruction, while the cause of his downfall, Lasca Sartoris, moves onto other conquests. In MacArthur and Sheldon's play, justice is served, and the toxic, flaming youth is snuffed out in the end.

In response to the black critics who were taken aback by the stereotypical and derogatory images, several white critics claimed that African Americans were being far "too sensitive." They did not think that it should be discussed as anything more than what it was: a piece of popular theater (and a not very good one at that). The *Herald Tribune*, for example, published a rebuttal to the claims of African Americans that the play was a "libel on their race," and "an unfair indictment of an entire people." The unnamed author concedes that, yes, black people have been oppressed, but they have made great strides in their artistic and cultural accomplishments, in which they rightly take "modest pride." He adds that they are not without help in their pursuits either: "Aiding them in their endeavor to justify themselves is a band of New York white folks, who, led by Carl Van Vechten and other intrepid abolitionists, clasp them hand in hand and help them over the rough places."[78] He also agrees that the portrait of black life as represented by Lenore Ulric is not "pleasant propaganda." On stage at the Belasco Theatre, "she is a smart viper, weaving her cankerous way from Harlem to Paris. . . . 'Lulu Belle' is not a pretty picture of a lady of color, or of the circles in which she wiggles." But this is no reason to protest, he says, for the history of the world's stage is filled with unpleasant images of every race, religion, and ethnic group. He cites examples including *Cradle Snatchers,* which "exceeds in its traduction of blonde life"; *The Shanghai Gesture,* "a bitter, unjust lampoon of the Chinese character and practices"; and "the Scandinavians may well consider themselves insulted by *Hamlet* and *Hedda Gabler,* and the Jews and Irish by *Abie's Irish Rose*"; and so on. He closes with the following rejoinder: "So the Negroes, like other persons, should take the abuses of the drama laughingly, and not waste their time in protest."[79]

Lenore Ulric herself commented on the objections to the play and her performance, stating that the work was not meant to be scandalous, but "socially constructive." In an interview following the opening, she argued in defense of *Lulu Belle,* saying that it had higher purposes than mere melodrama. Audiences could learn from the character and how Lulu Belle responds to her given circumstances, which would socially improve the spectators by seeing her "type" represented on stage naturalistically. She saw in the character a universal significance that people of all the races could identify and might therefore understand better.[80] This understanding could lead to better relations between (and among) the races and sexes. She explained:

> The character of Lulu Belle increases our knowledge of life, and therefore creates tolerance and sympathy. . . . No matter how much we disapprove of the type, we must admit that there are real Lulu Belles in the world and that they're not all mustard-colored, either. A study of the emotional reactions of such a woman broadens our own horizons, and I believe that anything which adds to our knowledge makes us better. I never yet knew a person with understanding

who hadn't a higher character than one who remained good merely through living in a shell of ignorance.[81]

The play was not intended to cast aspersions upon the lives of African Americans at all, according to Ulric; rather it was meant to provide enlightenment for its Broadway audiences.

The most vocal objections in the press to *Lulu Belle* did not involve the play's unfavorable representations of African Americans, but its blatant depravity. In its tryout run in Philadelphia, for example, the play's "vulgar language" incited calls for censorship, especially because a woman committed the transgressions.[82] A few of the more egregious offenses cited in the press included Lulu Belle's sexually suggestive lines: "Did you ever have your momma run her hand down your neck, down your spine, and around your solar plexus?"; and "If I were to take my Saturday bath in champagne, would you stick your head in and drink it up with me?"[83] These lines were subsequently cut. After its Broadway run, the play toured the United States, but, as reported in the *Amsterdam News, Lulu Belle* was banned in Boston. The mayor of the city refused to grant a license to the Colonial Theatre because the play was deemed indecent and immoral.[84]

Particularly offensive to some critics was the integration of Blacks and whites on the same stage, and similarly, in the same nightclub. Conservative opponents of the Harlem nightclubs cited the immoral sexual behavior that seemed to result from the intermingling of the races. Black and white critics and moralists suggested that allowing the two races to mix socially would invariably lead to any number of possible couplings between races and genders. Issues of purity of race usually delineated the arguments, but just below the surface were concerns that racial intermingling might lead to deviant sexuality. In their reasoning, interracial desire, a form of sexual perversion, was only one step removed from same-sex desire. Out of control and unregulated, Harlem became the arena in which whites experimented with such activities, and *Lulu Belle* metaphorically reflected this trend.

This is evident in the most vitriolic response to *Lulu Belle,* Arthur Hornblow's review in *Theatre* magazine (April 1926). Aligning it with two other controversial plays on Broadway, *The Glass Slipper* (1925) and *The Shanghai Gesture* (the three of them together forming "an unholy trinity of theatrical filth"), Hornblow rants: "All the ordures of brutal concupiscence, the noisome scrapings of the sexual garbage can, the shameless, abandoned jargon of the brothel, raucous ribaldry, rape, lewdness, the whole gamut of depravity and lechery—

such is the putrescent drama served to-day for the entertainment of your sons, and daughters, not secretly, furtively in some obscure East Side dive, but openly, brazenly in Broadway theatres of the first class."[85] He singles out *Lulu Belle* as particularly reprehensible amid the other "erotic exhibitions of its kind." At least previous "bawdy" shows had casts "confined to white players," so "if indecencies of dialogue or situation were committed, at least it was among one's own, in the family so to speak." "But now," he says, "emulating the example of certain cabarets, where black-and-tan performers draw the midnight pleasure seekers, an added thrill is sought at the Belasco by mixing the colors."[86]

Harlem's small speakeasies and integrated nightclubs particularly riled social and religious conservatives. As a result, committees were formed and social scientists were interviewed to determine the long-term social effects these cabarets might have. The *Hartford Times*, for example, analyzed the trend in the article "Harlem Negroes Run Dives for White Folks" (July 23, 1927). It contends that because of plays like *Lulu Belle*, "cabarets, with a suggestion of abandoned wickedness" have sprung up in astonishing numbers. And worse, "These places have multiplied so rapidly that they are virtually unregulated and unsupervised," with "grave social evils as a possible result of this haphazard mingling of races."[87] The "grave social evils" are not mentioned by name (perhaps because they are unmentionable), but prostitution and sexual deviance are the implied outcome of whites interacting with African Americans. This moral depravity that nonsegregated clubs caused was thought to stem from the "primitive" or "savage" urges that Blacks released in whites. While mixing with African Americans and taking part in their "Dionysian" dances, Caucasians discarded their layers of civilization and social constraints. As James Weldon Johnson noted, Harlem was a place where whites took a "moral vacation." He wrote:

> At these times, the Negro drags his captors captive. On occasions, I have been amazed and amused watching white people dancing to a Negro band in a Harlem cabaret; attempting to throw off the crusts and layers of inhibitions laid on by sophisticated civilization; striving to yield to the feel and experience of abandon; seeking to recapture a taste of primitive joy in life and living; trying to work their way back into that jungle which was the original Garden of Eden; in a word, doing their best to pass for colored.[88]

Harlem became a playground in which whites could indulge their passion to experiment with racial taboos. The nightclubs offered the possibility of transcending the socially codified barriers of race and class, and this experimentation resulted in the arousal of sexual pleasure.

Magnus Hirschfeld, "the Einstein of Sex," and cofounder of the World League for Sex Reform with Havelock Ellis, forwarded this argument in the press. In an interview that appeared in the *Chicago Herald and Examiner,* Hirschfeld, a German sexologist and proponent of homosexuality, discussed the reasons why white patrons attended black clubs and the erotic desire these clubs stimulated. Black erotic desire, however, is not included in his Freudian analysis. As is typical of the attitudes of the time, Blacks are the objects upon which whites cast their fantasies and are not in control of their own sexuality:

> The white man or the white woman who seeks love beyond the border line of color is thrilled by the sense of being subjugated by the more savage passions, the more dynamic life urge of a primitive race. In the man who thus surrenders his race pride it bespeaks a somewhat feminine attitude toward love. In a woman it is clearly an exaggeration of the normal desire for subordination.[89]

Within this framework, sexuality is intricately linked to race and gender. Hirschfeld equates black and female with the "primitive" (i.e., subordinate), and associates white and male with the "civilized" (i.e., superior). He classifies sexual desire as either active (civilized/white/male) or passive (primitive/black/female). If one extends this formula to the Harlem nightclubs, then it becomes clear how a mixing of the races leads to moral depravity. Because whites submitted to their "primitive" and "feminine" urges (compare this to the earlier discussion surrounding the presumed weaknesses and uncontrollability of single black women), "grave social evils" were sure to follow. Interest in sexual perversion was a natural corollary of whites' rejection of middle-class morality. And to satisfy this curiosity, the more adventurous whites frequented drag balls and clubs that featured gay and lesbian acts.

Within Harlem's world of drag balls and gay nightclubs, the title character, or in the words of the hit song from the show, the "mad-cap baby, called Lulu Belle," deserved a special tribute. In homage to her, the gay community named the Lulu Belle Club at 341 Lenox Avenue, near 127th Street, in Harlem after her. Black poet, artist, and actor Bruce Nugent, one of the few openly gay black intellectuals of the period, recalled "Lulu Belle's" as a hangout for "female impersonators," which catered to a primarily working-class clientele.[90] And Carl Van Vechten visited the club on at least three separate occasions in 1928, as his di-

aries document. The club shut down for a period that year as a result of numerous raids. The *New York Times,* for instance, reported that sixty-three
people were arrested during a raid of the club on January 29, 1928. According to
the article, "Most of those arrested were white persons who said they had been
'slumming.'"[91] The proprietor of the club was issued a summons for "operating
a dance hall without a license." The club reopened by the summer, since on August 16, Van Vechten indicated that he went to the "reopened Lulu Belle" with
Louis Cole, a black entertainer who sometimes appeared in drag. According to
his diary entry, he found it as "spirited as ever," and Van Vechten and Cole
stayed there until after three in the morning.[92]

A story on the front page of the *Amsterdam News* in February 1928 confirms
the club's notoriety. The report explains that within a two-week period, more
than thirty men in drag had been arrested there. One particular evening, two
undercover police detectives were dining at the club when five men dressed as
women approached them and invited them to "take an auto ride." The detectives agreed and "told the 'girls' they knew a 'nice place' at 152nd street and Amsterdam Avenue." When the group arrived there, "the 'girls' were horrified to
learn they had driven to the police station." With a wryness typical of the press,
the reporter explains: "[The five defendants] confronted the Lieutenant in silk
stockings, sleeveless evening gowns of soft-tinted crepe de chine and light fur
wraps."[93] Unlike the character Lulu Belle, the five men were unable to use "feminine wiles" and avoid the inevitable: They were sent to jail because they could
not pay the twenty-five-dollar fine.

In a notable parallel, *Strange Brother* contains an account of a young man
arrested for wearing drag. A plainclothes police officer visits a club (that bears
striking resemblance to Lulu Belle's) where he entraps a young man named
"Nelly." In night court, the officer explains that while at the club he saw "a
bunch o' fairies. A whole nest o' them."[94] The novel also includes information
about prison conditions for men convicted of homosexual-related crimes like
those arrested at Lulu Belle's might have faced. Near the end of the book, "Lilly-
Marie," a young man who had been arrested for wearing women's clothing, describes his experiences. He states that on Welfare Island the men with such pro-
clivities were segregated from the other male convicts. But he notes that he and
his consorts took especial pride in decorating their jail cells with ornaments
and pictures, and many of the inmates hung curtains made from paper or
cheesecloth over the metal bars. Among this group of "girls," as they referred to
themselves, the prisoners adopted the names of Broadway show characters,

movie actresses, and opera singers. One of the "girls," he informs the protagonist, was called "Lulu Belle."[95]

Lulu Belle's status as a gay icon is not hard to imagine, and her place in American theater history needs to be reclaimed. The gay community's appropriation of the character demonstrates the manner in which the subculture reinterpreted elements from the dominant culture and used them to bolster their position in that world. Just as imperious screen star Gloria Swanson was a popular figure for parody in the 1920s (as Joan Crawford and Bette Davis would become in the following decades), Lulu Belle's parodic appeal to the drag subculture stemmed from her defiance in the face of attempts to conform her to religious and social expectations. The critical denunciation of the play on the grounds that Lulu Belle posed a moral threat to society surely added to her popularity, as did Lenore Ulric's portrayal. Indeed, as a white actress, playing a black working-class single woman, who is also sexually liberated and wears gorgeous frocks, Lenore Ulric gave the ultimate drag performance.

Unfortunately, *Lulu Belle*'s notoriety, like the title character's, was short-lived. Perhaps it was inevitable that Lulu Belle would be punished and destroyed for violating convention and assaulting middle-class ideals, but she remains obstinate to the end. Immediately after George chokes her, the stage directions in the play state: "Lulu Belle screaming ha-ha, crawls out of bed, picks flowers up from floor and throws them at George, then drops dead."[96] If Lulu Belle has to be punished and destroyed for violating convention, she will go without a single regret. In her demise, she is remorseless, brazen, and—bedecked in ermine and diamonds—exceedingly glamorous. And as the participants at the Rockland drag and patrons at the Lulu Belle Club would have agreed, that is exactly as it should be.

"Hottentot Potentates": The Potent and Hot Performances of Florence Mills and Ethel Waters

All the crown heads of Europe have trouble with their throne;
But I got a kingdom in the hollow of my hand:
I'm the Empress Jones;
Hail from Harlem!
Settled here, knocked this Congo on its ear,
I came, I saw, and I conquered a nation with my trickeration.

I brought my bottle of Chanel with me,
I took along a script of Lulu Belle *with me;*
I win 'em all, but, oh, it raises hell with me,
The Hottentot Potentate. *

"YOU CAN'T DO WHAT THE LAST MAN DID"

Throughout the 1920s, Lulu Belle proved to be a remarkably durable and malleable persona. The darling of the gay subculture, which embraced her outrageousness and rebelliousness, she was also associated with the most prominent African American performers of the era. Almost immediately after *Lulu Belle* opened on Broadway, rumors began to circulate that the fictional title character was based on one of the most popular black entertainers of the time, Florence Mills. On February 19, 1926, the *New York Times* printed an advertisement with the provocative heading: "Was 'Lulu Belle' Written from the Life of Florence Mills?" Capitalizing on the success of the show and encouraging people to see the reputed real-life counterpart, the advertisement says, "That is a question theatre-goers are asking each other in New York to-day. This powerful Belasco triumph has caused more talk than fifty average shows put together."[1] The ad provides information about how one can see Florence Mills's show at the Plantation, a postshow nightclub on Broadway and Fiftieth Street. Mills, who had been considered for the title role in *Lulu Belle,* promptly refuted the allegation. In an interview with the *New York Graphic,* she said:

> Though I have not seen "'Lulu Belle" yet, I have read the script of the play. It is not founded on the story of my life. That has nothing to do with my refusal of the part now played so splendidly by Lenore Ulric. What would my people think if I took the lead in a production which paints the negro race in such a light?[2]

Even with nothing to support it, the rumor persisted, and "Lulu Belle" became shorthand for any suddenly successful black woman like Florence Mills.[3]

In 1927, Ethel Waters, a fast-rising star on Broadway, resuscitated the character and fanned the gossip flame that another hugely successful black woman, Josephine Baker, was a real-life Lulu Belle. Waters's musical revue *Africana* included a comedy sketch called "Harlem Transplanted to Paris," in which she satirized Baker's sensational stardom in Europe. Baker had made a splash on Broadway in *Shuffle Along* (1921) and *Chocolate Dandies* (1924) and then moved to Paris, where she became a sensation in *La Revue Negre* at the Théâtre des Champs-Élysées two years before Waters's send-up. Adding an ironic edge to the sketch, Waters performed the role as it might have been performed by Lenore Ulric in *Lulu Belle.* In a complicated intermingling of cultural references, Waters appeared in the scene wearing diamonds and furs, the accoutrements of fame and fortune for Baker and Lulu Belle. Women in the chorus (dubbed "banana maidens" in the program) garbed in banana headdresses and garishly exotic costumes, trademarks of Baker's own act, surrounded Ethel Waters on stage. In the scene, Waters wooed a dignified count, played by Louis Douglas, an act that parodied the *fictional* Lulu Belle's marriage to a count and *real-life* Baker's marriage to a *fictional* count. The centerpiece of the sketch was Waters's performance of the song "You Can't Do What the Last Man Did." As Waters explains in *His Eye Is on the Sparrow,* she parodied Lenore Ulric, who "played a Negro trollop who works her way up to a count and a boudoir in Paris by her diligent whoring."[4] Adding yet another layer of irony, the sketch alluded to Ulric's crossed-race performance of working-class blackness (and Baker's performance of aristocratic whiteness?). According to the critic of the *New York World Telegram,* the biggest laugh in the entire show came during the scene "when one of the comics asked Miss Waters if she were trying to 'pass.'"[5]

Lulu Belle's crossover act, this time to the black musical revue, reflects the continual circulation and cross-pollination of socially and artistically constructed images of blackness. In fact, the black musical revue with its loose structure, cartoonish settings, and anything-goes spirit was the perfect site for Lulu Belle's drag. The revues of the 1920s offered an assorted concoction of music, dance, comedy, and sentimentality, and were variously set among palm trees, watermelon moons, and high-class mansions. A costume list for a typical show would further demonstrate the theatrical contradictions. The leading lady, for instance, might be called upon to wear a stylized bandanna and apron in one scene, a jungle-like grass skirt and fright wig in the next, and a man's black tuxedo in another. The continuously shifting parade of racial and sexual identities might rival any at a Rockland Ball.

There has not been a great deal written about black musical revues, except in the ways in which the success of *Shuffle Along* (1921) helped create a new theatrical genre, and, as Langston Hughes famously wrote, "gave a scintillating send-off to that Negro vogue in Manhattan."[6] While the revue was one of the few theatrical arenas where an African American performer might find a modicum of success in the white-dominated popular theater of the 1920s, the shows recycled blackface comedy and structural elements left over from minstrelsy. The form upheld stereotypical notions about black womanhood as well. In such musical revues as *Put and Take* (1921), *Strut Miss Lizzie* (1922), *Blackbirds of 1928* (1928), and *Hot Chocolates* (1929), black women were generally represented as either exotic, primitive African natives; smiling, subservient "mammies"; or as sexually voracious, social-climbing "Lulu Belles." As David Krasner writes, "Black musicals could be both a blessing and a curse. They broke barriers and yet perpetuated stereotypes."[7] Nevertheless, the careers of some of the most illustrious black women performers of the early twentieth century, including Florence Mills, Ethel Waters, Josephine Baker, and Adelaide Hall, all developed from their appearances in musical revues.

A defining feature of the shows is their "blackness." They were, after all, the theatrical cousin to the "white" revues of the era, including Ziegfeld's *Follies*, George White's *Scandals*, and the Shuberts' *Artists and Models* series. Critics often compared the black revues to these shows, remarking, for instance, that by 1930 Lew Leslie's *Blackbirds* series relied too much on "the white man's formula for stage diversion."[8] Yet in 1930, black actors were still "blacking-up," or putting on the minstrel mask, which according to Nathan Irvin Huggins allowed them "to move in and out of the white world with safety and profit."[9] The minstrel mask, Huggins claimed, made African Americans far less intimidating for many white Americans.

This is no doubt true, but it ignores the fact that many of the revues, or similarly designed vaudeville shows, were not written and performed exclusively for white audiences. Black musical revues, which contained blackface comics like Apus Brooks, Izzy Rhinegold, and Sandy Burns, also performed for primarily black audiences in Harlem. These shows played such theaters as the Lafayette, Alhambra, and Lincoln, where they might precede a movie. They were also performed across the country in theaters and tents that catered to working-class African American audiences. Sometimes these shows (or revised versions of them) played Broadway, but more often than not, they played limited engagements in vaudeville houses on the TOBA (Theater Owners' Booking Association) circuit.[10] Black audiences apparently adored the familiar chicken-stealing sketches, minimally dressed jungle maidens, and slow-witted, malaprop-spouting comedians. Black critic Theophilus Lewis pointed to the stereotypical content in the shows and argued that black audiences were complicit in their perpetuation. According to Lewis, African American performers did not *have* to perform derogatory images of blackness within these venues. In an essay for *The Messenger* in June 1927, he wrote:

> If we do not like the social ugliness we see on the stage, the remedy is not to close the theatre or bawl the actors out, but to change our way of living. When people pack a theatre every night, it is a sign that they like the social behavior they see reflected there. When they cease to like it they will stay away from the theatre and the producer will alter his entertainment to suit the changed taste of the public.[11]

Black vaudevillian and playwright Salem Tutt Whitney weighed in on the argument, saying that in the precarious world of show business, producers and actors "must give the public what it wants" if they intend to make a living.[12] It seems clear from Lewis's statements and the unremitting lineup of black musical revues in the 1920s that the representations of blackness were just as popular and ingrained with African American audiences as they were with white.

Two of the most famous black women entertainers of the Harlem Renaissance, Florence Mills and Ethel Waters, gained fame and fortune as a result of their work in black revues of the 1920s. While the black revue in musical theater and African American history tends to be footnoted as a series of *Shuffle Along* rip-offs or else apologetically described as a hybrid minstrel / *Ziegfeld Follies* show, it deserves greater attention. This is especially true in the case of the shows starring Mills and Waters, who were acclaimed by both black and white audiences, and, in very different ways, exposed the contradictory yet intertwined elements of blackness and whiteness that the revues encompassed. Responses to Mills's performance in *Dixie to Broadway* (1924) and Waters's in *Africana* (1927), *Blackbirds of 1930* (1930), and *At Home Abroad* (1935), their most significant Broadway appearances in musical revues, indicate that these performers negotiated the racial and sexual stereotypes while gesturing toward a truly pluralist art form. Their performances, perhaps more so than those of other musical stars of the era, helped resolve the tension between pleasure and disdain evoked by the black musical revue, a genre that both affirmed and unhinged racial and sexual stereotypes. In performances that call to mind Lenore Ulric's in *Lulu Belle,* Mills and Waters allude to the masquerade of race, class, and gender, which they often applied on stage.

"PUT YOUR OLD BANDANNA ON"

One of the most successful revues of the period, *Dixie to Broadway,* is perhaps best remembered as the show that catapulted Florence Mills, already famous in Europe, to stardom in the United States. The show was particularly notable because for the first time, a black revue was constructed to showcase the talents of a woman and not designed around two blackface male comedians. Even more impressively, it played the Broadhurst Theatre, a respectable, choice house in the "very heart of Broadway," rather than "on the fringe of the theatrical district" as all-black shows tended to play (*Shuffle Along,* for instance, played at Daly's on Sixty-third Street).[13] *Dixie to Broadway* was quite successful, garnering generally excellent reviews and running seventy-seven performances on Broadway, which makes it also noteworthy as the first black revue to "pay back its cost."[14] In addition to the accolades awarded Florence Mills, the show established white producer-director Lew Leslie as a major presence on Broadway, one who "capitalized on the growing interest of New York's elite in the culture and history of black Manhattan."[15]

  Dixie to Broadway began as an entertainment that catered to a white, middle-class audience and for the most part remained so (except a two-week stint at the Lafayette). Its first appearance was in a New York nightclub setting, then on a European tour, and finally on Broadway, opening October 29, 1924. Reviewers praised Florence Mills wherever she played, and Leslie sought to use her

European popularity when he brought the revue back to the States. Although its run of seventy-seven performances is quite short by today's standards, the show was an unqualified success. The unanimously favorable notices accorded Florence Mills, billed "The Sensation of Two Continents" in program listings and newspaper advertisements, are responsible for the profit the revue turned. The show was Mills's third Broadway appearance, and regrettably, it was also her last.

Florence Mills was born in Washington, DC, in 1896, and by the age of three, she was already making a name for herself in show business. As "Baby Florence Mills," she entertained Washington diplomats in their drawing rooms, performing an adroit cakewalk and singing such songs as "Don't Cry, My Little Pickaninny." At eight, she made her professional stage debut in a road-show version of the Bert Williams and George Walker musical *Sons of Ham,* in which she received a rave notice from the *Washington Star* that noted, "As an extra attraction is Baby Florence Mills singing 'Hannah from Savannah.' Baby Florence made a big hit and was encored for dancing."[16] After touring with this show briefly, Mills and her two sisters, Olivia and Maude, put together a vaudeville act, and the Mills Sisters or the Mills Trio, as they were variously known, traversed the country. She joined legendary cabaret owner Ada "Bricktop" Smith and dancer Cora Green in 1914, and they billed themselves as the Panama Trio after the Chicago club in which they performed.[17] In 1916, she joined the Tennessee Ten, which was then playing the influential Keith vaudeville circuit. While appearing with this act, she met dancer U.S. "Slow Kid" Thompson, whom she later married, and as Theophilus Lewis wrote, "They were considered one of the most happily married couples in the profession."[18]

Her big break, though, came in 1921 when she replaced Gertrude Saunders in *Shuffle Along.* Almost immediately, Mills captured the attention of director-producer Lew Leslie, who cast her in his *Plantation Revue* at his newly opened Plantation Club. A very young Paul Robeson was part of this show and wrote, "How thrilling it was to listen to Florence Mills sing nightly—'Down Among the Sleepy Hills of Tennessee.'"[19] In addition to her acclaim on Broadway and in London, Mills also has the distinction of being the first African American to "headline" at New York's Palace Theatre, the most prestigious vaudeville venue of its day.[20] A year later in 1926, she made a rather surprising debut at the Aeolian Hall in New York, which was primarily known for its programs featuring operatic and classical selections, and occasionally traditional black spirituals sung by individuals like Robeson and Roland Hayes.

Mills's magnificent career came to an untimely end, though. While readying Lew Leslie's *Blackbirds of 1928* for Broadway, she was struck with acute appendicitis, and she died on November 1, 1927. She was thirty-one. As James Weldon Johnson wrote, "It is not an exaggeration to say that her death shocked the theatrical world."[21] Five thousand mourners packed the Mother Zion Church in Harlem for her funeral—the church could comfortably fit only about two thousand—and over 150,000 people lined Lenox and Seventh Avenues to pay respects as the procession took her body to Woodlawn Cemetery. The newspapers reported that Harlem had never seen such a public outpouring of grief as it had during this funeral, and all were amazed at the spectacle of the occasion.[22] Thirty women from the various choruses of Mills's shows served as flower girls leading the coffin out of the church, and eight notable female stars from the black theater, including Ethel Waters, Gertrude Saunders, and Cora Green, were honorary pallbearers. Celebrities and family members eulogized her, read poems, and sang hymns to her memory. And presumably because of the overcrowded conditions combined with the heightened emotion, about fifty people fainted in grief. The papers also reported that a cornet player in the band "collapsed from heart disease on Seventh Avenue and died before an ambulance surgeon arrived."[23] But by all accounts, the coup de grâce occurred when lyricist Andy Razaf dedicated his song, written with J. C. Johnson, "All the World Is Lonely (for Our Little Blackbird)" to her, and a thousand blackbirds were released from a plane overhead.[24] It was a breathtaking and stunning tribute to a young woman who had been hailed "the pride of the race."

The last flourish was a reference to Mills's trademark song, "I'm a Little Blackbird Looking for a Bluebird," which she sang to great enthusiasm in *Dixie to Broadway*. Although she had appeared on Broadway before, this was the show that sealed Mills's success in show business and confirmed her as a source of pride for African Americans. As James Weldon Johnson wrote about her, "She had made a name in *Shuffle Along*, but in *Dixie to Broadway* she was recognized for her full worth."[25] In fact, with the opening of *Dixie to Broadway*, Florence Mills emerged as both an extraordinary entertainer and as a national spokesperson for her race. For her performance, she was hailed as a unique and forceful new talent on Broadway, and her sudden fame allowed her the opportunity to publicly speak out against racial prejudice. And although Mills portrayed well-worn representations of black women in the show, donning both the jungle and plantation costumes, she also assumed the images of bourgeoisie romanticism and aristocratic refinement. Taken as a whole, her performance represents the modernist tension between savagery and civilization, and it also demonstrates the manner in which Mills playfully, with the collaboration of the show's white creators, demolished the stereotypical associations with black womanhood.

A script for the revue is not available, but it is possible to glean the overall effect of the show on the basis of the reviews and program listings of the New York production. In his biography of Florence Mills, Bill Egan is especially thorough in his description and reconstruction of the show, act by act and song by song.[26] The act and song titles are in fact indicative of the milieu the show evoked. The production's prologue, "Evolution of the Colored Race," was intended to introduce a motif for the entire show, and it shoehorned in references to Salome, Madame Butterfly, and Abraham Lincoln. After the first few numbers, including "Put Your Old Bandanna On" and "Dixie Dreams," the show dropped this framing device. Familiar features of the black musical revue followed, such as a haunted house sketch, "Treasure Castle," which played upon the notion of superstitious, easily spooked black people. There were several big, energetic dance numbers, such as "Jazz Time Came from the South" and "Darkest Russia." And the show included a customary "Oriental" skit, called "The Sailor and the Chink," performed by Henry Winfred and Billy C. Brown, or as one critic described the team, "the former being vaudeville's best known Chinese portrayer and the latter a 'cork' artist [i.e., a performer in blackface] of class and a vocalist of ability."[27]

The New York critics tended to focus on particular numbers more than others. Several reviews single out dancer Johnny Nit, whose first significant appearance in the show was as part of a trio of dancers chained together by the ankles in "Prisoners Up-to-Date." Alexander Woollcott of the *New York Sun* referred to this former vaudevillian as the "dark Mr. Nit with the toothful smile," and claims that "the lisp of his feet on the floor is rhythm's self, and it was out of the efforts of the honky-tonk pianists to bend their measures to the likes of him that the thing called ragtime was born."[28] The critics praised other dancers as well, including Willie Covan and Mills's husband U. S. Thompson, for their remarkable energy. Gilbert Gabriel of the *Telegram and Evening Mail* wrote that Covan and Thompson "shuffle up to a hysteria of motion, bouncing and cavorting on every inch of their bodies that will afford a landing place."[29] Another highpoint was the homage to and imitation of such performers as George M. Cohan ("Georgia Cohans"), Eva Tanguay, and Walker and Williams in the "If My Dreams Came True" segment.

But the focus of attention was clearly on twenty-eight-year-old Florence Mills, who had six numbers in the show. From her first appearance in the show to her last, audiences responded rapturously to this unlikely new star. Often describing her as "birdlike," "beautiful," and "grotesque," the critics went to some pains to explain Mills's mysterious but undeniable appeal and unique talents. Mills's unexplainable charm produced by these contradictory qualities is perhaps best exemplified by Heywood Broun's description in the *New York World:*

> Curiously enough there are not particularly good voices in *Dixie to Broadway* but there is a striking one. The method of Florence Mills is like that of no one else. She does not precisely sing but she makes strange high noises which seem to fit somehow with a rapidfire sort of sculpture. Sometimes the intent is the creation of the grotesque and then it fades into lines of amazing beauty. Now I have seen grace.[30]

Others described her as a "nimble microbe," "intensely lively, and agile, and industrious," "strung on fine and tremulous wires," and "a flashing and beautiful woman who lights up like a Christmas tree when she dances and is quite as festive."[31]

In general, the critics applauded numbers set in plantations or among glittery jungle backdrops, and they singled out such scenes for their "authenticity" and warm nostalgia. For example, in two of the most successful numbers in *Dixie to Broadway,* Mills and her chorus-girl ensemble, the "Plantation Chocolate Drops," paid tribute to a romanticized pre–Civil War South. At these moments, Mills and her ensemble energetically re-created the representations of singing and dancing "darkies" for the amusement of the Broadway audiences.

It is important to remember that the majority of the audiences at *Dixie to Broadway* tended to be white and middle class. Although the Broadway theaters were no longer formally segregated at this time, few blacks attended the productions. Of course, there would be a greater number at the black revues than there would be at standard white fare, but the percentage was still rather small. In a 1928 article written for *The Messenger,* a monthly black periodical, Randolph Edmonds described the usual composition of a Broadway show audience: "There is very little, if any prejudice on Broadway now. But if the managers suddenly decide to put us in the gallery, there will be too few of us to make any difference, for we pay very little of the thousands of dollars necessary to run them for a year."[32] In addition, the white audiences who frequented the Broadway shows were often the same audiences who traveled uptown to sample the talent in the Harlem clubs.[33] So even though this was the first musical on Broadway that Florence Mills headlined, many in the audience were familiar with her work from other venues.

Androgynously dressed, wearing stylized tramp's clothing, including loose-fitting, brightly striped short pants, a baggy white shirt, a beggar's hat, and toting an over-the-shoulder hobo's kit bag (i.e., a handkerchief-bundle tied to a stick), Mills made her first appearance singing "Dixie Dreams." The bittersweet song evokes the tradition of Stephen Foster, recalling such standards as "Old Folks at Home" and "My Old Kentucky Home." Similar in tone and style to those songs, "Dixie Dreams" begins with the lyric, "Dear Old Dixieland, how I long for your sunshine, / Gee, I'm sorry I ever started to roam," and it includes references to "sunny southern bowers," "fields of white" (i.e., cotton), and nostalgic recollections of "mammy's songs and stories."[34] Set on a plantation with the ensemble wearing straw hats, the number reflects the show's unabashed lineage to minstrelsy. In fact, "Plantation Melodies," as Eric Lott describes the songs of this genre, were integral to minstrel shows of the nineteenth century. In these numbers, blackface entertainers pined for the carefree, rustic, and far less complicated life of slavery. The South was posited as wholesome and familial, and the North, where the narrators in these songs had regretfully arrived, was corrupt and lonely. Lott claims that these numbers often elicited a sentimental yearning to return to the South or to slavery.[35] Blackface performers generally had great success touching a collective emotional nerve in their urban audiences by lamenting the missed pleasures of "de ol' plantation." According to Lott, the songs metaphorically played upon the desire to return to an insouciant childhood, as well as helped mollify white guilt over the treatment of black people.

In the "Dixie Dreams" number, Mills recapitulated, or—to employ Gates's terminology—"signified on," the simple, sentimental minstrel caricature. As a woman taking on the formerly male persona, she also demonstrated the remarkable malleability and fluidity of the minstrel mask. Invented by white male performers in blackface, adopted and perfected by African American male performers in blackface, including Williams and Walker who billed themselves as "two real coons," the minstrel mask took on a new veneer with Mills's rendition. As one critic remarked, her performance evoked the sentimental and comical persona that Bert Williams evinced on stage. He wrote, "She is the lithe embodiment of the song and sorrow, the poetry and the pathos, and the rich comedy of her race."[36] To other critics, Mills's next number in *Dixie to Broadway* produced a similar transitory experience.

In a bizarre merging of representations of the African savage and the antebellum "mammy," Mills and the Plantation Chocolate Drops performed an exuberant dance number called "Jungle Nights in Dixieland." The dancers wore colorful grass skirts and large white wigs, and they shuffled, shimmied, and shook accordingly. Beneath the grotesquerie of the costumes and dancing, though, several critics pointed to the glimpses of a presumed black authenticity that the number offered. To them, "Jungle Nights in Dixieland" provided a transparent view of the supposedly "real" cultural distinctions between the races. That is, although Florence Mills was born in Washington, DC, thirty years after slavery was abolished, and although, as she stated, she had "never visited a jungle,"[37] she could effectively tap into a seemingly collective black consciousness. And according to one critic at least, Florence Mills embodied the entire history of her race within "Jungle Nights in Dixieland." He wrote: "[Mills] can shift from the frenzied war whoops that takes one back to the days of her ancestors on the Congo to the soft easy dribbles of hummed speech that were intoned on the plantations back in those dear old southern times before the war."[38]

Responses from the black community to the production reflect the widely divergent opinions on the depictions of the primitive and the folk in African American arts. Many of the young Harlem Renaissance writers presented these elements in their own work, offering them as a defining feature of black artistic expression. Granted, for many artists this was a way to appeal to white patronage, but it also represented an aesthetic to which they could lay claim. Langston Hughes, for instance, encouraged other writers to listen to "the tom-tom cries and tom-tom laughs" and to celebrate the dialect poetry and folk tales of Paul Laurence Dunbar and Charles Chesnutt.[39] In "How It Feels to Be Colored Me," Zora Neale Hurston writes about the African savage that arises within her when she hears a jazz orchestra begin to play. In a description that does not sound too far removed from the over-the-top performance of "Jungle Nights in Dixieland," she writes:

> I dance wildly inside myself; I yell within, I whoop; I shake my assegai above my head, I hurl it true to the mark *yeeeeooww!* I am in the jungle and living in the jungle way. My face is painted red and yellow and my body is painted blue. My pulse is throbbing like a war drum. I want to slaughter something—give pain, give death to what, I do not know.[40]

For many of the black writers, primitivism was regarded as an affirmative element, reflecting an idea that African Americans were closer to "nature" and as a result were more instinctual, unconstrained, and more elementally alive than whites who were trapped in industrialization and modern life.[41]

This helps explain why *Variety*'s George Bell, who was invited as a "Negro first nighter" to review the show, called it a "credit to the colored race, rather than a ridicule."[42] Tony Langston, drama critic of the African American paper the *Chicago Defender,* had only raves for the show, referring to it as "The great review [*sic*] is one of the best shows of its kind ever seen in a Loop theater. It surpasses everything of the type shown in Chicago in the past several years."[43] And the *Amsterdam News* remarked on Mills's ability to transport her audience to a peaceful southern setting in the "Dixie Dreams" number: "Her singing, coupled with the music of Bill Vodery's Plantation Orchestra, unfurls to your gaze filled with wonder Aurora Borealis rising over yon distant green hill in old Virginny and the sweet nectar of roses wafted to you on zephyric breeze, and you are only released from your hypnotic state at the volume of applause which crashes about you as Florence leaves the scene, though forced to come back again and again."[44]

Other African American critics were less than complimentary of the tone of the show (although they praised the performance of Florence Mills). The attitude mirrored the other side of the artistic debate in which individuals like W. E. B. Du Bois vehemently opposed the perpetuation of racial stereotypes. Du Bois argued that such shows confirmed derogatory black representations for white audiences and increased attitudes of black inferiority. He argued that the ridicule of blacks was evident in the musicals by the "loud ejaculations and guffaws of laughter [that] broke out in the wrong places."[45] Similarly, critics in the *Messenger* and *Opportunity* reflected this standpoint. Never a big fan of Lew Leslie's shows or black musical revues in general, Theophilus Lewis of the *Messenger* stated, "Mr. Leslie impudently thrusts his show forward as an apologist for the Negro race."[46] Roger Didier of *Opportunity* was also offended by the stereotypical nature of the production, which to him was evident even in the scenery:

> There is not only a repetition of the threadbare stereotypes of defunct minstrelsy but something which comes dangerously near to obscenity. The drop used throughout the show, gaudy and indecorous, pictures on one side a "comic strip" Negro stealing a chicken and on the other similar Negroes playing at dice. The overused razor crops up as the show goes on.[47]

While the diverse reactions to the *Dixie to Broadway* reflect the conflicting attitudes toward representations of African Americans in the arts, the responses to the show and Mills's defense of it hinted at yet another prevalent view of artistic expression, *cultural pluralism.*

In his advancement of cultural pluralism, Alain Locke emphasized the importance of "race cooperation" and "constructive participation" in order for the New Negro to ultimately "celebrate his full initiation into American democracy."[48] In his essays "The Concept of Race as Applied to Culture" (1924) and "The New Negro," Locke does not minimize the importance of racial self-determination and individuality, as they were crucial elements in the development of "race consciousness." The resultant artistic output is the by-product of this collective group expression, which distinguishes one cultural group from one another. To Locke, a culture is defined by its artistic creations, including literature, art, and theater. Yet although he wrote about the particular "traditions" and "values" of a particular race that are necessary components of a culture's artwork, Locke did not see them as stable entities. To Locke, race and culture are not fixed entities that separate one group from another. They evolve as a result of migration, historical circumstances, and contact with other groups. Therefore, it is imperative in Locke's philosophy that races not only respect and "study" the cultural output of other racial groups, but that they also share their own artworks with other groups. To Locke, an enlightened civilization depends upon the exchange and distribution of these cultural products, which he saw as a fundamental duty of the New Negro in the advancement of a truly integrated American society. He writes, "To all of this the New Negro is keenly responsive as an augury of a new democracy in American culture. He is contributing his share to the new social understanding."[49] In order to demonstrate "race loyalty," artists need to put the needs of their culture over their own efforts at personal success and advancement. Locke believed that such cultural connections were already being wrought through the work of the artists in Harlem.

Whether or not Florence Mills had read Locke's work and consciously set out to embody his philosophy of cultural pluralism in the musical revue is not certain. It is certain, however, that she saw herself as a spokesperson for the race, and she forwarded many of the ideals of the New Negro in interviews. In a statement during her pre-Broadway engagement of *Dixie* that appeared in the black newspaper *Chicago Defender,* Mills explained why she did not accept an offer from Florenz Ziegfeld to appear in an edition of his hugely successful *Follies* series. Although the *Follies* were almost exclusively white except for an occasional featured black artist, the opportunity would allow her to follow in the tradition of Bert Williams, the first black performer in the *Follies.* It would surely bring her to an altogether new height of stardom in the white theater. She explained:

I felt . . . that since Williams established the Colored performer in association with a well-known revue, that I could best serve the Colored actor by accepting Mr. Leslie's offer, since he had promised to make this revue as sumptuous and gorgeous in production and costume as Ziegfeld's Follies, White's Scandals or the Greenwich Village Follies, at the same time using an all-Colored cast. I felt that if this revue turned out successfully a permanent institution would have been created for the Colored artists and an opportunity created for the glorification of the American High-Brown. My wish and Mr. Leslie's promise have been fulfilled in *Dixie to Broadway.*[50]

Adopting Locke's view of racial loyalty, Mills saw the black musical revue, particularly *Dixie to Broadway,* as an effort to strengthen black culture rather than as a means of purely personal gain. For Florence Mills, the black musical revue represented a form of social uplift that epitomized the ideals of the New Negro and gave African Americans an international presence. On her death, the *Amsterdam News* alluded to this fact when the editorial page stated, "It is not too much to say that her popularity in Paris helped to soften anti-American feeling in France."[51]

Paradoxically, the show that Mills regarded as an emblem of cultural empowerment was not written by African Americans. *Dixie to Broadway,* like many of the black revues of the 1920s, was written and produced by a contingent of white men.[52] While the black comics would have written their own material for the show, and the dance teams would have done their own choreography, the white composers and authors would have written the connective material and Mills's sketches. In fact, the juxtaposition was somewhat jarring for some of the critics, who faulted the show for its overpowering "whiteness." When the material pulled away from plantation settings, jungle costumes, and tap-dancing chain gangs, and the cast performed in elegant evening wear and in front of an oversized, white grand piano, critics accused the show and the performers as trying to "pass" for white. The most noteworthy example is during the "Mandy Make Up Your Mind" number. The segment appeared near the end of the first act of the show, and it strongly recalls the spectacular wedding finales of the *Ziegfeld Follies.*[53] Lew Leslie and Florence Mills, however, put their own spin on it. In this version, Mills, who was known for cross-dressed roles (for instance as Sammy, the Dixie waif, she performed in the "Dixie Dreams" number), played the groom and was surrounded by a full, formally dressed wedding party as she sang to the reluctant bride:

Marchin' down the aisle,
Your style will make 'em all stare.
With a little black-eyed Susan
Stuck in your hair.
Gee, but your candy, Mandy
Won't you decide?[54]

Not only does the act conjure images of the "white" wedding Ziegfeld motif, but the dignified costumes contrast sharply with the bandannas, convict outfits, and grass skirts worn by the cast earlier in the show. A complete role reversal had been accomplished by the conclusion of this act. In "Jungle Nights in Dixieland," Mills performed the picture of a displaced jubilant African woman celebrating the joys of plantation life; in "Mandy," she depicted the image of a sedate, sophisticated, and domineering white, upper middle-class American man.

The transition from the frenetic jungle savage to the boyish plantation wanderer to the aristocratic gentleman reveals a form of cultural evolution from primitivism to modernism. The shifting images also imply that the representation of the jungle dancer is as much an act as the aristocratic white man. For some critics this merging of cultural images was particularly off-putting. George Jean Nathan referred to it as "a music show miscegenation."[55] The critic from the *American* was similarly distressed by the cultural hybridity of the show:

> In these colored entertainments there is a growing tendency to obliterate race peculiarities as much as possible and to "make-up" white. I think that a pity. After all, we go to these entertainments for the sake of differences—just as we travel to find something alien to our own customs. But of course there are still qualities that cannot be deleted, and on these we can bank.[56]

Florence Mills herself alluded to the cross-pollination of cultural images when she explained in the *Defender* interview that she and Lew Leslie were attempting to create a new entertainment institution that combined black vaudeville (read "low-brow") with the white *Follies* (read "high-brow") to form a middle-class, "American High-Brown" revue. The form of entertainment Mills prescribed was much more refined and bourgeoisie than what one might see in Harlem nightclubs and vaudeville. Her performances at the Palace Theatre on Broadway and at the Aeolian Hall affirm her desire to reach a middle- and up-

FIG. 7. Florence Mills as the groom and Alma Smith as the bride in "Mandy, Make Up Your Mind" from *Dixie to Broadway* (1924). © White Studio. (Billy Rose Theatre Division, The New York Public Library for the Performing Arts, Astor, Lenox and Tilden Foundations.)

per-class audience. The method in which she and Leslie pursued their American High-Brown revue appears as if it were explicitly modeled on Lockean philosophy of cultural pluralism.

Florence Mills's big number in the show, and the song for which she would be forever identified, "I'm a Little Blackbird Looking for a Bluebird," is in the tradition of Bert Williams's portrayal of the melancholic, every(black)man. His songs, both as written and in his languid, despondent delivery in his resonant bass voice, summoned the sadness and weariness of living a lonely existence within circumstances he is powerless to change. Williams's most famous songs, "Nobody" and "Jonah Man," articulate the pain and dejection of being black and vulnerable in a white man's world. Mills's version of "Blackbird" created a similar effect through the lyric:

> Never had no happiness
> Never felt no one's caress
> Just a lonesome bit of humanity
> Born on a Friday, I guess
> Blue as anyone can be
> Clouds are all I ever see
> If the sun forgets no one,
> Why don't it shine for me?[57]

The song's lyric is relentlessly sentimental, and the rhymes are undeniably simplistic. The melody, which was suited to Mills's "birdlike" voice, contributes to the song's perceived syrupy melancholy. The grammatically incorrect lines make it even more jarring on the ear. There are, however, specific references to race in the song, such as "Tho' I'm of a darker hue, I've a heart the same as you,"[58] and the lyric takes on greater social significance and increased empathy.

The tone of the song shifts somewhat in the middle. While the first part focuses on a universal sense of isolation that African Americans face, the second part is much more closely linked to the singer's gender. The lyric demurely highlights the singer's desire for male companionship and love. The bluesy folk tradition in the first stanza leads into a love ballad in the Tin-Pan Alley tradition. Previously in the song the singer comes across as abandoned and destitute, but by the end she is downright coy and presents herself as a jazz baby:

> I'm a little blackbird looking for a little bluebird, too.
> You know little blackbirds get a little lonesome, too, and blue.

I've been all over from east to west.
In search of someone to feather my nest.
Why don't I find one the same as you do?
The answer must be that I am a hoo-doo
I'm a little jazz-bo
Looking for a rainbow too.[59]

It sounds not unlike a song that Lulu Belle might perform. But in fact, Mills believed that this, her signature song, had a deeper social significance than simply the lament of a lonely woman looking for the love of a man. Although it is not strongly evident in the song, she tried to convey the antiracist argument in her performance. Writing for London's *Sun Chronicle,* she claimed that "Blackbird" profoundly articulated the "Negro's attitude towards life." In a short essay called "The Soul of the Negro," Mills compares the plight of black people in the United States to "a small boy flattening his nose against a pastry-cook's window and longing for all the good things on the other side of the pane."[60]

The conflicting images and structure of the song are the result of a merge of different music traditions, a cultural pluralism. Mills indicated this aspect when asked about the white authorship of the songs and how this fact could potentially undercut the truthfulness of the message she hoped to convey. In one interview, for instance, she was reminded that her onstage performance of a presumably authentic lived black experience was filtered through the composition of two Jewish men. She responded:

That's true. . . . But then I always say that the Negroes and the Jews are, in art, brother peoples. They are two of the three most ancient races in the world, they've retained their national characteristics right through thousands of years. Both have a fund of natural simplicity and love of art to draw on.[61]

Her comments parallel Locke's own words when he referred to Harlem as "the home of the Negro's 'Zionism,'" and wrote, "As with the Jew, persecution is making the Negro international."[62] For Florence Mills, the combined traditions and values could indeed create a powerful and new form of artistic expression. Understanding, appreciating, and incorporating Jewish culture in her own creative work was a way of realizing the goals of the New Negro. (In 1926, at the final performance of *Blackbirds* in London, she further demonstrated her solidarity with Jewish culture by singing the hymn "Eli-Eli.")[63]

The combination of Florence Mills's innate performance ability and her commitment to social progress helped make the song a musical phenomenon. Although a recording of Mills performing the song does not exist (indeed the great misfortune is that none of her songs had been recorded), based on the descriptions of her singing it, one can understand to some extent how she could, with this simple song, manage to "so quickly[,] so certainly and so electrically get an audience into her grip and keep it [t]here."[64] The contradictory elements of the song lyric, such as the racial protest set against sexual desire and the sentimentality that is pitted against the coyness, made perfect sense in her rendition. Her performance capitalized on the song's contradictions, and she used her high-pitched birdlike tones to emphasize the sadness and highlight the comic aspects. These qualities are especially evident in the description by Theophilus Lewis, who generally disdained the black musical revue form. Even he had to concede Mills's mesmeric power as a performer:

> [Florence Mills] has perfect control of both the technique of restraint and the technique of abandon. In the early scenes of *From Dixie to Broadway* she employs restraint. But when she sings her song "I'm a Little Blackbird," she lets herself out, and—My God! Man, I've never seen anything like it! Not only that, I never imagined such a tempestuous blend of humor and passion could be poured into the singing of a song. I never expect to see anything like it again, unless I become gifted with second sight and behold a Valkyr riding ahead of a thunderstorm. Or see Florence Mills singing another song.[65]

Mills's offstage persona was similarly contradictory. While she forwarded the ideals of the New Negro, she frequently referred to herself as a "pickaninny," and in interviews and essays for the press, Mills often performed this stereotypical caricature. In an article for London's *Sun Chronicle* titled "The Soul of the Negro" (which calls to mind Du Bois's *The Souls of Black Folk*), Mills incorporates the language of folk poetry and slave narratives. For example, she defends black people by denoting their "childish trust" and "white to the core" feelings, and attesting that although they "may not be so sophisticated, so developed as the white man," they do not deserve to be treated as social outcasts. Pathos and mawkishness nearly overburden her plea for acceptance; the strains of a Dixie melody seem to underscore the writing. She writes, for example, "When I was born I was just a poor pickaninny, with no prospects but a whole legacy of sorrow." Cannily, Mills seemed to recognize that in order to make people listen to a young black woman's appeal for racial equality, she had to do it from behind a familiar, nonthreatening guise. She writes: "In America, despite the very real prejudice that exists, the Negro race is rearing its head in all branches of social life. In England where the color line is practically nonexistent, Negroes have achieved a virtual equality."[66] Her performance of the unthreatening and simple "pickanniny" role both on stage and off helps explain why she was so successful as a black spokesperson. It granted her a platform that otherwise might have eluded her, and once she had it, she was able to register her racial protest.

Yet while she exuded a good-willed, ever-cheerful, and nonmalicious spirit, she also, depending upon the audience, used her position for more pointed attacks at racism. In an article appearing in the *Amsterdam News*, a black newspaper, Mills was more direct in her criticism of the color barrier in the United States. She said, "There are many colored boys in America who, after being trained as lawyers and doctors, have to become train attendants because they are black and there is no place for them." And addressing the incongruity of racism in the United States, she told the interviewer, "If a white person in a theatre is put next to a Negro, the white person objects. Yet the same white person will eat food cooked by a colored person and be waited on by another Negro."[67] Unlike other black performers, who did not risk their careers on speaking out against social injustices, Florence Mills believed that doing so was her duty as a public figure.

The technique by which Florence Mills strove for racial tolerance was based on her ability to ingratiate herself with her public. She once remarked, "The stage is the quickest way to get to the people. My own success makes people think better of other colored folks."[68] Mills's performance strategies were notable for applying exaggerated images of racial stereotypes to the material written for her. While overplaying these stereotypes, she showed that they were associated with cultural performance traditions rather than as defining features of her race. This inflection is evident in a review by George Jean Nathan, who described her performance of multiple images associated with her race:

> When Florence Mills sings, the voice of her Negro people is in that singing, even when the lyrics of her songs are out of the Yiddo-American Broadway music publishers' shop. When she dances, the feet of all the pickaninnies since the Civil War are in her shoes. And when, in the argot of her own people, she struts her stuff, you get in her the spirit of our colored Americans off on a gala holiday. She is surely worth seeing.[69]

Indeed as the proclaimed toast of Broadway and the ambassador of her race, Florence Mills was surely worth seeing.

Mills's contemporary and a celebrated Broadway performer in her own right, Ethel Waters, also used her star status to critique black representations. In her performance of the songs "Stormy Weather" and especially "Supper Time," Waters could strike a forceful blow against the dehumanizing effects of racism. Unlike Mills, however, Waters's predominant stage persona was not characterized by innocence and androgyny, but by mischievousness and sexual playfulness. While Mills intentionally eliminated, or at the very least downplayed, the bawdiness of the musical revue material—James Weldon Johnson wrote that it was "impossible for [Florence Mills] to be vulgar, for she possessed a naïveté that was alchemic"[70]—Waters often nudged the boundaries of decorum with her "blue" songs, or those with risqué or double entendre lyrics. Like Florence Mills, Waters at times adopted stereotypical representations, but in her demeanor and vocal style, she distanced herself from these images. Applying the raucous performance style she developed in front of working-class black audiences, Ethel Waters called attention to the ludicrousness of the stereotypical depictions through satire and mock sentimentality, thereby draining them of their potency.

"SHAKE THAT THING"

Although today is she is primarily known for her film work in the late 1940s and early 1950s, including *Pinky* (1949) and *The Member of the Wedding* (1952), and while she is best remembered as a corpulent, spirituals-singing black woman, Ethel Waters was not always the embodiment of the familiar image of the matriarchal African American. In the 1920s and early 1930s, Waters was regarded as a sometimes glamorous, sometimes sexy, sometimes bawdy, and always original singer and comedienne. Her voice did not have the raw blues power of Bessie Smith or the distinctive birdlike quality of Florence Mills, but with her inimitable puckishness and impudence, she could put across a song like no one else. When she opened on Broadway in the mostly white 1935 musical revue *At Home Abroad,* the last revue in which she appeared, Brooks Atkinson of the *New York Times* described her as a "gleaming tower of dusky regality, who knows how to make a song stand on tip-toe."[71]

Born in Philadelphia in 1896 and out of wedlock—her mother, then twelve, was raped at knifepoint by her father, a man Ethel Waters never knew—Waters seemed an unlikely candidate for international stardom. In *His Eye Is on the Sparrow* (1951), Waters recounts the tumultuous early years of her life with unflinching candor. Upon reading a segment printed in a staid magazine prior

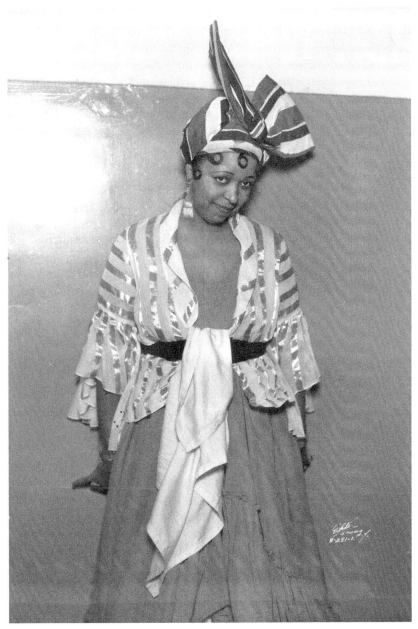

FIG. 8. A demure Ethel Waters (circa 1930) in typical attire of the black musical revues: plantation drab meets Broadway glitz. © White Studio. (Billy Rose Theatre Division, The New York Public Library for the Performing Arts, Astor, Lenox and Tilden Foundations.)

to the book's release, Carl Van Vechten wrote to painter and lithographer Prentiss Taylor: "The part of Miss Waters's Memoirs in the October issue of the *Ladies Home Journal* is sensational in all respects. How that cumbersome conservative magazine happened to publish all this rape and bastardy and adultery is beyond anybody, but they did."[72] Added to these shocking descriptions is her unembarrassed narration of a life filled with crime and hard luck. As a child, Waters stole and associated primarily with whores, thieves, and hardened criminals. And at thirteen, she was married for the first time to a man who brutally beat her. The marriage lasted barely a year.

Her lucky break came when she was seventeen. While supporting herself as a chambermaid, Waters performed at a Halloween party on a whim. Known as "Chippie" Waters to her friends at the time, she claims in her autobiography that she had become "a really agile shimmy shaker," and notes: "It was these completely mobile hips, not my voice, that won me friends and inspired admiration."[73] A pair of professional vaudevillians in the audience that night saw her and offered her the opportunity to perform with them in a small TOBA unit out of Baltimore. She reluctantly accepted and began a highly successful vaudeville career under the name "Sweet Mama Stringbean," in reference to her height and lanky frame. While touring—chiefly in the South—she quickly developed a following for her blues songs and "shake dancing," or the shimmy. Although the shimmy had explicit sexual connotations, Waters applied a playfulness that undercut the dance's potential lewdness. As William Gardner Smith points out, when Waters danced, it did not seem crude or base, impressions other women dancers often gave while performing in a similar manner. Smith explained in a profile written years after Waters had given up shimmying:

> She did the hottest shake dance of her, or any other day. She used to hold her arms far out from her body, to give the freest movement to all parts of her anatomy; she wore tassels on her hips sometimes, and a large buckle on her belt, to accentuate the movements of her body. She could squirm, twist, shake and vibrate in a way which was absolutely uncanny. And yet—who ever felt the slightest sense of vulgarity? One had the impression that she could bathe in mud and still remain clean.[74]

Her elfin grin and mischievous demeanor added a layer of innocence that made her sexy but not coarse. She made the shimmy almost respectable.

The shimmy was an appropriate dance for Waters, whose early career was based on her movement between working-class and middle-class venues. As

Rebecca A. Bryant explains, the dance, which emerged from "black and tans" (working-class cabarets and bars that catered to both white and black patrons) on the fringes of urban centers in the second decade of the century, gradually found its way onto vaudeville and Broadway stages.[75] On the one hand, the shimmy coincided with the emergence of the independent, modern woman. The isolated shaking of the torso, hips, and shoulders was a direct assault on the Victorian attitudes toward women, which were reflected in the formal social dancing of the nineteenth century. And as David Krasner notes, the pulsating, liberating movements of the shimmy provided a welcome release for working-class African Americans, who craved relief from the regularized rhythms of factory work.[76] The dance also had practical benefits. Since the dance floors in African American speakeasies and clubs tended to be miniscule, social dances that required extensive movement or travel would have been impossible. The shimmy could be done standing in one place. The dance gradually caught on, and performers like Sophie Tucker, Mae West, and Ethel Waters were responsible for the introduction of this dance to middle-class audiences and its assimilation into social dance styles and Broadway musical theater.

The shimmy was ideally suited for a Harlem nightclub like Edmond's Cellar, where Ethel Waters made a name for herself beginning in 1919. The club, located on 132nd Street and Fifth Avenue, was considered a dive in its day, but for Waters, it provided an entrée into New York's world of popular entertainment. Edmond's attracted a rough crowd. Prostitutes, drug dealers, ex-convicts, and numbers runners were the club's main patrons, and even though Broadway was just a few miles away, the entertainment worlds could have been in entirely different universes. The smoky nightclub had a particularly low ceiling, seated about 150 to 200 people, and had a "handkerchief-size dance floor."[77] If the audience appreciated the performer's act, they reflected it in tips that went into a kitty and were divided among all of the performers. If they did not, then it was most likely the end of the line. As Waters quipped, Edmond's was the "the last stop on the way down in show business. . . . After you had worked there, there was no place to go except into domestic service."[78] While performing jazz and blues songs such as "St. Louis Blues," "I Want to Be Somebody's Baby Doll So I Can Get My Lovin' All the Time," and her trademark shimmy number, "Shim-Me-Sha-Wabble," Waters was a huge hit with the crowd, and the kitty overflowed as Waters performed from night until dawn.

By the mid-1920s, Waters became a major recording star for Black Swan, a label that specialized in "race records." The act she perfected for the dicey crowd at Edmond's helped make her nationally known through records, but it proved to be quite controversial for the mainstream. Jazz music and the shimmy dance were associated with sexual depravity and baseness, and black and white conservatives wanted to eliminate them from popular entertainment. Although Waters's sexualized physicality naturally could not come across on her records, the connotations were often evident in her vocal delivery, and her rendition of "Shake That Thing" became the flashpoint for a cultural firestorm. The song is a string of coy sexual insinuations and double entendre, a form to which she returned to again and again. The title plays on the notion of a particular dance style called "shake that thing," in reference to the shimmy, but it also alludes to a sexual act between a man and a woman. The lyric includes references to "jellyroll," which was simultaneously associated with jazz (e.g., "Jelly Roll Morton") and sex. Bessie Smith, for instance, recorded "Nobody in Town Can Bake a Sweet Jelly Roll Like Mine," which included the lyric, "No other one in town can bake a sweet jelly roll so fine, so fine / It's worth lots of dough, the boys tell me so."[79] A good deal of the humor, and the controversy, in "Shake That Thing" stems from the fact that those who are "shaking that thing" are primarily older people, and they are teaching the young ones how to do it. The song flies in the face of respectability:

> Why, there's old Uncle Jack, the jellyroll king,
> He's got a hump in his back from shakin' that thing,
> Yet, he still shakes that thing,
> For an old man, how he can shake that thing!
> And he never gets tired of tellin' young folks: go out and shake that thing![80]

On the recording, Waters heightens the sexual connotations by elongating and seductively growling the "oh's" and "ooh's" that are used in the musical break. The throbbing, honky-tonk piano contributes to the erotic overtone. In addition, her back-of-the-throat delivery of this song contributes to an overt sense of sexual longing and desire. Yet Waters's characteristic sense of applied innocence is also evident. Indeed, there are moments in the song when she sings with such a level of sincerity—such as when she compares it to other dances, including the Charleston and the pigeon-wing—the listener questions whether or not Waters herself is in on the joke. James Weldon Johnson indicated this quality about her, which helps explain how Waters earned the title "Queen of Double Entendre." "Miss Waters," he writes in Black Manhattan, "has a disarming quality which enables her to sing some songs that many singers would not be able to get away with on the stage. Those who have heard her sing 'Shake

That Thing' will understand."[81] And William Gardner Smith remarked similarly on the way "she raised her full, clear voice in songs with triple-meanings without making the most sensitive souls among her audience withdraw."[82]

Others were not so convinced of Waters's ability to mask the sexual allusions in "Shake That Thing," and her presentation of the oversexualized black woman—not unlike the prototypical Lulu Belle—also received a great deal of criticism. Her recording of "Shake That Thing" may have sold more copies than any other for Columbia Records until that time, selling equally well among black and white audiences, but some were distressed by the trend that this success signaled. Conservative black writer George S. Schuyler, who wrote a weekly column for the *Pittsburgh Courier,* mockingly referred to the song as the "Negro's National Anthem" because to him it represented the basest form of entertainment for which Blacks seemed to yearn. Similarly, in August 1926, the *Amsterdam News* reprinted an article that first appeared in the *Chicago Bee* and castigated all those connected with the recording of "Shake That Thing" for pandering to the white and black public's insatiable taste for sexual content. The author writes, "The American people crave filth and dirt. They thrive on a diet of mud. Like microbes they grow in dark cavernous quarters. They relish artistic carrion. They are prurient for songs suggestive of the vulgar." The article goes on to say that this appetite explains the sensational success of Waters's recording, which, in the author's view, has no artistic merit:

> Here is the proof positive of it: For this popular song is about the most vulgar, sordidly suggestive, indecent in connotation which any company has put upon the market. Devoid of richness of rhythm, lacking beautiful music, unspeakably low in language—this song is a tawdry, musically cheap and linguistically common composition, compared with which "Yes, We Have No Bananas" was as a production from Bach or Beethoven.[83]

"Shake That Thing" may not have been Bach or Beethoven, but it pushed Ethel Waters to the highest echelon of mainstream entertainment: Broadway. Waters knew, however, that as a Broadway performer, she would need to tone down her shimmy and ease up on the sexual connotations. In short, she would have to be more like Florence Mills.

As performers, Mills and Waters had a good deal in common. Waters, like Mills, was as comfortable with up-tempo jazz numbers as she was with sentimental ballads. They were both resourceful comediennes and adept dancers, and they could convincingly play the standard roles of the black revue, including the Dixie waif, jungle maiden, and the New York sophisticate. Still, their stage personalities were quite different, and no one could confuse one with the other. Mills appealed to her audience through her endearing and sympathetic traits; Waters won them through her mischievous and devil-may-care qualities. Folk and Tin Pan Alley were the primary songs in Florence Mills's repertoire; blues and double entendre were in Ethel Waters's. While Florence Mills strove for respectability and hoped to raise the level of black musical performance by appealing to middle- and upper-class tastes, Ethel Waters retained her working-class roots and sensibility and poked fun at the notion of celebrity.

Following a career path comparable to Mills's, Waters worked her way from vaudeville and New York nightclubs and onto Broadway. In 1927 she opened in the musical revue *Africana*. Unlike most of the black musical revues of the 1920s, *Africana* was produced by an African American, Earl Dancer (her husband at the time), and it had songs by Donald Heywood, who was also black. When the show opened at Daly's, the theater that previously housed *Shuffle Along*, the *Amsterdam News* noted its "barbaric and primitive splendor,"[84] and other critics praised the show's "liveliness" and "swift pace." The *New York Times* called it "a simple corking Senegambian show that takes its place at once in the same category with 'Shuffle Along' and 'Runnin' Wild.' "[85] Not surprisingly, the show contained the standard features of the black revue. Waters sang, for instance, the obligatory "Wish I Were in Dixie" song, here called "I'm Coming Virginia" (which includes the lyric, "Beneath your bright southern moon, / Once more I'll croon / A dear old mammy tune"), and the "cotton bale" scene in which Waters sang "Here Comes My Show Boat."[86] Some of the critics complained about the unevenness of the show's numbers, particularly in a dance number that concluded the first act. "Pickaninny" Hill, advertised in the program as "the champion cakewalker of the world," led the company in "Old-Fashioned Cakewalk" that received particularly negative reactions. Hence, within the week, several of the numbers were dropped and new ones substituted.[87]

Notably present on opening night of *Africana* was Carl Van Vechten, who remained a good friend and champion of Ethel Waters for most of her career. On a sign outside of the theater was printed his endorsement, in which he said he "would rather hear Ethel Waters sing 'Dinah' than hear [Spanish singer] Raquel Miller sing her entire repertoire."[88] Several critics described Van Vechten's behavior during the show, which, according to at least one observer, was "embarrassing." Critic Bide Dudley wrote that Van Vechten clapped loudly and called out requests for songs during the performance. According to show business columnist Walter Winchell, Van Vechten "occupied a fourth-row-on-the-aisle chair" and shouted for Waters to sing "Dinah," which she did.[89] Robert Garland wrote that "Mr. Van Vechten did everything to prove that Miss Waters is his favorite colored girl and no fooling. There was the passion of possession in Mr. Van Vechten's claps and cheers."[90] For many, Van Vechten's presence was a reminder of Waters's connection to Harlem and her nightclub appearances in which audiences tended to be much more vocal and boisterous. This was not necessarily a good thing. While *her* performance seemed completely appropriate for Broadway, in their view, *his* was not. Broadway audiences tended to be much more reserved and decorous. In fact, Waters found the difference between black, working-class nightclub and vaudeville audiences and white, middle-class audiences quite striking. In an interview in the *Amsterdam News*, she stated, "Some of the white women in the audience with their husbands just sit there and glare at me and the poor man, much as he would like to show his appreciation, dare not move."[91]

In Waters's Broadway debut, the critics invariably compared the new star with Florence Mills. "Since Florence Mills first showed Broadway, in 'Shuffle Along,' what a gifted Negro comedienne could really do when she set her mind to it," Richard Watts, Jr. wrote, "no similar player has proved so ingratiating as did Miss Waters last night."[92] Rowland Field of the *New York Times* said that she "must be ranked on an equal footing with Florence Mills and Josephine Baker as a colored chanteuse."[93] But the elements that made Ethel Waters a vaudeville and nightclub headliner and a recording star also emerged in her performance in *Africana*. Because of her broad, outlandish humor along with a lanky frame and a few high kicks, a couple of critics compared Waters with Charlotte Greenwood, the white vaudeville and musical theater comedienne. Others wrote about her unpredictability, which the critic of the *New York World Telegram* succinctly described as the "hint of smouldering menace under her vast iridescent smile."[94] Several critics remarked on Waters's ability to perform off-color numbers and make them seem completely inoffensive. The critic for *Dance* magazine said that "her impish grimaces and her casual jollity slip over many a wisecrack that might be objectionable under less infectious guidance."[95]

As evident in these responses, Ethel Waters, like Florence Mills, rose above stereotypical stage depictions by revealing the masquerade of black womanhood. While Mills accomplished this representation through overplaying the images and exaggerating them, Waters detached herself from them. Performing the Dixie number in a bandanna and tramp costume, or shimmying in a scanty skirt and top, Waters seemed to wink from behind the representation of the pickaninny or the hypersexed black woman. She drew the audience into her game, and they were willing to participate in the amusement. Offstage, she could be just as mischievous. Whereas Florence Mills was terribly sincere and took her responsibilities as a celebrity very seriously, Ethel Waters often took a different approach, satirizing the image of a sophisticated starlet. In an interview that appeared in the *New York Herald Tribune,* for instance, she presented herself at the height of elegance, immersing herself in all of the trappings of a glamour goddess of the Broadway stage. Nowhere are there signs that she had been raised among prostitutes and thieves. She is described as wearing a black-and-white chiffon gown, white silk stockings, and Deauville sandals. Full of self-importance and dropping names all over the place, she is quoted as interrupting the interviewer to ask her husband, Earl Dancer, if he would inform her when it is 5:45 p.m. "This charming lady," she explains, "has asked me to talk about myself, and you know how I enjoy that. Carl Van Vechten and his wife are giving a dinner for me and I must keep track of the time." Later in the interview, she explains how she found herself in show business. It appears that her father, "a terribly respectable and serious man," had told the young Ethel that she was destined to be a "domestic," but the call of the stage was too strong. She continues to have fun at the interviewer's expense when Earl Dancer returns promptly at 5:45 p.m. to remind Waters of her dinner engagement. When the interviewer tells her how handsome Dancer is, Waters drops the primness and replies that Dancer's face shall remain beautiful only as long as he is true to her. With an almost demonic intensity, she shouts at the interviewer, "But, oh, I'm jealous, I'm wild, I'm fierce! I could kill for love—I'm primitive in my passions!" After a short laugh, she tells the interviewer, "Forgive me. I didn't mean it. I didn't, really."[96] And she resumes the interview as the archetypal glamorous starlet.

This unpredictability and outlandish humor were the hallmarks of Waters's Broadway career as she continued performing in a series of revues (some all-black, and some with a white cast). Waters continued to tease the limits of decorum, nowhere more than in her performance of black composer Eubie Blake and lyricist Andy Razaf's "My Handy Man Ain't Handy No More," which she introduced in *Lew Leslie's Blackbirds of 1930.* The show also starred Flournoy Miller, one of the stars and creators of *Shuffle Along.* Nevertheless, it was a critical and financial disappointment. As Waters quipped: "*Blackbirds* opened at a Forty-second Street theater right next to the flea circus. Our show was a flop, and the fleas outdrew us at every performance. The Depression came in and made our business worse. But it didn't dent the take of the flea circus at all."[97] In typical Lew Leslie fashion, the revue rehashed familiar settings, such as its opening number situated on a levee in Mississippi, an African jungle number in Mozambique, and of course, Harlem. The sketches consisted of parodies of *Green Pas-tures,* a black biblical retelling by white playwright Marc Connelly; *All Quiet on the Western Front,* here called "All Quiet on the Darkest Front"; and Shake-speare's *Othello,* in which Waters played Desdemona.[98] Naturally, the women in the large choral dance numbers were characteristically underdressed and suit-ably energetic. In his review, Percy Hammond acknowledged, "The dusky young women of the ensemble sing well and undress successfully; and the dancing is rhythmic and acrobatic."[99] All of the ingredients in the Leslie recipe were in place, but by 1930, the confection had lost all of its airiness and distinctive flavor.

A low point in the show was a sketch called "Aunt Jemima's Divorce Case," which combined all of the most degrading black stereotypes into one skit. Ac-cording to several critics, the jokes were tired, and the humor forced as it re-tread old minstrel show gags. The characters included Aunt Jemima; Cream of Wheat, her husband; The Ham What Am, the judge; and Sambo, the lawyer. To critics who had once applauded, or at least tolerated, the debased caricatures, the gags had worn out their welcome on Broadway. The images had been re-hearsed and replayed so often on stage in the musical revue that the comic ele-ments of the minstrel mask had all but dropped out. White critic Richard Lock-ridge of the *Sun* railed against Lew Leslie's perpetuation of exaggerated blackface humor as reflected in this sketch, which he said concealed a truly un-corrupted, and presumably untapped, African American talent. In a tirade about white culpability and black gullibility for the original construction of the "stage darkie" caricature, he wrote:

> It would be interesting to discover, and quietly murder, the man who first con-vinced Negro comedians that the way to be a comic lies in blacking brown faces. You take a Negro, who is apt to have naturally certain qualities which the white race cannot acquire, and black him up. You lay on his dialect with a trowel—and with no closer relationship with the actual dialect of the Negro than may be found in the phonetic idiosyncrasies of the average white writer about him. You tell him it is funny to twist words, using for example, "evict" in place of "con-vict," which ninety-nine times out of one hundred, it isn't. You make him, in short, a bad imitation of what was not a very good imitation in the first place, and you tell him to make the people laugh. He—and I shall never know why—believes you.[100]

Lockridge's argument is telling in that in an age when black performers had gained considerable artistic and commercial ground, the white assumption that

FIG. 9. The "Aunt Jemima's Divorce Case" from *Lew Leslie's Blackbirds of 1930*. © White Studio. (Billy Rose Theatre Division, The New York Public Library for the Performing Arts, Astor, Lenox and Tilden Foundations.)

African Americans were merely unwitting imitators and unoriginal pawns was still thriving. The attitude evokes Henry Louis Gates's discussion of the nineteenth-century notion that black writers were actually "mockingbird poets" because they were "generally thought to lack originality." African Americans supposedly "excelled," according to Gates and his charting of the widely held belief, "at mimicry, at what was called mindless imitation, repetition without sufficient revision."[101] Regarding the black musical revue, the recycled jokes, sketches, and musical numbers had become so commonplace on Broadway that the exotic appeal no longer impressed the mostly white audiences. New images of the "authentic" would need to be found.

Blackbirds of 1930 and its indefatigable fidelity to the old formula and its lack of originality anticipated the demise of the black musical revue on Broadway. Lew Leslie, the master of the form, would try to resuscitate the genre with two more editions, in 1933 and 1939, but with dismal results. (Leslie's immediate follow-up to *Blackbirds of 1930, Rhapsody in Black* in 1931, was moderately successful, but that show, which also starred Waters, had eliminated the typical format of the black musical revue and was structured more or less as a concert.) Theophilus Lewis once criticized Leslie for shamelessly recycling material from one show to another, stating, "Mr. Leslie seems to think that all you have to do to make a dance appear new is to change the costumes of the dancers. He has the same idea regarding a song."[102] The only salvation in the 1930 show was Ethel Waters, who provided respite from the tediousness of the over three-hour-long opening night show, and whom Lockridge himself referred to, with highest praise possible, as "endlessly original." To Lockridge, Waters was not simply a copy of incessantly reproduced images of blackness, but offered an animated spark lost among the lackluster proceedings.

Charles Darnton of the *Evening World* said that Waters was one of the few bright spots in the show, and added, "I don't know what we would have done without her."[103] Fortunately, she had some terrific Eubie Blake and Andy Razaf songs to sing, including "Lucky to Me" and "Memories of You." But the highlight was her rendition of the fiercely funny "My Handy Man Ain't Handy No More." To several critics, though, the song bordered on pornographic. Darnton called it "one of the frankest ballads of this free age"; Richard Lockridge referred to it as "so disturbing a mess of double meaning"; and the *New Yorker* said that only Waters's "innocence and cleansing quality" made the song "almost permissible."[104] "My Handy Man Ain't Handy No More" was actually a follow-up to a number Razaf had written and composed for Waters in 1928 titled "My Handy Man."[105] That earlier song offers a glowing tribute to a man who satisfies the singer's every domestic need. She relishes the way "He shakes my ashes, / Greases my griddle, / Churns my butter, / Strokes my fiddle"; and how "He threads my needle, / Creams my wheat, / Heats my heater, / Chops my meat." The sexual double-entendre also includes allusions to "Feed[ing] the horses in my stable" and "Trimming the rough edges off my lawn." But the last verse justifies why Barry Singer deems "My Handy Man" "a bawdy blues of such transcendent craft and consummate comic timing that it nearly overwhelmed all memory of its innumerable predecessors, becoming, on the instant, the genre's quintessential representative and remaining so till today."[106] Even on a recording, Waters's playful naughtiness mixed with haughty boastfulness is irresistible as she sings about her handy man:

My ice don't get a chance to melt away,
He sees that I get a nice, fresh piece every day.
My man is such a handy man.

The musical sequel to this song, composed two years later, revisits the same handy man, who, it turns out, does not gratify in the same way he used to.

"My Handy Man Ain't Handy No More" is, if anything, even funnier than the first installment, and it benefits from Blake's music, which has been described "as funny as Razaf's words."[107] The singer sets the mood by explaining that "Somethin' strange has happened to my Handy Man, / He's not the man he was before," and "He never hauls his ashes 'less I tell him to."[108] The lyric also visits a familiar domestic territory, once again subtly comparing parts of the woman singer's anatomy to a "stove," a "stable," and a "front lawn." In this version, the handy man's admirable abilities have all but disappeared, and he is absolutely useless to her:

Once he used to have so much endurance,
Now it looks like he needs life insurance;
I used to brag about my Handy Man's technique,
Around the house he was a perfect indoor sheik
But now "The spirit's willing but the flesh is weak":
My Handy Man ain't handy no more.

According to Allen Woll, the song's torrid, controversial lyric was enough to induce an "audible buzz" among the opening night audience and cause one critic to warily dub the show "Hot Stuff" in his review.[109]

Although "My Handy Man Ain't Handy No More" was written by two black men, it has a great deal in common with the songs of the 1920s "blueswomen," including Bessie Smith, Gertrude "Ma" Rainey, and Alberta Hunter. On one level Blake and Razaff's song may be regarded as uncomfortably stereotypical as it rehearses the familiar image of the sex-mad African American woman. But on another, the song, like many blues songs, offered a space for resistance. The blues was a productive site for protesting oppressive social and political ideologies concerning black women. First, by exaggerating and undermining the singer's references to various household duties, "My Handy Man Ain't Handy No More" reverses and subverts cultural presumptions surrounding black gender and sexual roles. In Razaf's lyric, the (presumably) black man is responsible for carrying out domestic duties, and the woman is entrusted with the power to make sure they are completed. As the decision maker, she is the one who calls the shots in the relationship. And in a switch from the common criticism that might have been directed at a black woman housekeeper whose abilities to keep an orderly home had begun to slip, the handy man "has lost his domestic science / And he's lost his self-reliance." The song also debunks the traditional middle-class notion of home in which a woman accedes her independence to marriage, domesticity, and the will of her husband. And even more radically, it inverts the image of the stereotypically macho and hypersexualized black man. Here the handy man is sexually enervated and rendered impotent (the cliché "the spirit's willing but the flesh is weak" takes on a whole new provocative meaning in Waters's delivery), while the woman is represented as the aggressive partner.

Thus, the setting of "My Handy Man Ain't Handy No More" may represent a familiar place for a black woman, but the singer has transformed it into an arena in which she is both empowered and has sexual autonomy. In this domestic, although eroticized, scene, the handy man is only useful to her when he can provide services that fulfill the singer's needs. Yet flying in the face of current discourse surrounding black women's morality, she unapologetically rejects middle-class sentiments about chastity and fidelity. This was, after all, an age when black women needed to constantly protect themselves from attacks against their supposed depravity. But as Angela Davis explains, "In the process of defending black women's moral integrity and sexual purity, they [were] almost entirely denied sexual agency."[110] The blues, however, were a site of resistance where black women could proclaim their assertiveness and independence. For as Hazel Carby convincingly argues in her analysis of women blues singers, the blues opened a space of resistance for black women to unashamedly present themselves as "sexual beings," thus affirming their freedom and individuality.[111] Drawing upon the blues tradition of sexual liberation while performing this song, Ethel Waters, along with composers Blake and Razaf, effectively "redefined women's 'place'" and constructed "a space in which the coercions of bourgeois notions of sexual purity and 'true womanhood' were absent."[112]

Sexual allusions of the blues were standard in the 1920s rent parties, honkytonks, and after-hours Harlem clubs, but with the enforced decency laws on Broadway, a song like "My Handy Man Ain't Handy No More" could force a show to close. The fact that the song did not meet with a wrathful censor was most likely due in large part to its uncanny delivery by Ethel Waters. Vocally, she offered a more refined presentation than her "blues mama" contemporaries such as Bessie Smith and Gertrude "Ma" Rainey. As Barry Singer explains, "Blessed with bell-like vocal timbre that was complemented by a vaudeville-derived conscientiousness about enunciation, Waters, unlike the rawer, more rural belters, delivered the blues with urbane elegance and a lilting melodicism."[113] But even more importantly, Waters had by now perfected a complex style in which she could appear to accommodate the image of the stereotypical images of black femininity while at the same time undermining this image in her delivery of double-entendre songs. Not only was she adept at using her voice to convey the multiple meanings of a lyric, but she used her expressive face and lanky body to accomplish the same effect. The second-string *Times* critic summed it up perfectly when he wrote, "Every gesture, every grimace counts. In the rolling of her eyes, the exaggerated showing of her teeth, the comic shrugging of her shoulders, there is a multitude of meanings."[114]

By the 1920s, double-entendre songs had become part of a popular black cultural tradition. Mel Watkins traces the development of this brand of African American humor back to slave songs. Comical irony, subterfuge, and contradiction, Watkins posits, were "the central means of coping with slavery."[115] According to Giles Oakley, blues and their often oblique denunciation of whites evolved from black work songs, and while singing under the watchful eye of white overseers, the seditious implications in the songs would go unheeded.[116] Subsequently, black comics had become adept at "masking" their true feelings and intentions in the face of white oppression by employing elusive or culturally acceptable terms that white audiences did not always "get." In a method similar to the literary metaphor defined by Henry Louis Gates as "double voicedness," as well as to Du Bois's "double consciousness," black humor often contained dual connotations. Therefore, as a form of double-voicedness, double entendre may be regarded as a strategy of black resistance. In these songs, performers and lyricists call attention to the slipperiness and "mutability" of the language of the oppressor, and intentionally displace the "white term" with a distinctively black connotation.[117] Encoded, layered with new or reversed meanings, and manipulated, words in black double-entendre lose their power to debase and demean. In other words, on the surface, a song could appear to be a middle-class household elegy about a man who no longer works efficiently around the house, but underneath it could describe the sexual dissatisfaction of a working-class black woman who craves frequent and stimulating sexual intercourse. In a Broadway theater, the song, particularly with Waters's exaggeratedly innocent delivery, had the *air* of respectability, for as Charles Darnton wrote, she sang "My Handy Man Ain't Handy No More" with "all the innocence of a domestic lament."[118] But like the skimpy outfits that black chorus girls wore, the literal meanings just barely concealed the eroticized and titillating images underneath.

A final example of Ethel Waters's skillful ability to nudge the boundaries of decorum and play with cultural representations occurred in the nonblack musical revue *At Home Abroad*, which opened in 1935. The hit show, directed and designed by famed MGM director Vincente Minnelli, also starred British comedienne Beatrice Lillie, tap dancer Eleanor Powell, and vaudeville song and dance man Eddie Foy, Jr. Structured as a musical "travelogue," *At Home Abroad* included sketches and numbers set in locales such as Paris, Vienna, Russia, Jamaica, and Africa. Not surprisingly, the last two provided the backdrops for two of Waters's numbers. The New York critics lauded the show for its cleverness and arch sophistication, and hailed white composer and lyricist Arthur Schwartz and Howard Dietz's score, which included the hilarious "Paree" sung by Lillie and the now-standard "What a Wonderful World," as "amusing," "swell," and "luxurious."[119] But as the sole black star of the revue, Waters was expected to provide the evening's exotica, which she did dazzlingly with the help of Minnelli's costumes and set design. As Atkinson wrote, "[Minnelli] has set her in a jungle scene that is laden with magic, dressing her in gold bands and a star-struck gown of blue, and put her in a Jamaican set that looks like a modern painting. Miss Waters is decorative as well as magnetic."[120] Indeed, few could make the jungle seem as alluring, enchanting, and as amusing as Ethel Waters while at the same time pointing to the artifice and the artistry surrounding her.

In *At Home Abroad*, the black segments contrasted sharply with the droll songs and sketches predominantly set in Europe, though these moments reintroduced images of a glittering black savagery back to an increasingly white Broadway. This is particularly evident in the review by Percy Hammond of the *New York Tribune,* who wrote, "Miss Ethel Waters, the Negro prima donna, again brings the jungle to Times Square efficiently."[121] Backed by a chorus of black men and women dancers in her big African and Jamaican numbers, including "Hottentot Potentate" and "Steamboat Whistle," Waters represented the merging of familiar black stereotypes with Tin Pan Alley music and lyrics along with polished Broadway showmanship. Of course, the inhabitants of Minnelli's "jungle" in *At Home Abroad* were Broadway's version of "savage": Scantily dressed in sequins, satin, and chintz, the black chorus danced suggestively not to tom-toms and bongoes, but to the jazzy strains of a piano and muted trumpet.[122] The effect was not completely unlike the grotesquerie evoked by

Florence Mills and her "Chocolate Drops" in "Jungle Nights in Dixieland" from *Dixie to Broadway*. Yet as was characteristic of Waters's performance style in the 1920s and early 1930s, she rendered these images with a knowing wink and a sly smile. Writing for *Women's Wear Daily*, for example, Kelcey Allen notes Waters's remarkable ability to "sell" her songs in this show, and Brooks Atkinson described the "enormous lurking vitality" she applied to her numbers.[123]

These qualities were particularly evident in her performance of "Hottentot Potentate," in which Waters not only challenged popular conceptions about black womanhood, but also created a space that recognized and accepted the gay community.[124] In this, her "African" number in the show, Waters sings about becoming the ruler of Harlem and bending the will of the people to serve her. À la Julius Caesar, the Hottentot Potentate "came," "saw," and "conquered" this "Congo" kingdom, and the residents easily submitted to her "trickeration." Much of the song's humor, though, derives from the unabashed joy she receives from the worship the denizens bestow upon her:

> My witchcraft made them make a crown for me;
> The natives do a lot of bowing down for me,
> And any one of them would go to town for me,
> The Hottentot Potentate.

On one level, the song is a parody of *Emperor Jones* (here she refers to herself as "the Empress Jones"), Eugene O'Neill's 1920 play about a Pullman porter who becomes the revered (then reviled) ruler of a barbaric, unnamed West Indies tribe. In that play, Brutus Jones, with O'Neill's own allusion to Caesar, exploits his black subjects who later bring about his descent into madness and suicide. Hazel Carby reads the play as an enactment of the Caucasian fear of black insurrection and "retribution" for slavery. An escaped convict and murderer, Jones "tricks" the natives into believing he is godlike by playing upon their fears and superstitions, and he uses his brute strength to intimidate them further. According to Carby, Jones symbolizes whites' "historical nightmare" of enslavement by "those they had enslaved." The play provides an outlet for those ingrained apprehensions. Carby writes: "Within the dominant cultural imagination, *The Emperor Jones* plays an important ideological role in the displacement of social and political anxieties of black rebellion, revolution, and revenge."[125] In "Hottentot Potentate," Dietz, Schwartz, and Waters push the image inside out. Sex and sophistication, rather than fear and force, are the tools of oppression for the "hot and potent, potent and hot, Hottentot Potentate."

In addition to the popular cultural allusion to *The Emperor Jones,* the specter of Lulu Belle haunts the song at every turn. Nearly ten years after *Lulu Belle* opened on Broadway, the sordid tale of Harlem's most famous hussy had not faded from cultural consciousness. As with Lulu Belle, the tantalizing charms of the black temptress in Schwartz and Dietz's song are irresistible and inescapable. In fact, the song makes direct reference to Sheldon and McArthur's play: "I brought my bottle of Chanel with me, / I took along a script of *Lulu Belle* with me." And playing on the title character of that play, not only does the Hottentot Potentate set a snare for the unwitting natives, she revels in her conquests, which bring her tremendous wealth and prestige. The Hottentot Potentate reflects the ease in which she is able to bewitch the credulous natives and capitalize on their particular fears of enslavement. On the recording of the song, Waters purrs with just the right amount of slyness and seduction:

> I fool 'em, fool 'em, playing a part,
> And I rule 'em, rule 'em, I've got an art,
> And I ghoul 'em, ghoul 'em, right from the start,
> I gave 'em that hotcha, je ne sais quoicha.

Like Lulu Belle, who beguiles an unsuspecting French count, it is fairly obvious that the Hottentot Potentate's selective command of French comes in pretty handy as well. In this comic parody, though, the Lulu Belle figure is not a harbinger of destruction, but of unyielding, joyful subjugation.

This element in *At Home Abroad* aroused the indignation of at least one critic reviewing the show. A *New York Times* critic, who attended the show's out-of-town tryout in Boston, found the show "approach[ing] vulgarity" at certain intervals, and he dismissed Waters's rendition of "Hottentot Potentate" as "not worth her trouble."[126] To those accustomed to seeing black women performers embodying images of, to use Sterling Brown's phrase, the "exotic primitive," her performance must have been unsettling. Instead of reinscribing the familiar representation of black womanhood, she exaggerated it, inverted it, and made it laughable. In this particular number, Waters blatantly turns on its head the culturally accepted proposition that assumes a black woman on stage must be represented as a primitive, eroticized African maiden, a sex-mad Lulu Belle, or a desexed mammy figure. Here not only is the Hottentot Potentate known for her "trickery" and "hotcha," both familiar images associated with the stereotypical black woman, but more importantly, she is ultra chic with her "drawing room technique," "modern improvement," and as she proudly proclaims: "The heathens live upon a bed of roses now, / And Cartier rings they're wearing in their noses now." Savagery and oppression of O'Neill's original vision in *The Emperor Jones* have been replaced by glamour and modernity.

As Mel Watkins explains, this form of reversal was a common method for black performers in confronting an especially degrading image. He explains, "There was no other way of dealing with it except to make fun of it and reverse the joke."[127] With her inimitable, comedic style, expensive dress, and sinewy voice, not to mention the assistance of Dietz's witty lyrics, Waters separated herself from the stereotypical image. Rather than reinscribing the image or being trapped by it, or indeed performing it with exquisite grace and artistry as Florence Mills had in her own career, Waters distanced herself from it. And by doing so, she pointed to the artifice of the representations, which is highlighted by the lyric's numerous implications about theater, art, and "playing a part."

Another aspect of the song is the way in which it reflects a space that can accommodate nonheterosexual identities as well. Like the Harlem neighborhood itself, the environment articulated in the lyrics of "Hottentot Potentate" is not only comprised of contested black representations, but it also offers a space for gay inclusion. While the song's references to *Lulu Belle* point to customary stereotypes about black women, they also signal not-so-veiled nods to the gay community that adopted the title character of Sheldon and MacArthur's play as its icon. At one point, the Hottentot Potentate comically warns that certain kinds of behavior will not be tolerated in her utopian society. She sings: "The new name for the Congo's stamping ground / Is Empress Jones's Africana vamping ground; / I don't allow no camping on my camping ground!" But just a few verses later she seems to recant, and she takes pride in the fact that she has made of this land a much less barbaric and virile atmosphere:

> This wild and savage, open airy land
> With lions and with tigers was a scary land
> Until I made of it a savoir *fairy*land.

On the recording, Waters feigns shock at her verbal slip with an inflected "Dear!" By doing so, she not so subtly winks at the coterie of "male queers" who often saw her perform. As she notes in her autobiography, when she performed at Edmond's it was not uncommon for gay men to "beg me to let them wear my best gowns for the evening so they could compete for the grand prizes" in various Harlem drag balls.[128]

For gay men in the Broadway theater, the comical allusions to "Lulu Belle," "vamping," "camping," and "savoir *fairy*land" meant that Waters affirmed and publicly recognized their existence in a site that by law prohibited lesbian and gay subject matter. The raids of *The Captive* and *The Drag* in the same year that *Lulu Belle* premiered were authoritative admonitions of this fact. Thus, in a mode of resistance similar to the racial double-entendre of the blues, Waters acknowledged a clandestine gay community with coded language. While heterosexual members of an audience might not necessarily have grasped the significance of certain terms, the gay community traditionally delighted in sly references to its lifestyle. As George Chauncey documents, singers in the 1920s and 1930s who presented lyrics with gay-inflected subtexts generally attracted a huge following of homosexual men. In particular, Chauncey notes Beatrice Lillie, who was the featured star of *At Home Abroad*, and a fixture of Harlem's gay and lesbian nightlife, as a popular attraction among the gay community. Her comic song "There Are Fairies at the Bottom of the Garden" was a "camp classic" for gay men, and as one of her fans later recalled, "The Palace was just packed with queers, for weeks at a time, when Lillie performed."[129] Moreover, Chauncey insightfully describes the communal effect such an occasion offers gay men in a non-gay-identified space: "Whether or not the other members in the audience noticed them, *they* were aware of their numbers in the audience and often shared in the collective excitement of transforming such a public gathering into a 'gay space,' no matter how covertly."[130] It is not unreasonable to imagine, then, that when Ethel Waters sang "Hotentot Potentate," she created a space for surreptitious community-building among gay men. During the brief span of the song, Waters regally and unabashedly evoked an environment that was not ruled by a predominantly racist, sexist, and homophobic ideology, but was inclusive and liberating. That is, in this number, the sexually emancipated, "hot and potent, potent and hot" Hottentot Potentate presided over an "Africana vamping ground" in which cultural representations of race, gender, and sexuality were subverted and reimagined.

At Home Abroad was one of the last musical revues in which Ethel Waters would appear. She had scored terrific notices in *Rhapsody in Black* (1931), and especially Irving Berlin's nonblack revue *As Thousands Cheer* (1933), in which she introduced the powerful antilynching song "Supper Time." But the all-black, Broadway musical revue trend had all but run its course by 1935, and Waters's appearance in the otherwise white *At Home Abroad* offered a nostalgic throwback to the glitzy jungle scenes from the revues of the 1920s. In the 1930s, minstrel shows, vaudeville, and musical revues were no longer all the rage. With the emergence on stage and film of the "integrated" musical, or one in which the songs are (generally) connected directly with the plot and character, variety shows were more likely to be found on the radio. African Americans were not generally "integrated" into these new musicals, so the roster of black musical performers diminished considerably.[131] By the middle to late 1930s, the black musical theater had entered a "period of exile." And as Allen Woll explains, with the Depression and a preponderance of integrated book musicals and black plays depicting social realism, "A once thriving cultural tradition faded to a mere whimper on Broadway. Black-performed musical shows did not disappear during the next twenty years, but they existed on the fringes of Broadway as oddities, exotica, or nostalgic reveries."[132]

By all accounts, Waters had a remarkable career, which spanned seven decades. She was one of the few black Broadway stars of the 1920s, along with Josephine Baker and Bill Robinson, who continued to find work after—to paraphrase Langston Hughes—the Negro was no longer in vogue. In her later career, Waters gradually replaced her sexy, vamping, and often risqué image—indeed, Waters was known for her dramatic image changes—with the one for which she is best known today. Beginning in the late thirties, as she got older and heavier, and parts for middle-aged black women were fewer and farther between, she accepted roles that required her to be matriarchal and pious. This was first evident in her dramatic debut as Hagar in Dorothy and DuBose Heyward's *Mamba's Daughters* (1939). Roles in *Cabin in the Sky* (1940), *Pinky* (1949), for which she earned an Academy Award nomination,[133] *Member of the Wedding* (1952), and a brief stint as a maid in the television series *Beulah* followed. She continued to sing, notably with the Billy Graham Crusades, up until her death in 1977.

The contributions that Ethel Waters and Florence Mills made to Broadway and musical theater should not be overlooked. The black musical revues of the 1920s and early 1930s are problematic, and they will never be considered among the great works of the American stage. The sketches and musical numbers often recycled offensive stereotypes, and they were built around individual talents, so the shows rarely could be successfully recast with different performers. Although the genre produced a number of musical standards, such as "I'm Just Wild about Harry," "Black and Blue," and "I Can't Give You Anything but Love," just as many songs, like "Juba Dance," "Oriental Blues," and "That Brownskin Flapper," could never make a convincing case for rescue from oblivion. And although it is tempting to dismiss the revues because they were often produced, directed, and written by white men for chiefly white Broadway audiences, this response oversimplifies the issue. The performances of Florence Mills and Ethel

Waters, who perfected their acts in predominantly black venues, demonstrate the complex interconnections of race, gender, and class identifications. And without denying the commercial motivation behind the revues, the shows embodied the contradictory social and artistic attitudes of the 1920s and early 1930s. Mills and Waters simultaneously played the stereotypes to the enjoyment of both black and white audiences, and with the assistance of their white or black creators, they often satirized, exaggerated, and poked fun at these depictions. They merged elements of primitivism and modernism and attempted to realize the goals of cultural pluralism and racial uplift. In the process, they forged new possibilities for images of African Americans, and opened spaces for working-class sensibilities and a recognition of a gay and lesbian subculture. Above all, Waters and Mills were unapologetically resilient and outspoken in an era when neither of these qualities was popularly acceptable for black women.

CHAPTER 5

"In My Well of Loneliness": Gladys Bentley's Bulldykin' Blues

What make you men folk treat us women like you do?
What make you men folk treat us women like you do?
I don't want no man that I got to give my money to.

Call me a leper giving nothin', but I know.
Call me a leper giving nothin', but I know.
'Cause right back I told him, man, I ain't no billy goat.

Give my man everything from a diamond ring or dough.
Give my man everything from a diamond ring or dough.
The next thing I'm gonna' give him six feet in the cold, cold ground.

—GLADYS BENTLEY, "WORRIED BLUES"*

SEXUAL PERVERTS ON PARADE

With the enforcement of the Wales Padlock Law and stricter censorship of Broadway plays, musicals, and revues, lesbians and gay men in mainstream theater audiences had to content themselves with sly allusions and coded innuendo. In the late 1920s and early 1930s, Broadway performers like Ethel Waters teased the limits of decency with double meanings that the censor politely ignored, but the city made it very clear that it would no longer tolerate blatant sexuality or "perversity" on its public stages. Standing behind the rationale that New York City was the entertainment capital of the world, state and city elected officials were intent on promoting a respectable, wholesome image of Broadway and taking back New York City's mantle as "the most moral city in the universe."[1] Thus, police batons and political crackdowns on obscenity charges kept the New York theater's closet door rather securely closed, and only coy references to homosexuality, such as indirect suggestions and questionable character traits, escaped the vigilant public censor.

Up in Harlem, however, where drag balls continued to attract thousands of spectators, and cross-dressed men and women could be spotted daily on the streets, many of the nightclub floor shows and theater revues—although officially held accountable under the same state censorship laws—were as coarse and rowdy as ever. Female impersonators, "bulldykin' women," and "freakish men" appeared on stage with great regularity during this era, and although there were sporadic efforts to clean up Harlem's reputation, tourists demanded that the neighborhood live up to its image as a place of racial and sexual exotica. Because one of the functions of the ghetto is to provide a controlled site for a certain amount of lawlessness—A. B. Christa Schwarz refers to Harlem of the 1920s and 1930s as "New York's premier red-light district"[2]—city authorities had a far more relaxed legal attitude in Harlem than they did in Midtown. It should come as no surprise, then, that some of the best-known Harlem acts were those that flaunted the qualities deemed impermissible on Broadway. As *New York Age* writer Marcus Wright reported in his weekly "Talk of the Town" column in 1934, some of Harlem's most popular entertainers included a bawdy lesbian comic, Jackie "Moms" Mabley, and a pair of female impersonators, the Sepia Mae West and the Sepia Gloria Swanson.[3]

If the Sepia Swanson and West were Harlem's queens of risqué performance, then a young black performer named Gladys Bentley, also included in Wright's list, was Harlem's king. Bentley, a 250-pound black lesbian, was, if possible, even more scandalous than Swanson and West. Like those performers, Bentley aroused the ire of several critics with her ribald performance, and she pushed the boundaries of stage decency to their limits with her nightclub act. Bentley, an avowed "bulldagger," was famous for her suggestive songs and masculine appearance.

In the late 1920s, Bentley began her career as a pianist, playing the rent party circuit and then in Harlem's swankest nightclubs. Performing in her trademark white tuxedo, she was best known for taking popular, mainstream songs and substituting the lyrics with her own off-color treatment. "[S]o adept was she at this art," Wilbur Young wrote, "that she could take the most tender ballad and convert it into a new low with her filthy lyrics." He added, "In fact, some of these lyrics would be so rank that the house lady would look on in despair while Gladys, not content with merely singing them herself . . . would encourage the paying guests to join in on the chorus which they did willingly. At this stage, it was just a matter of time before the house got raided."[4] Off stage, Bentley's persona was similarly ignominious. She only wore men's clothing in public, and she married a white woman in a highly publicized New Jersey civil ceremony.[5]

Indeed, by the mid-1930s, Bentley was known as much as a neighborhood personality as she was a performer. In March 1936, for instance, the *New York Times* described her as "not only a fixture at Harlem's Ubangi Club but a figure in the community."[6] Yet she was not relegated to the fringes of Harlem's social and entertainment worlds. Her nightclub act regularly transferred to the neighborhood's large theaters, though the critics often disparaged her for her suggestive songs and the chorus of "pansies" who accompanied her. Writing about a show Bentley headlined at Harlem's Opera House, one critic described it as "one of the rankest revues this commentator has witnessed in many a moon." Remarking that a group of novelty musicians called the Washboard Serenaders[7] was the only redeeming performance on the program, the critic vehemently urged audiences to stop paying to see entertainments that featured repugnant acts like the one Gladys Bentley presented:

> If patrons would refrain from attending shows of the nature of the current Opera House revue, probably the management wouldn't embarrass us by parading sexual perverts and double entendre jokes crackers. I have no fault to find of "men" earning their living as "chorus girls," but why glorify them on the stage of a theatre patronized supposedly by respectable people?[8]

But people did not stay away. Throughout much of the 1930s, Gladys Bentley continued to pack people, both black and white, into Harlem's largest theaters and most fashionable nightclubs with her outrageous and frank performances.

But this is only part of the story. Indeed, Gladys Bentley was quite conventional in many respects. She recorded a number of blues songs, including "Worried Blues," "Moanful Wailin' Blues," and "How Much Can I Stand?" that depict a woman wronged by a man. In her later years she cast off her characteristic tuxedo, claimed to be from Port-of-Spain, Trinidad—although she was born and raised in Philadelphia—and wore flowers in her hair, dresses, and pearls while performing jazz and blues standards. She is, to say the least, a complex figure in the Harlem Renaissance even though she is often regarded in performance studies and lesbian and gay history as the ultimate symbol of defiance against prevailing images of femininity and heterosexuality. This is quite understandable when one looks at the photos of her in her white tuxedo and reads the sensational eyewitness accounts (along with Eric Garber's excellent 1988 biographical overview of her in *Out/Look*). But on the other hand, the principal artifacts of her career—an autobiographical apologia for *Ebony* magazine, a handful of blues recordings, and an appearance on Groucho Marx's *You Bet Your Life*—depict her as a woman-who-loves-men blues singer (of considerable talent), who never joined the ranks of other blueswomen with the likes of Bessie Smith, Gertrude "Ma" Rainey, and Alberta Hunter. These contradictions in Bentley's public and performance persona are what make her particularly intriguing. Examining the creative output of her career as well as contemporary accounts of her personal and professional life, one sees that Bentley toyed with and manipulated the social, sexual, and artistic conventions of her era. At times parodying these norms and at others embracing them, Gladys Bentley simultaneously subverted the rigid dualities of male/female, hetero/homosexual, and black/white. "She was," as Langston Hughes said, "something worth discovering."[9]

IF THIS BE SIN

In 1928, the year that Gladys Bentley began her performance career in New York, another lesbian narrative was playing out on the international arts scene. Radclyffe Hall's *The Well of Loneliness* was the subject of a literary and legal melee in the United Kingdom, and the novel was banned for its "offense against public decency."[10] Nevertheless, the novel, which focuses on Stephen Gordon, a "mannish lesbian" and her unfortunate relationships with other women, received a great deal of support from England's literati. In October 1928, customs officials in the United Kingdom seized copies of the book that had been published by a French company, and "literary giants" H. G. Wells and George Bernard Shaw spoke out against the action. Shaw stated, "I read it, and read it again, and I repeat that it ought not have been withdrawn. It speaks of things people ought to know about."[11] And although she did not think the book should have been published because it might cause people to speculate about "unmarried women living alone," Virginia Woolf wrote in a letter dated September 2, 1928, to her sister that "much of Miss Radclyffe Hall's book is rather beautiful."[12] The presumed or actual merit of the novel notwithstanding, the literariness was precisely why magistrate Sir Charles Biron ordered police officers to destroy the seized copies. He argued, "It must appear to every one of intelligence that the better an obscene book is written the greater is the public to whom it is likely to appeal. The more palatable the poison, the more insidious it is."[13]

Released in the United States in December 1928 by the Covici-Friede Publishing Corporation, the novel met with a similar response. In January 1929, John S. Sumner, secretary of the New York Society for the Suppression of Vice, filed injunctions against the publishers for violating "Section 1141 of the Penal Code relating to the circulation of indecent literature."[14] The case was eventually dropped in April of that year, but the legal attention certainly did not hurt sales. The book was an immediate best seller and sold an impressive 20,000 copies in its first month of release.[15] *The Well of Loneliness* received favorable responses as well from Harlem's prominent literary figures. Richard Bruce Nugent considered it "a superbly written and conceived work," and Alain Locke stated that he did not know "whether to admire more its beauty or its quiet bravery."[16] The novel's success, either as a result of its literary merits or the controversy surrounding the subject matter, ensured its standing as the quintessential lesbian narrative, helping to define the ways in which lesbians were presented and viewed for much of the twentieth century. That is, while the fictional character Stephen Gordon put forward a sympathetic and heroic portrayal of a lesbian, ironically, the magistrate who claimed that the novel would have a powerful effect on its readers was at least partially right. Stephen Gordon became *the* archetype for lesbians in the popular culture and social consciousness.[17]

Knowingly or unknowingly, Gladys Bentley drew on the notoriety of Radclyffe Hall's novel as she created her own iconic persona. Before examining Bentley's theatrical and performance career in depth, it is useful to examine the ways in which Bentley, at least on reflection in her later years, framed and constructed her own public representation. Her *performance* of the mannish woman, to apply Judith Butler psychoanalytic literary theory with the historical terminology for a butch lesbian, seems to derive from Bentley's own (close) reading of *The Well of Loneliness*. Bentley certainly knew of Hall's novel since she performed a number called "In My Well of Loneliness" in the musical revue *Brevities in Bronze* (1937).[18] And in 1952, as a preview of a full-length memoir entitled *If This Be Sin*,[19] she wrote an autobiographical piece for *Ebony* called "I Am a Woman Again" in which she claimed that one of her primary reasons for writing was to "help people who are trapped in a modern-day 'well of loneliness.' "[20] Bentley herself seems trapped in the narrative arc of *The Well of Loneliness* because she rehearses several of the key plot points, especially when writing about her childhood and adolescence. Her relationship with her parents, her attraction to male clothing, and her own sexual awakening, which preceded her rise to fame as a performer, are all sensationally recounted in the *Ebony* article. In the essay, Bentley alternates between boasting about her career and bemoaning her miserable existence, but the narrative thrust mimics the Bildungsroman of fictional Stephen Gordon, albeit with significant differences.

The essential differences between the subjects are their race and social class. While Stephen Gordon was born to white British aristocrats (Sir Philip and Lady Anna Gordon), Gladys Bentley was born in 1907 to black working-class Philadelphians (George L. Bentley and Mary C. Mote). The conditions of their births, according to the two texts, however, are remarkably similar. Stephen's parents desperately hoped and assumed that their child would be a boy. In fact, so sure of the sex of the child were they that they named the infant before birth. The narrator says, "When the child stirred within [Lady Anna] she would think it stirred strongly because of the gallant male creature she was hiding; then her spirit grew large with a mighty new courage, because a man-child would be born."[21] According to Bentley, a similar willfulness and obsessiveness was evident in her mother's desire for a boy, but the distinctions of class and race underscore the Gordons' and Bentleys' gender preference. This is apparent in Bentley's own memoir as she details her parents' (especially her mother's) basis for wanting a son so strongly. While the aristocratic Gordons represent the Victorian desire for a male heir to carry on the family name and provide "complete fulfillment,"[22] Mary Bentley demonstrates a widespread attitude held by mostly whites, but also by some African Americans, that working-class, black women were naturally drawn to immorality and corruption. Perhaps in response to publications such as the one by mulatto schoolteacher William Hannibal Thomas, who declared that "innate modesty is not a characteristic of the American Negro woman" and who spoke of their "bestial instinct,"[23] Bentley's mother zealously prayed for a son. According to Gladys Bentley, "Girls," her mother believed, "were fated for trouble."[24] In both cases, whatever the cause for wanting a boy over a girl, the "gender inversion" of both children is an implied result of their parents' yearning, ardent prayer, and visualization of the coveted son.

Just as Stephen Gordon's relationship with her mother is fraught with disagreement and misunderstanding, Gladys Bentley places much of the blame for her own childhood unhappiness on her mother, who would not touch the child and refused to nurse her for the first six months. In both narratives, clothing represents the primary cause of conflict between the mothers and daughters. Hence, male attire assumes central importance as a site of gender assertiveness and filial revolt. *The Well of Loneliness* depicts the struggle between Lady Anna and Stephen:

These days there was constant warfare between them on the subject of clothes; quite a seemly warfare, for Stephen was learning to control her hot temper, and Anna was seldom anything but gentle. Nevertheless it was open warfare, the inevitable clash of two opposing natures who sought to express themselves in apparel, since clothes, after all, are a form of self expression.[25]

Likewise, Bentley explains that she used to wear her four younger brothers' suits to school. She endured the scorn of her teachers and her classmates, who taunted her for not wearing dresses on her "large and stocky" body. Describing the contretemps with her parents over the issue, she says, "Now, I tried to withstand my parents, but they got after me so often that we finally compromised, agreeing that I would wear middy blouses and skirts."[26] For both young women, their clothes, as it were, make the man. Stephen and Gladys are uncomfortable with their ungainly and chaotic bodies, which are both biologically feminine and structurally masculine. Only by donning the outer effects of manhood are they able to rectify the gender confusion for themselves.

Gender is not the only identity construction at play here, but as recent and not-so-recent critiques of *The Well of Loneliness* show,[27] Radclyffe Hall conflates gender categorization with sexual preference, and the author intermingles various theories of sexual orientation that were floating around at the time. For instance, she merges Sigmund Freud, who forwarded a notion of the psychological origin of sexuality; Havelock Ellis (who provided a short prefatory commentary for the novel), who argued that one's sexual disposition is inborn; and notably, German sexologist Richard von Krafft-Ebing, who equated one's gender role with one's sexual desires and behaviors.[28] As a result, there is a certain amount of confusion about where the authors (Hall and Bentley) position themselves. On the one hand, they seem to be advocating understanding based on the subjects' innate characteristics. On the other, they seem to fault the child-rearing habits of the parents. As Laura Green notes in her analysis of Stephen Gordon, "The confused origin story that Hall gives Stephen is to some degree emblematic of a more general confusion, during the period, of how to conceptualize and represent identities."[29] Indeed, Bentley reiterates this confusion in her own narrative through her explanation of her inborn masculine leanings, which are matched by fervent desires to be a boy that are at odds with her repudiation of men.

Yet young Stephen and Gladys are sexual creatures as well, and they both have sexual awakenings at an early age. For seven-year-old Stephen, the object of her desire is the young housemaid Collins, whom the very thought of makes

Stephen "go hot down her spine."[30] The culmination of Stephen's preadolescent desire occurs when Collins rolls down her stocking and allows the young girl to touch her knee, which is swollen with fluid as a result of scrubbing hard wooden floors. The moment is charged with sexual tension when Collins "displayed the afflicted member," and "Stephen's eyes filled with quick, anxious tears as she touched the knee with her finger."[31] Thus, the child becomes not only male-identified in temperament and behavior, but also in her sexual preference. Similarly, young Gladys realized her own sexual attraction to women at a young age. According to her *Ebony* article, she was attracted to one of her teachers, recalling:

> During recess, I stayed in the class and helped her, dusting and arranging things on her desk, cleaning blackboards. Sometimes she would let me comb her long, beautiful hair. In class I sat for hours watching her and wondering why I was so attracted to her. At night I dreamed of her. I didn't understand the meaning of those dreams until later.[32]

In this passage, Gladys Bentley complicates her identity, which during her career as a performer both her critics and admirers tended to reduce her to her indeterminate gender ("mannish") and size ("ample"). In the autobiographical essay, she declares for herself a sexual preference based on physical attraction to another woman. In 1952, this was a brave act.

The naive sexual encounters experienced by Stephen Gordon and Gladys Bentley have a deeper significance as well. The description of the young women's inner desires (manifested in physical sensations and dreams) and innocuous physical realizations of those desires (touching Collins's knee and combing the teacher's hair) help point to the "naturalness" of the women's sexuality. Because the childlike sexual feelings are intuitive and reflexive, they deflect labels of sinfulness and immorality. Heike Bauer explains that the discussion of sexuality in children was a new phenomenon at the turn of the twentieth century, but it changed the way in which psychologists discussed sexuality. Both Sigmund Freud in his *Three Essays on Sexuality* (1905) and Krafft-Ebing in his *Psychopathia Sexualis* (1886) point to sexual desire (or as Krafft-Ebing describes "sexual instinct") in preadolescence, which implies that it is an inherent personal attribute.[33] Rather than something adults actively choose, then, sexual preference resides in the person from at least childhood. Since their depictions of sexuality are positioned as instinctive or psychologically rooted, the narratives of Stephen Gordon and Gladys Bentley, with their emphasis on sexual innocence and gender blamelessness, register as a call for tolerance and under-standing. Yet in neither narrative does the protagonist experience tolerance and understanding. Instead, the central figures of the texts come across as martyrs; they are destined to live lives filled with loneliness and unhappiness.

Both Stephen and Gladys Bentley advance through childhood and adoles-cence not comprehending the basis of their unhappiness. In the novel, Stephen's father "understands" his daughter's difference (which he does not share with her) from reading Krafft-Ebing. At age twenty-one, Stephen comes across her dead father's notes in the book, and she is horrified by what she reads. She suddenly recognizes herself as one of the "thousands of miserable, unwanted people, who have no right to love."[34] Bentley, on the other hand, ex-plains that her parents took her "from doctor to doctor" to cure her of her pro-clivities. Nothing seemed to work, but she points out that her mother and fa-ther "meant well." "They just didn't know," she claims, "how to cope with a situation which to them was at once startling and disgraceful."[35] For both women, eventual knowledge of their "inversion" is associated with bodily afflic-tion, which they merge with early-twentieth-century psychoanalysis and Chris-tian notions of sinfulness. They claim for themselves martyrdom based on their inborn "faults." For Stephen, God has made her "hideously maimed and ugly," and she wears the "mark upon Cain."[36] For Bentley, the diagnosis of her "differ-ence" is a "malignant growth festering inside [her]," which long undetected causes her to become a "victim of her own sins."[37] In true heroic fashion, the recognition of their plight leads to a casting out and a break from the commu-nity in which they were raised. For Stephen Gordon, exile from her parents' es-tate would lead her to London. For Gladys Bentley, the destination was New York City.

It is important to remember that Gladys Bentley's rewriting of *The Well of Loneliness* took place eight years before she died, most likely to resuscitate her moribund career. Yet the text serves as a fitting foundation for scrutinizing her performances on stage and off during the Harlem Renaissance. Bentley's recep-tion, both critically and socially, was similar to that of the novel. While she had many fervent admirers, who praised her for her talents as a musician and singer, she had as many detractors, who reproached her for her vulgarity and sexual immorality. These responses echo the social tension over homosexuality, which was becoming increasingly visible on the stages and streets of Harlem in the 1920s and early 1930s.

For good or ill, Gladys Bentley's tuxedo-clad persona reinforced the stereotypical image of the bulldagger and strengthened the alliance of lesbianism and masculinity (and the resultant and inevitable sadness). As Esther Newton writes about Stephen Gordon, the depiction of the "mannish lesbian" fuses gender identity with sexual preference, thereby bolstering the homosexual as invert model.[38] Nearly twenty-five years after the novel was published, Bentley reinvigorated the language of early sexology to tell her own story and proved the durability of the familiar mannish lesbian character. The character had not changed much in that quarter century, and Bentley mimics—only slightly revising—the destitution of her literary sister, Stephen Gordon.

To make matters more confusing, the fictional character was based in part on real-life figures, having her origin in the author's own lived experience and in psychological case studies of "female inverts." Krafft-Ebing's delineation of "the extreme grade of degenerative homosexuality," whose only "feminine qualities" are "the genital organs,"[39] finds its way into both *The Well of Loneliness* and Bentley's "I Am a Woman Again." Krafft-Ebing refers to the female invert as a member of a "third sex" who cannot be defined as either male or female. Describing Stephen's feelings of solitude, for instance, Hall writes, "She had not yet learnt that the loneliest place in this world is the no-man's-land of sex."[40] Bentley's version is only slightly different: "For many years I lived in a personal hell. Like a great number of lost souls, I inhabited that half-shadow no man's land which exists between the boundaries of the two sexes."[41] This highlights the interplay between reality and fiction in Gladys Bentley's memoir. Intertwining her life with Stephen Gordon, Bentley's own identity has many levels of recycled images and conflicting stances on homosexuality that are grounded in personal experience, popular fiction, and scientific case studies. As a result, she is like the shadows in Plato's cave: determining the real Gladys Bentley is a nearly impossible proposition.

Descriptions of and responses to Gladys Bentley's New York performances in the late 1920s through the mid-1930s indicate that she was indeed nearly impossible to categorize as well. As a singer of the blues, in which she first made her mark as a performer, she posits the image of a down-on-her luck, sexually starved woman who has been treated badly by a man. In her nightclub and theater act, she offered a very different image. In her trademark tuxedo, she gave the impression of an independent, self-assured, and sexually empowered individual. Her multiple personae teased the boundaries between male and female; homosexual and heterosexual; aristocrat and working class; and white and black. In short, Gladys Bentley seemed to revel in occupying an identity in the entertainment world that could only be described as a "half-shadow no man's land."

HOW MUCH CAN I STAND?

Although there is no record of Gladys Bentley in Harlem before 1928, she claims that she left home in 1923 to go to New York City. This would have made her sixteen years old. Other accounts, however, suggest that she arrived in Harlem around 1925.[42] But whenever she got there, Harlem was the perfect place for a disenfranchised young woman like Gladys Bentley. As Eric Garber writes, "It was within [Harlem's] nocturnal milieu of illicit sexuality, gambling, and drugs that Gladys Bentley found a place where she could be herself."[43] Playing piano in the Harlem rent party circuit, she quickly established herself as a highly proficient pianist and secured a modest living. Although black male musicians dominated the circuit, Bentley earned a formidable reputation as a pianist and singer, and she was soon playing, first as a substitute then as a featured performer, in small nightclubs in Jungle Alley. Her first break came when a friend told her that a club on 133rd Street, called the Mad House, was looking for a pianist right away. "But," he informed her, "they want a boy." Without missing a beat, Bentley replied, "There's no better time for them to start using a girl."[44] She rushed over, persuaded the reluctant owner to give her a chance, and immediately wowed the audience. Starting at $35 a week, she was soon making $125 plus tips, which was an impressive salary for a black woman entertainer in the 1920s.

As a result of her burgeoning notoriety as a pianist and singer, a recording contract seemed imminent, and in 1928 record producers were willing to take a chance on Harlem's new talent. She signed with an agent, and in 1928 and 1929, Bentley recorded a total of eight sides (or what today would be called "singles"). In this era of 78 RPM records, a singer would release two songs at a time, one on each side of the record, which sold for about seventy-five cents. Bentley recorded with OKeh Race Records, the white-owned studio that gave a jolt to the music industry when it took a chance on an unknown blues singer, Mamie Smith (no relation to Bessie), in 1920. In 1926, the powerhouse recording company Columbia Records acquired OKeh. On August 8 and 31, 1928, Bentley recorded her first four sides, "Ground Hog Blues," "Worried Blues," "How Long—How Long Blues" and "Moanful Wailin' Blues." She recorded her last four sides with OKeh, "Wild Geese Blues," "How Much Can I Stand?" "Big Gorilla Man," and "Red Beans and Rice," on November 15, 1928, and March 26, 1929.[45] Because blues records sold particularly well among black consumers, the records were primarily promoted in the major black newspapers.[46] The first two records must have sold reasonably well to warrant a follow-up, but either because of her scandalous image or because her records never found a huge audience, Bentley did not record any other songs for OKeh.

Like the blueswomen who came before her, Gladys Bentley often used the musical form to counter the common perception that black women were merely objects to be controlled, degraded, or looked down upon. A great deal has been written about this aspect of the blueswomen songs of the 1920s, especially about some of the biggest names of the era, including Bessie Smith, Gertrude "Ma" Rainey, and Alberta Hunter. Sandra Leib, Hazel Carby, and Angela Davis in their own studies have all pointed to the empowerment that the blues afforded black women, which they see as an early form of black feminism. Looking at the songs as forms of social and political protest, they argue that the blues provided one of the few public arenas in which black women, representing working-class sensibilities, could speak out against widespread injustice, such as prejudice, financial hardship, and domestic violence. Angela Davis, for instance, building on the ideas of Hazel Carby, argues that many of the songs of "Ma" Rainey and Bessie Smith "begin to articulate a consciousness that takes into account social exploitation, racism, and male dominance as seen through the lenses of the complex emotional responses of black female subjects."[47] Indeed, resisting the popular images of black women as asexual and domestic (i.e., the mammy representation) or exotic and uncontrollably sexualized (i.e., the banana-adorned, savage figure), the blues songs affirmed black women as rational, complicated individuals, who are very much in control of—and empowered by—their sexual desires and emotions.

In many ways, these attitudes are strongly evident in several of the songs Gladys Bentley recorded, and in some cases wrote, in the late 1920s. She drew upon such social issues as domestic violence, abandonment, and exploitation. But Bentley's songs are not all about social and political assertion. In a not uncommon (but not often discussed) aspect of the blues by women performers, Bentley's songs also can be defeatist, self-pitying, and (by our own standards) anti-feminist. I would argue, however, that Bentley, rather than undermining and limiting the social and sexual agency of the blueswomen, expands upon the images of black women, presenting an even more complex view of black experiences, concerns, and sexuality.[48]

"Worried Blues," one of Bentley's earliest compositions, signifies on—to use Henry Louis Gates's term—the blues advice song—to use Angela Davis's classification. A blues advice song speaks directly to a presumed audience, offering guidance and warnings based on personal experience. When singing about male-female relations, for instance, the singers often challenged men for their actions and counseled women on how to recognize warning signs in a relationship and what to do if a male lover treats them poorly. "Worried Blues" urges women to be alert both because of men's natural weaknesses and the influence of calculating, immoral women. In a warning that reflects the Lulu Belle motif, the song highlights the effects of a bad woman on a good man, explaining how difficult it is to "keep a real good man nowadays" because "any young chippie gal has got so many doggone ways." At the same time the song highlights the dangers of weak men, but it also pits women against other women.

Bentley's lyric represents the quintessence of the formidable woman blues song. The tone is defiant and cautionary, and depicts a female subject who is to be both respected and feared. The lyric begins with a rhetorical question concerning the treatment of women by men. The singer positions herself as both a victim of male oppression and as one speaking out against it: "What make you men folk treat us women like you do? / What make you men folk treat us women like you do?" The third line, which is typically the "response" to the first two lines in a classic blues stanza, answers this question by avowing a personal stance. In the process, the singer articulates her financial independence and refusal to be financially exploited by relationship: "I don't want no man that I got to give my money to." In the following stanzas, the singer reiterates the this economic exploitation of women by the man, speaking out against the parasitic "sweetman."

The third and fourth stanzas continue the discursive shift of the song's focus and intended audience. While in the first stanza the singer speaks on behalf of all women and from a shared experience, in the second, the singer registers a personal complaint against a particular man: "Give my man everything from a diamond ring or dough." Emphasizing the awesome power of the wronged woman as well as a warning to anyone who crosses her, the singer responds: "The next thing I'm gonna' give him six feet in the cold, cold ground." The threat of violence underscores the singer's fearlessness and refusal to submit to subjugation, which is a rather common motif in blues songs. As Paul Oliver writes, the violence that is often evident in the blues helps to convey and encourage resilience among the listeners "by emphasizing assertiveness and unwillingness to submit to repression."[49]

At the end of the song, the lyric once again reaches out to a wider audience. Yet rather than directing it to "you men folk" as in the first stanza, the moral is intended for young women, who may not be able to resist the sexual pull (as presumably the singer was unable to) of the men who prey upon them: "You can never tell what an old, old man can do. / You can never tell what an old, old man can do. / Keep your eyes open, girls, 'cause he'll put that thing on you." While the sweetman of the singer's own experience metonymically represents the possible dangers of all men, the lyric points to the sexual weakness of women, who often give in to the sexual temptations of men. The title of the song, "Worried Blues," underscores the subtextual sexual anxiety of the singer. By the end of the song, it appears as if the aggressive and confident singer is "worried" that she will yield to her own sexual desires.

Bentley's performance of the song on record intensifies this overtly sexual interplay and erotic tension. Her growling, rumbling vocal delivery is complemented by the pounding, sultry piano (which she is playing). In addition, her high-pitched muted-trumpet-like scatting—one of Bentley's most distinctive musical features—in the song's musical breaks adds a feminine quality to the song. While speaking out against male-female sexual attraction, the song itself is seductive and arousing in its delineation of pure heterosexuality.

The images and themes Bentley introduces in "Worried Blues" weave throughout her other songs as well. "Ground Hog Blues" is the lament of a woman who bemoans (literally, in terms of the guttural groaning and moaning in which Bentley prefaces the song) the fact that she is a "low-down dog" because her man is both taking her money and cheating on her. As in "Worried Blues," the singer is financially independent and respectable, but she feels used and cheated. In this song, the singer emphasizes her moral respectability as well, claiming at one point that she "went to church / Like all good women do." At the same time, "How Long—How Long Blues" and "Moanful Wailin' Blues" emphasize the sexual yearning of the singer. These recordings feature Eddie Lang on guitar with Bentley singing and accompanying herself on piano. The twanging acoustical guitar punctuates the lyric, responding to and reinforcing the singer's melancholic complaint. In "Red Beans and Rice," the only double-entendre song Bentley recorded, the sexual yearning is even more pronounced. The singer's sexual hunger, as it were, is evident through the abundant food imagery and Bentley's leering vocal rendition. In the song, the singer must live on a diet of rice and beans without meat (stating regretfully, she "don't get no chicken"). As with most of her songs, she financially supports her man, whom she suspects has "some outside gal." He is so stingy, though, he will not even "buy no sugar to sweeten his own tea." At the end of the song, she announces her sexual frustrations, declaring that she "can't keep working with only rice and beans in sight." The playfulness of the double entendre is accentuated by the sudden hastening tempos during the musical breaks that just as quickly revert to a mock somberness during the blues accompaniment. The song hints at what Bentley's scandalous reputation as a performer might have been like.

The bleakest of Bentley's songs is "Wild Geese Blues," which is as close to an existential nightmare as a lyric can get. The initial stanzas introduce nature's unsympathetic relation to the singer's dejection. The "wild geese" of the title mock her sentiments of entrapment, and the image of the "weeping willows swaying" metaphorically reflects her own sorrows. Furthermore, the application of the classic blues structure with its repeated two-line "call" followed by the third-line "response" effectively emphasizes the main themes of the song. Despair and loneliness are ever present and unending in the singer's world: "Heard that lonesome music just about the break of day, / Heard that lonesome music just about the break of day, / Wash my feet in molasses tryin' to keep bad luck away." Even as she tries to find solace by ventilating her sadness and attempting to release her sense of abandonment, nature itself seems to conspire against her: "Threw my window open just to air these loves of mine, / Threw my window open just to air these loves of mine, / Groundhog saw his shadow, six more weeks of wintertime." In the last stanza, the song switches from a focus on lost love to the grim realities of being poor and destitute. While many of Bentley's songs portray an independent woman, here the singer faces an uncompromising and cruel existence: "Hard coal in my cellar, only got to shovel more, / Hard coal in my cellar, only got to shovel more, / Can't get no more credit from butcher or the grocery store." Many African Americans of the era would recognize their own struggles in this song, and as Daphne Duval Harrison explains, this is one of the points of the blues. One of the primary functions of the blues, according to Harrison, is to articulate the "agony and pain of life as experienced by blacks in America."[50]

"Wild Geese Blues" incorporates several prominent themes often revisited in the blues. Particularly among the blueswomen of the 1920s, abandonment, loneliness, financial destitution, and uncertainty about the future are evoked in the songs. In "How Much Can I Stand?" and "Big Gorilla Man" Bentley introduces another unfortunate reality: domestic violence. "How Much Can I Stand?" is unique among Bentley's blues in that it is grounded in the psychological development of a particular woman. In musical theater terms, it would be classified as a "character song" because the lyric charts the emotional growth of the singer. She moves from complete dependence on a man, who used to be attentive and caring, "but now he treats [her] like a darn stepchild," to contemplation of suicide as a result of the physical and mental abuse, to sexual and emotional autonomy of the woman as she announces that she will not fall into the same pattern again.

The song includes the repeated refrain, "How much of that stuff can I stand?" which takes on more urgency as the song progresses. Early in the song, for instance, the singer reiterates the cheating man motif (along with the food/sex connotation): "One time he said my sugar was oh, so sweet, / But now for his dessert he goes across the street. / How much of that stuff can I stand?" A few stanzas later, the song powerfully and poetically evokes the horror of domestic abuse: "Said I was an angel, he was born to treat me right. / Who the devil heard of an angel that gets beat up every night? / How much of that stuff can I stand?" The refrain is employed differently in the next stanza when it relates directly to issues of life and death as the singer considers suicide (or is it murder?): "Went down to the drugstore, asked the clerk for a dose, / But when I received the poison, I eyed it very close, / How much of this stuff can I stand?" At the end of the song, however, the singer does not swear off men completely. Not only does she state her intention of getting another man, but while asserting her own respectability, the singer claims she will marry him. The lyric concludes: "The next man I get must be guaranteed, / When I walk down the aisle, you're gonna' hear me scream, / How much of this stuff can I stand?" The lyric represents a process of self-realization as the singer announces her determination to continue to love men, yet the application of the final refrain indicates that the abusiveness of men is inevitable.

Frank references to physical abuse were not uncommon in the women's blues songs of the 1920s. The responses to it, however, were complicated and contradictory by today's standards. In some of the songs, women stand up to it or take revenge on the abusers. In "Blood Hound Blues," for example, Victoria Spivey sings about escaping from prison after poisoning her abusive lover, lamenting, "I know I've done wrong, but he beat me and blacked my eye, / But if the blood hounds don't get me, in the electric chair I'll die."[51] Similarly, Ma Rainey's recording of "Black Eye Blues" concerns a woman who resolutely says that she will "hang around" even as her man beats her and cheats on her, but she waits for the day when she gets revenge after catching him with his "britches down."[52] In other cases, though, women submitted to the abuse either out of necessity or because it was a fact of life. Bessie Smith's "Outside of That" gestures toward this attitude. The singer claims that her man "blackened my eye," and "knocked out both my teeth," she contends, "Outside of that, he's all right with me."[53]

Gladys Bentley's recording of "Big Gorilla Man" pushes this notion of acceptance a bit further. The singer recognizes the violence of the titular figure, admitting that he "makes [her] scared." And when she sees his eyes "gleaming," she begins "screaming." But she is unable to extricate herself from the abusive relationship because of the sexual fulfillment the "big gorilla" provides. The song begins:

> That big gorilla, a woman killa',
> And I ought to know.
> He mistreats me, knocks and beats me,
> Still I love him so,
> 'Cause he's got that something that I need so bad.

It is clearly not fear that keeps her in the relationship, but her own need for sex, which she stresses with the repeated line, "'Cause he's got that something that I need so bad." On the recording, Bentley further enhances the primal sexuality of the song by groaning, scatting, and intensifying the sense of urgency of the repeated line. As with many of the blues songs, "Big Gorilla Man" offers the view of an emotionally complex woman who knows that on one level she is in an unhealthy relationship, but on another receives a great deal of sexual gratification. In this case, sex trumps security.

In "Sexuality, Authenticity and the Making of the Blues Tradition," Marybeth Hamilton says that the early race records of the blues were located "in a nexus of sex, commerce and urbanism."[54] Bentley's recordings, with their emphasis on sexual attractions, financial support/independence, and the competition posed by young, single women ("chippies") in the urban context, fit squarely in this tradition. They do not, however, fit the image of the cross-dressed, butch lesbian, which one normally associates with the performer. One might assume that that is because the issue was taboo in this musical genre, but lesbianism was not uncharted territory in the blues. The most famous of these songs is Ma Rainey's "Prove It On Me Blues." Recorded just a few months before Bentley recorded her first two sides in 1928, "Prove It On Me Blues" is sung from the point of view of a woman who dresses in "a collar and tie" and can "talk to the gals just like any old man." Yet even as the singer flaunts her lesbian appearance and mannerisms (Rainey's own attraction to women was well known), she defies anyone to prove her sexual preference:

> They said I do it, ain't nobody caught me
> Sure got to prove it on me
> Went out last night with a crowd of my friends
> They must've been women, 'cause I don't like no men.[55]

Simultaneously obvious and hidden, public and private, she is a sexual desperado tauntingly floating between genders. The singer is deliberately evasive, because to her, sexual desire is a matter of personal choice. In another famous lesbian blues song, Lucille Bogan's "B.D. Women's Blues" (which she recorded as Bessie Jackson), men are represented as dispensable in their roles as both sexual partners and monetary supporters. The song contains the following lyric: "Comin' a time, B.D. womens ain't gonna need no men, / Comin' a time, B.D. womens ain't gonna need no men, / The way they treat us is a lowdown and dirty sin."[56]

It is tempting (and perhaps possible) to read into Bentley's own compositions, as well as her selection of songs by others, a decidedly lesbian point of view. Her deep, forceful voice and her indelicate way with a piano keyboard match the cultural depictions of a bulldyker. The songs also all share in common a negative portrayal of men, a sentiment Bentley herself expresses in her autobiographical essay.[57] There are no "good men" in the songs, only exploiters, abusers, and cheaters. The only usefulness of these men is the sexual gratification they provide. Otherwise, they cause heartbreak, loneliness, and animosity among women. Yet the songs are undeniably and audaciously heterosexual. Granted, the songs were recorded before Bentley created her signature cross-dressed, proudly lesbian persona, but the women in these songs define themselves in relation to men. There is not even a hint of female companionship. Even so, I would argue that there is a transgressive element in the collective performances.

Through much of the twentieth century, the blues were considered a truly African American art form, or as Ann DuCille describes, "the metonym for authentic blackness."[58] Evoking the class-based view of black "realness," James Weldon Johnson referred to the blues as "folk-poetry," which in his estimation offered an unmediated view of the struggles and concerns of working-class African Americans.[59] Similarly, W. C. Handy, who is regarded as the "Father of the Blues," referred to the blues as the black "mother tongue" in his 1941 autobiography, and as an art form that could be imitated by non-Blacks but one that could not be "delegated outside of the blood."[60] And Amiri Baraka describes the "native American music" as "the product of the black man in this country," emphasizing that the "blues could not exist if the African captives had not become American captives."[61] Read all together and against her autobiographical essay, Bentley's blues recordings point to the performative nature of race.

The recordings embody the struggles and obstacles African American women continually encountered in the United States, but one must keep in mind that Bentley's blues were produced and distributed by a white-owned company.[62] The result is black artistic expression with the intervention of white marketing and commercialism. In addition, the lyrics convey the strength, determination, and articulate protest of black women—indeed, a form of protofeminism, as Carby and Davis indicate. Yet Bentley's overly (hetero)sexualized portrayal makes even this come across as an act. I do not wish to imply that the image of an empowered black woman in the 1920s was based on fiction. Certainly, history and personal accounts by black women demonstrate that financial exploitation, abandonment, and domestic violence were are all too real. Nevertheless, read through her literary mannish-lesbian performance in the *Ebony* article, Gladys Bentley's blueswoman performances—and recognition of them *as* performances—reflect the inability to synthesize a black woman's experience into a single, universal experience. Examining Bentley's career as a Harlem fixture, nightclub performer, and headline attraction in a series of black revues, in which she merged her opposing images, one may see how Bentley opened a space for additional representations of black women.

LORD, HOW I ADORED IT

While other lesbian and bisexual performers such as Ethel Waters, Ma Rainey, and Jackie Mabley did not publicly flaunt their sexuality, or at least dared others to "prove it on them," Bentley made it an essential part of her early career. Both on stage and off, she was the epitome of masculine swagger and braggadocio. Although she was sometimes referred to as a male impersonator, a term she used to describe herself in the *Ebony* article, in modern language Bentley's signature performance would more appropriately be called a "butch lesbian."[63] Differing from the traditional male impersonator, or drag king, in the popular theater, Gladys Bentley did not try to "pass" as a man, nor did she playfully try to deceive her audience into believing she was biologically male. Instead, she exerted a "black female masculinity," to use Judith Halberstam's terminology, that troubled the distinctions between black and white and masculine and feminine. Through her manipulation of gender and racial identities, she demonstrated the constraints of those cultural binaries.[64]

Both Bentley's success and her controversy as a performer in the Harlem clubs and theaters of the 1920s and 1930s were a result of her parodying and exaggerating the socially concretized demarcations between gender, race, and class. This larger-than-life quality of Bentley's persona was symbolically attached to her weight, which most of her critics emphasized in their reviews. A critic quipped about one of her theatrical performances that she and her enormous bulk "threaten[ed] the floor by tap dancing—a little."[65] Wilbur Young begins his biographical sketch, "Huge voluptuous chocolate colored Gladys Bentley," and later compares her to "an overstuffed beer barrel."[66] Variously referred to as "ample," "buxom," "portly," "large and ungainly," Gladys Bentley reversed the stereotype of the ideal woman as frail, or, at the very most, shapely (à la Mae West). Bentley was a hyperbolic response to the black woman representing the "world's body,"[67] and she resisted and subverted a Freudian and Lacanian notion of woman as lack, symbolically absent in phallocentric subjectivity. Her extreme corporeality, though, was the opposite of deficient; it was a sign of surplus and hyperpresence. Hence, Bentley's overstated performance and appearance destabilized the conventional identity roles assigned within the divisions of black/white, woman/man, high class / low class, and homo-/heterosexual and reflected the possibility of, in Marjorie Garber's words, a "category crisis."[68]

Bentley developed her cross-dressed, mannish persona on the rent party circuit and in private gatherings in the late 1920s. She quickly became well known for her parodies of popular songs, turning bourgeois love songs into scatological odes. Simultaneously mocking "high" class imagery with "low" class humor, she applied aspects of the sexually charged "black" blues to demure, romantic "white" ballads, creating a culture clash between these two musical forms. None of these parodies was recorded, most likely because they far exceeded the bounds of decency and also because to record them would violate copyright laws. One of the lyrics, a lampoon on "Sweet Georgia Brown" and "My Alice Blue Gown," familiar Broadway show tunes of the day, survives. Bentley's version became an homage to anal sex:

And he said, "Dearie, please turn around"
And he shoved that big thing up my brown.
He tore it. I bored it. Lord, how I adored it.
My sweet little Alice Blue Gown.[69]

Although reactions to Bentley's version are not available, it seems fairly clear why such a song would be the catalyst for a raid of the club, an effect that, according to Wilbur Young, Bentley's performances often had.

The song's allusions to sexual gratification and preference establish a connection with the blueswomen of the 1920s.[70] Like the women who ironically sang about loving the men who blackened their eyes and knocked out their teeth, the singer's enjoyment of the violent sexual act is a way of accentuating her own sexual choices. In addition, the song registers a direct affinity with male homosexuality. Dressed in masculine clothing, Bentley's acknowledgment of the pleasures of anal intercourse could be an activity between two men. In fact, one of the most controversial features of Bentley's act was her allusion to homosexuality, which she made a central part of her act. For individuals who looked to Harlem to fulfill their longings for the taboo, Gladys Bentley more than fit the bill.

By 1929, Bentley had become a mainstay of Harlem cabarets and speakeasies, especially at the Mad House and Harry Hansberry's Clam House, both of which were in Jungle Alley. She appealed to both white and black audiences, but she was a particular favorite of white patrons, who, according to an *Amsterdam News* columnist, went to Harlem precisely to "engage in vices which they would not attempt in their own communities."[71] This is evident in an entry in a 1931 Harlem guidebook by Charles G. Shaw, a *Vanity Fair* columnist. He described the Clam House as

> A narrow room in Jungle Alley, catering to a large white patronage and featuring Gladys Bentley, pianist and torrid warbler. A popular house for revelers but not for the innocent young. Best after 1 A.M. and open until all hours.[72]

With her deep, rumbling voice, closely cropped, greased down hair, and masculine clothes (she was not wearing full tuxedos yet, but a variation on her schoolgirl outfit including skirts, dress shirts, and bow ties), she was an intriguing sight.

Her unique appearance and expert musicianship attracted celebrities and artists alike, who were drawn to her blend of blues and scandalous banter. Eslanda Robeson, the wife of actor Paul Robeson, gushed, "Gladys Bentley is grand. I heard her three nights, and will never be the same."[73] Langston Hughes had a similar reaction when Bentley first started out as a performer in small clubs:

For two or three amazing years, Miss Bentley sat, and played a piano all night long, literally all night, without stopping—singing songs like "The St. James Infirmary," from ten in the evening until dawn, with scarcely a break between the notes, sliding from one song to another, with a powerful and continuous underbeat of jungle rhythm. Miss Bentley was an amazing exhibition of musical energy—a large, dark, masculine lady, whose feet pounded the floor while her fingers pounded the keyboard—a perfect piece of African sculpture, animated by her own rhythm.[74]

At other times, Bentley's performance could be exceedingly moving, as indicated by Harlem schoolteacher Harold Jackman in a letter to poet Countee Cullen. Jackman remarked, "When Gladys sings 'Saint James Infirmary,' it makes you weep your heart out."[75]

The contradictory descriptions of Bentley are typical of those who saw her perform. Merging cultural expectations of blackness, she seemed to exude a throbbing, primal Africanness that Hughes pinpoints, as well as a soul-stirring vocal delivery derived from spirituals and gospel music. This image collided with her representations of whiteness, specifically through her high-class, masculine appearance and Broadway elegance. Therefore, writers like Hughes denoted her primitive, "jungle"-like qualities as the basis of her wide appeal, and others described her sophistication, which she accentuated by her "immaculate white full dress shirts with stiff collars, small bow ties and skirts, oxfords, short Elton jackets and hair cut straight back."[76] She seemed to represent a clash of low and highbrow cultures in one body: At one moment she appeared to be the model of refinement and restraint, but then the next she erupted into a display of blues and raunch. Although Bentley refined her act in small clubs and speakeasies in Harlem, by the end of the 1920s, she was the toast of New York's cosmopolitan set.

One of the first people to discover Bentley was author and socialite Carl Van Vechten, who was intrigued by her. He religiously went to see her perform at the Clam House between 1929 and 1930, and in his 1930 novel, *Parties,* he included a reference to her in the guise of a peculiar night club pianist. In the novel, one of the characters persuades another to go with him to Harlem, urging, "There's a girl up there now you oughta hear. She does her hair up so her head looks like a wet seal and when she pounds the piano the dawn comes up like thunder."[77] In truth, Van Vechten was enthralled by Bentley, and as evident in separate diary entries of 1929 through 1930, he saw her perform on nearly

FIG. 10. Gladys Bentley, artist Prentiss Taylor, and singer Nora Holt, who was the inspiration for Lasca Sartoris in Carl Van Vechten's *Nigger Heaven*. This photo was taken in Harlem in February 1932. © Carl Van Vechten. (Van Vechten Trust, Bruce Kellner Successor Trustee, and Beinecke Rare Book and Manuscript Library, Yale University.)

twenty different occasions at the Clam House and at private parties. In November 1929, for example, he gave a cocktail party and supper for twelve, which included Cecil Beaton and Langston Hughes, and Bentley played piano, sang, and danced.[78] A few weeks later he saw her at a party thrown by blues singer Clara Smith, and then again at another party hosted by wealthy sophisticate Eddie Wasserman, and at which Van Vechten met Cole Porter.[79] According to gossip columnist Louis Sobol, Van Vechten's appreciation for the singer even extended to his bestowing upon her a gift that would become her trademark, a white tuxedo.[80]

In 1930, Gladys Bentley had her own weekly radio program in which she performed jazz and blues standards,[81] and by 1933, her star was still rising. She moved from playing private parties, speakeasies, and the radio to nightclubs and legitimate theaters. After making a name for herself in Harlem's nightclub scene, she headlined a series of musical revues, first at King's Terrace, an after-theater nightclub on Fifty-second Street near Broadway, and her performance was considered even more shocking in Manhattan's Midtown. In March 1934, for instance, Bentley's "dirty songs" led to a formal complaint against the management of the King's Terrace, for presenting what the police commissioner dubbed "vile" entertainment.[82] One of the songs in Bentley's repertoire was "It's a Helluva Situation Up at Yale," which includes the lyrical limerick:

> It's a helluva situation up at Yale.
> It's a helluva situation up at Yale.
> As a means of recreation,
> They rely on masturbation.
> It's a helluva situation up at Yale.[83]

Bentley was supported by a chorus of pansies, described as "eight liberally painted male sepians with effeminate voices and gestures," who "assisted the singer in throwing this piece of filth at a blushing audience." According to one observer, the lewd stage show was not the biggest offense on the audience's senses. "The chief and filthiest offering of the evening, however, is a personal tour of the tables by Miss Bentley. At each table she stopped to sing one or more verses of a seemingly endless song in which every word known to vulgar profanity is used."[84]

A few weeks later the police padlocked the King's Terrace, presumably as a result of "the masculine-garbed, smut-singing entertainer," Gladys Bentley.[85] Undeterred, Bentley took her act back up to Harlem, and her *King Terrace Revue* transferred to the Lafayette Theatre, where it played for a limited engagement of a week. A publicity photo for the show depicts Bentley wearing her immaculately tailored white tuxedo standing suavely behind a group of kneeling black men in sailor suits, who are described as "the six 'Favorites of the King."[86] The billing plays on the familiar drag king/queen nomenclature, but it also amusingly, and not so subtly, points to the blatant homosexual content of the act. The picture of the sailor chorus surely was a reference to the gay subculture, which transformed New York's waterfront into a legendary homosexual cruising spot. For gay men, the sailor on leave was a symbol of masculine eroticism, pent-up sexuality, and rough trade.[87]

The homosexual content may have been coded in advertisements for this, Bentley's first show in a Harlem proscenium house, but it was even less subtle in performance. The theater critic for the *New York Age,* Vere Johns, mockingly referred to the revue as a "'fairy' good show," but he was actually quite put off by the production's cross-gender representations and the allusions to "perverse" sexuality.

A large and ungainly woman (if I may say so), who cuts her hair and dresses in tuxedos and calls herself Gladys Bentley, albeit that her troupe of six refer to her as a "gorgeous man" is supposed to be the headline attraction at the Lafayette this week. And she refers to her six boys as "fellows" and then apologizes to them for so doing. As a matter of fact if these boys were put into dresses they would be indistinguishable from the chorines. I, personally, could not enjoy their part of the show as I had a burning desire to rush out and get an ambulance backed up against the stage door to take them all to Bellevue for the alienists to work on.[88]

The critic did, however, enjoy an act by Consuelo Harris and her dance partner. Unfortunately, Gladys Bentley sabotaged his enjoyment of that act as well. In his review, he asked, "Won't someone please chase Gladys Bentley off the stage when Consuelo and partner are doing their dance?"[89] In the next several years Bentley continued to nurture this outrageous and controversial persona in a succession of revues at the Ubangi Club.

When the popular Connie's Inn, which fostered the talents of Louis Armstrong and Thomas "Fats" Waller, moved to Midtown, the space had trouble keeping a tenant. The Harlem Tavern and the Harlem Club both folded rather quickly, but when it reopened in April 1934 as the Ubangi Club, the neighborhood had a new major attraction. With a name intended to evoke associations with Africa and "the suggestion of voodooism,"[90] the Ubangi Club traded on the taste for the exotic that tourists craved from Harlem. Its shows were frequently reviewed in the major black papers, including the *Amsterdam News*, *Chicago Defender*, and *Pittsburgh Courier*, but there were some rumblings that the club barred black customers, or at least those attending in mixed racial parties.[91] In its "Night Club Notes" column the *New York Times* refuted this claim in 1936, stating, "The Ubangi still draws a mixed crowd, is noisy and intimate and gay—altogether Harlem, in short."[92]

Shortly after the club's opening in June 1934, Bentley headlined a revue, and continued to do so for the following three years. In fact, her name became synonymous with the club, as indicated by another announcement in another *New York Times* column: "The Ubangi Club, Harlem's reigning hot spot, will offer a brand new revue tomorrow evening, featuring (of course) Gladys Bentley."[93] Bentley's series of revues included such fairly big names as comedian Jackie Mabley, bandleader Willie Bryant, and singer-dancer Avon Long. The shows were built around her formidable reputation and talents, and included such titles as *Club Ubangi Revue* (1934), *The Ubangi Club Follies* (six editions in

1935–36), *High, Wide and Handsome* (1936), *Round the World in Swing Tempo* (1937), and *Brevities in Bronze* (1937).[94]

In general, the reviews for the shows were positive, and she attracted sizable crowds. Writing about her show in 1934, one columnist reported that she was a huge hit with the crowd and was "solidly breaking them down" with her risqué entertainment.[95] In 1935, the *Ubangi Club Follies* played a one-week engagement at the Apollo, where it preceded the Warner Baxter film vehicle *Under the Pampas Moon*. Lou Layne of the *New York Age* found the live entertainment enjoyable but thought that, at ninety-nine minutes, it "could be cut without impairing the show." He did, however, have high praise for Bentley, stating that she "sings, dances and plays the piano in typical night-club fashion, delighting her listeners every moment she's on-stage."[96] By the end of 1935, Bentley's Ubangi Club show had made her a bona fide Harlem celebrity. In December of that year, for instance, she appeared in a star-studded benefit for "Harlem's Needy" at the Rockland Palace. The "Monster Breakfast Dance," as it was called, began at 10:00 p.m. and went until dawn, and it featured such bandleaders as Fletcher Henderson, Willie Bryant, and Duke Ellington. Guest appearances included world-champion boxers Jim Braddock, Jack Dempsey, and Joe Louis, along with stage and screen stars Jimmy Durante and Lew Clayton.[97]

As Bentley's celebrity grew, double entendre and gender play remained a central feature of her act, but she discarded her "King" designation. Perhaps poking fun at regal star designations, like Bessie Smith's identification "Empress of the Blues," or in an effort to establish her own mainstream imperial status, Bentley took on a new title. When her Ubangi Club show played the Harlem Opera House in 1935, she appeared in her familiar white tux, and although she never played a Broadway house, she went under the ironic billing "Broadway's Queen of Song and Jazz." Around town she was also popularly known as "La Bentley," causing one critic to remark on the confusing gendered article, implying that "Le" might be more appropriate.[98] Consistently toying with and undermining gender classifications, Bentley seemed to enjoy the bafflement she caused.

By 1936, Bentley was the headliner of Harlem's biggest nightclub floor show. The *New York Times* said that it "continues to hold its ground and turn out its sizzling entertainment."[99] But at this point, Bentley was better known as a teaser of the limits of propriety than as a musical performer. For example, the title of one of her club editions, *High, Wide and Handsome,* called attention to the star's image (tall, heavy, and masculine) rather than the evening of songs and dances the show contained. And even though she introduced a few new songs

FIG. 11. A regal Gladys Bentley in her trademark top hat and tuxedo. Photographer unknown. (From collection of the author.)

for each edition of her nightclub show with provocative titles like "The Devil Trucks His Rounds," the *New York Times* said she was "no great shakes as a singer but who seems to have ample personality."[100] She continued to annoy some critics, who often found her act offensive, but her popularity with audiences could not be denied. About her Ubangi Club show that transferred to the Apollo Theatre in 1936, a critic from the *Age* wrote that Bentley was still plying her sexually laden songs to the audience's acclaim:

You know what Gladys Bentley does, something suggestive as usual. Somehow, I've never learned to appreciate her work but that doesn't stop her from being a prime favorite with the mob. After all, how much do I know?[101]

Later in the same year when she returned to the Apollo, the same critic wrote dismissively, "Ample Gladys Bentley, who is as much part of the Ubangi Club as the scenery, delivers a couple of those songs that have come to be identified with her, dual meaning lyrics that really have only one."[102]

A mark of Gladys Bentley's success is her regular appearance in the gossip columns of the 1930s. Whether or not it was a calculated performance, her off-stage persona received as much attention as her onstage act. She attracted attention as a regal presence, hobnobbing with New York's elite. Columnist Marcus Wright, for instance, reported that "Gladys Bentley and her sophisticated group were seen in Jones's Bar and Grill on last Wednesday night. They solidly beat it up, and carried on."[103] She also made a very public display of her lesbian identity, making it an essential part of her image both on stage and off. Wilbur Young, writing in 1939, stated:

> As Gladys grew in popularity, rumors had it that she was queer and even sported a girl friend. To add to these whispers, she could be seen any day marching down Seventh Avenue attired in men's clothes and she seemed to thrive on the fact that her odd habits was the subject of much tongue wagging.[104]

She was often seen with a host of young women, who appeared to be smitten by her masculine charms. Gossip columnist Archie Seale, for example, reported seeing "the buxom Gladys Bentley entering the Alhambra [Theatre] late Saturday afternoon while three chicks stood amazed."[105] And as an ultimate act of heterosexual repudiation, she married a white woman in a New Jersey civil ceremony. Louis Sobol, a gossip columnist for the *New York Evening Graphic*, recalled Bentley approaching him and telling him: "'I'm getting married tomorrow and you're invited.' When Sobol asked who the lucky man was to be, she giggled and replied: 'Man? Why boy you're crazy. I'm marryin' ———' and she named another woman singer."[106]

By 1937, however, Bentley's act seemed to have lost much of its potency. Her shows seemed slick and stagy, and what had once seemed daring and impertinent was now self-conscious and deliberate. She had already dropped one of the most effective elements of her performance, her piano playing, and sang while someone else accompanied her. Although she still sang double-entendre numbers, her shows emphasized the superficial glitz of "respectable" Broadway fare. As Langston Hughes claimed, when "she got famous," Bentley "acquired an accompanist, specifically written material, and conscious vulgarity."[107] Her final show in Harlem, *Brevities in Bronze,* a rousing, blues-inflected revue that originated at the Ubangi Club, was much like a polished Cotton Club show. The revue was aimed at an audience that expected a nightclub confection to be one part naughtiness, one part rhythm and jazz, and one part downtown sophistication. In *Brevities in Bronze,* Bentley was backed not by a chorus of "pansies" but the Ubangettes, a chorus of black women, who were dubbed "The Gorgeous Fast Stepping Sepians." She sang her obligatory double-entendre songs, and also on view was a woman striptease artist who went by "Gypsy Rose Lee in Bronze." The reviews for the show were mostly positive, but it is evident that the show lacked the spontaneity that Bentley's performance had once conveyed. *Brevities in Bronze* seems to have been created with the express purpose of shocking for the sake of shocking. The *Amsterdam News* called it a "diverting bit of entertainment," and said that it was "carefully gauged to suit the sensibilities of night club goers, who love their entertainment to center on the risqué."[108] The *Sun* wrote that *Brevities in Bronze* "is a big revue that sets out to be shocking and succeeds nobly."[109] The critic of the *World Telegram* called it "the kind of show one expects from the bronze belt; fast, robust, dancing across—and through—the thin ice of good taste with a laugh and a leer."[110]

But in an appropriate coda to her provocative Harlem performances, Bentley's big number in *Brevities in Bronze* articulated her defiant stance against social expectations. In this number, fittingly called "Gladys Isn't Gratis Any More," and just as she did in her blues songs almost ten years before, she proclaimed her economic, social, and sexual independence. With music and lyrics by Donald Heywood, the song perfectly articulated Bentley's unwillingness to fit into the assumed category of what an African American black woman should be. The *New York World Telegram* claimed, "Portly Gladys Bentley, in white tails, gives her number all she has (about 300 pounds)."[111]

Just as the thirty-year-old Bentley was being discovered by the major New York papers, unfortunately, the public's fascination with Harlem was severely on the wane. Harlem was not the tourist attraction it had once been, and Midtown was ensuring its status as the world's entertainment epicenter. As the *New York Times* reported in 1936, "Harlem's moon has gone into something of an eclipse more recently, what with downtown activity speeding up and the Cotton Club moving to Broadway."[112] In 1937, the Ubangi Club closed, and *Brevi-*

ties in Bronze transferred for a brief run to the Plantation Club, the former home of the Cotton Club.[113] By 1938 there were judgments and tax liens against the Ubangi Club.[114] In 1944 the club tried to recapture its former glory by re-opening—sans Bentley—in Midtown (right around the corner from the site of the old King's Terrace, Bentley's former haunt). Even with floor shows with titles like *Top Hats and Tom Toms* that drew on the familiar cultural collisions of white and black entertainment, the nightclub only lasted two years.[115]

Many of Harlem's largest clubs and theaters persevered for a time with the onslaught of the Great Depression. It even managed to retain some of its appeal with the repeal of Prohibition, which removed much of the exuberant lawlessness that the neighborhood seemed to offer. As James Hatch explains, the Depression was the great leveler, transforming the optimism of the 1920s "into a movement concerned with social problems and leftist politics."[116] In addition, Harlem's riots of 1935, which Claude McKay described as "the gesture of despair of a bewildered, baffled, and disillusioned people," shattered Harlem's sense of optimism.[117] In a time when a large percentage of the population was spending much of its time on relief lines and breadlines, Gladys Bentley's nightclub act seemed inappropriate and strangely naive.

But Bentley's own relatively brief Harlem career can in no way be termed a failure. In the 1920s and 1930s she defiantly demanded respect as an African American, a woman, and a butch lesbian. Her blues songs named and called attention to issues affecting working-class people, and her exaggerated, larger-than-life appearances on stage and off poked fun at cultural ideologies associated with race, class, gender, and sexual orientation. Bentley's refusal to capitulate would exact a terrific price in the 1950s, but in the 1920s and 1930s, she represented one possible model of black womanhood, who was at once robust, self-supporting, and sexually liberated.

"IN THE TWILIGHT ZONE OF SEX"

In May 1958, Gladys Bentley appeared on Groucho Marx's television game show, *You Bet Your Life*, which is apparently the only extant video of her.[118] Wearing a plain-colored, short-sleeve blouse, a matching skirt falling below her ankles, pearl necklaces (two), pearl bracelets, large daisy-like earrings, and flowers in her scooped-up and scooped-back hair, Bentley presents a very different image from the one she did twenty-five years before in the Harlem nightclubs. On the show, she is partnered with a Nigerian man, who wears traditional African clothing, including a brightly colored fila (round cap) and buba (long-sleeved, oversized blouse). Underneath the Nigerian attire, however, he wears a gray suit, white dress shirt, and a plain tie. The pair makes for an exotic duo, which is clearly the intent. The rest of the contestants and the entire audience (or at least those who are visible when the camera pans the studio) are white. The cultural and racial distinctions are highlighted by Groucho's remarks in an aside to the live-studio audience. "One thing about our show," he quips, "you never see any unusual people." Groucho continues to riff on the foreignness of the participants, particularly in his interview with the Nigerian man. He mock-bungles his name, asks him "what part of Nebraska [is he] from," and invites the man to talk about Nigeria (especially about the culturally acceptable polygamy). Groucho eventually turns his attention to Gladys Bentley, apologizing for not engaging her sooner, but, as Groucho jokes, "It isn't often we get a charming lad from Guatemala."

Bentley, perhaps not to be outdone by her game show partner, claims that she too is foreign. She says she is from Port-of-Spain, Trinidad (which, incidentally, is her mother's country of origin). In the brief interview that follows, Bentley's main intention for appearing on the show is to plug her upcoming book and club appearances.

> GROUCHO MARX: Do you have a job, Gladys?
> GLADYS BENTLEY: Yes, I'm an entertainer. I sing and play for a living in nightclubs all over the country. And I just finished a book called *If This Be Sin*.
> GM: Well, what is it about? Is it about geometry?
> GB: My life story.
> GM: Your life story. You're *the* Gladys Bentley.
> GB: Yes, that's right.
> GM: I thought your name sounded vaguely familiar. Gladys, how long have you been singing in nightclubs around the country?
> GB: For about forty years.
> GM: What kind of songs do you sing?
> GB: Well, I do everything—all kinds of songs.

Looking somewhat older than her fifty-one years—claiming that she had been performing in nightclubs for the last forty years (starting then presumably when she was eleven) does not help—Bentley's manner in the interview is professional and cool. The image of the bawdy, mannish lesbian of her youth is nowhere to be seen, and the once torrid blues singer comes across on television as surprisingly matronly.

Groucho invites Bentley to perform, but in the process, he also gets in a joke about her weight, cautioning, "Watch that [piano] stool" as she takes a seat. But then Bentley performs a jazzy and rousing version of "Them There Eyes," made famous by Billie Holiday, and the years seem to disappear. Her voice is in fine form, recalling her characteristic interplay of a throaty alto with her improvisational trumpet-like notes that seem to pop out of the top of her head. While her fingers fly over the piano keys with ferocious speed and vigor, one is reminded of Langston Hughes's description of her as an "amazing exhibition of musical energy." And in what might be considered a portent of Hughes's connection to her as "a perfect piece of African sculpture," her Nigerian game show partner begins dancing to the music. The man's polycentric dance movements, including vibrating hands, pelvis, and pulsating feet evoke images of ritualistic images of African celebration. To the audience's delight, Groucho, his trademark cigar firmly clamped on the side of his mouth, joins in with his own imitation of African dance while whooping for her to increase the already hot tempo.

At the end of her performance, Bentley is greeted with enthusiastic applause, and Groucho tells her, "You sang 'Them There Eyes' so realistically, I could see the contact lenses." At this point in the show, the contestants take part in the actual game, and they correctly identify four tunes and win $1,000. Groucho tells them that they would have the option to wager this money on the opportunity to win more. Later in the show, the pair returns saying that that they will not risk losing the money they have won by spinning the wheel for a chance at $10,000. Then, there is a revealing moment in which the audience gets a glimpse of Bentley's legendary toughness and swagger. She defiantly shakes her head and tells Groucho, "I don't want no part of that wheel."

This is the last record of Gladys Bentley, and while she continued to perform in clubs across the country, there is not a great deal of information about her between her final show at the Ubangi Club and her death in 1960. In 1938 Bentley left New York and eventually settled in East Los Angeles, where she lived with her mother in a small home on South Crawford Avenue. Over the next twenty years, Bentley had tried several times to rejuvenate her singing career but with mixed success. She appeared at the Paradise and Swanee Clubs in Los Angeles in 1938 and 1939, but Los Angeles in the 1940s and 1950s was far less tolerant of a 250-pound butch lesbian than New York City in the 1920s. Her career was directly affected by the rising tide of conservatism that took hold in the 1940s and continued into the 1950s. During an engagement at Joaquin's El Rancho in February 1940, the nightclub had to file for a special police permit that would allow her to appear in pants rather than a skirt.[119] Yet Bentley persisted.

FIG. 12. Gladys Bentley performs "Them There Eyes" on the Groucho Marx game show, *You Bet Your Life* (1958). © National Broadcasting Company, Inc. (Shout Factory DVD and NBC Home Entertainment.)

She performed occasionally at Mona's, San Francisco's well-known lesbian bar. In 1942, for instance, she appeared on a bill as "America's Greatest Sepia Piano Artist" and the "Brown Bomber of Sophisticated Songs."[120] She also made a handful of recordings in the 1940s, notably with Excelsior under "Gladys Bentley and her Quintette," such as "Boogie'n My Woogie" and "Thrill Me Till I Get My Fill."[121] In September 1944 she returned to New York City and opened at Tondaleyos nightclub, and according to press reports, Bentley was not only a versatile entertainer but also a gifted "linguist and composer," and her act included songs performed in French, Spanish, and Yiddish.[122] The following year she was once more a headliner at the Apollo on a bill that included trumpeter Oran "Hot Lips" Page. The *Amsterdam News* indicated that Bentley was still worth watching and carried with her an "international reputation." The review states, "Despite her weight she is a clever and nimble dancer. But her fame rests upon the originality of her own songs."[123] Bentley was back on the West Coast by 1946 and performing at the Cobra Club in downtown Los Angeles.

In the 1950s she recorded a handful of songs, including a Christmas song, "Jingle Jangle Jump" with jazz saxophonist Dexter Gordon.[124] At about the same time she recorded "Before Midnight" for Flame Records, a jazz record that did not have a lyric, just a series of doo-wahs and scatting. Still, it is a good match for the resonant blues quality she developed in the late 1920s.[125] She even tried her hand at marriage—to a man—but, according to one reporter, "she returned to her old ways."[126] Supposedly, a friend of the writer visited Bentley shortly after the wedding and noticed two photos, one of a man and the other a woman, on Bentley's bureau. When the writer's friend asked about the identities of the individuals, Bentley reportedly responded, "Oh. That's my husband (pointing to the male) and that's my wife."[127] She was divorced a short time later.

Sadly, Bentley never replicated the fame she had achieved headlining at such nightclubs as the Clam House, Kings Terrace, and the Ubangi Club. And she never again attracted the audiences that packed the Lafayette, Apollo, and Harlem Opera House. Before her death from the Asian flu in 1960 (she was fifty-two), she invested a good deal of her energy in evangelism, and she was a prominent member at the Temple of Love in Christ Church, Inc., where she was ordained a minister just a few weeks before her death.[128] On January 23, 1960, with her mother making all of the necessary arrangements, Gladys Bentley was buried at Lincoln Memorial Park in Carson, California.[129] According to gossip columnist Dorothy Kilgallen, Bentley had completed her autobiography, which might have strengthened her legacy, but she hadn't found a publisher.[130]

Gladys Bentley's descent into obscurity is particularly unfortunate because beginning in the late 1950s, the United States witnessed a renewed interest in blues and folk songs. Corresponding with the civil rights movement and an attention to the plight of downtrodden people, whom these singers represented, many of the classic blueswomen were coaxed out of retirement, and they attracted a whole new audience. Performing in smoky Greenwich Village clubs, folk festivals, and blues concerts, these women introduced the form to a new generation of music fans. Alberta Hunter, Ida Cox, Ada "Bricktop" Smith, Sippie Wallace, Victoria Spivey, and Edith Wilson all benefited from the revival and brought to their songs an added layer of toughness and a deeper affirmation of survival. Even more unfortunate for Gladys Bentley is that she did not live long enough to celebrate the revolutionary temperament of lesbian and gay pride that the Stonewall Riots initiated in 1969.

Harlem of the 1920s and 1930s may have tolerated a butch lesbian like Gladys Bentley, but in the McCarthy era of the late 1940s and early 1950s, she would have been perceived as something of a national menace. The "excess" of Bentley's persona, as marked by her flagrant violation of acceptable female behavior, appearance, and desire, challenged the presupposed notion of femininity and necessarily had to be reclaimed by patriarchy. In her 1952 *Ebony* article, "I Am a Woman Again," Bentley renounced her previous identity and "the sex underworld in which [she] once lived," presumably as an attempt to resuscitate her moribund career. But even in this article, Bentley once again appears to be the ultimate chameleon. Like a gifted, adaptable actor, Bentley sheds the costumes, dialogue, and props of one role and sets the scene for a new dramatic interpretation. Yet rather than completely concealing her former self within the new characterization, Bentley occasionally offers privileged, unmistakable glimpses of the performer within the role, presenting the impossibility of locating the "real" Gladys Bentley and affirming the impossible task of finding the truth behind the portrayal.

Bentley's denunciation in the 1950s of her former life was a reflection of the prevalent cultural attitude of the era. David Savran shows that the image of the American nuclear family offered a comforting refuge from "an increasingly anxiety-producing and dangerous world" torn apart by World War II and confronted by the Cold War. Within this representative image "was the strict prescription of masculine and feminine roles defined by the interrelationship of both men and women in both home and marketplace."[131] Gay men and lesbians posed a direct threat to this picture of safety and tranquility, because they could corrupt and potentially destroy the sanctity of the American family with their perversity. The postwar United States was intent on reflecting an idyllic scene of harmony and impenetrability founded on the notion that men and women had particular roles to play.[132] If Bentley wanted to be a part of this stolid new vision of the United States, which had no room for a sexually and economically independent black woman, she necessarily had to change her public and private act. In short, she had to be domesticated.

To this end, she describes her previous life as "tragic," a "living hell," and a "strange, heart-twisting existence," but she refers in loving detail to her former apparel, including "tailor-made clothes, top hat and tails, with a cane to match each costume, stiff-bosomed shirt, wing collar tie and matching shoes."[133] She talks about her luxurious "$300-a-month apartment," the servants who attended to her, and her beautiful car. These images are a far cry from the drab, shapeless white housedress covering her huge body that she wears in the article's pictures. Throughout the article are photographs of Bentley appearing domesticated: "Turning back cover of bed to make homecoming husband comfortable," "taste-testing dinner for her husband," and "making selection from jewel case for an evening out." Whereas she lived amid New York's splendor, the photo captions state that she now lives in a "modest, tastefully appointed home directly in rear of a similar home she purchased for her mother."[134] One is forced to wonder which life indeed is the "personal hell" that she describes.

Whereas in the 1920s and 1930s, Bentley proclaimed her sexual and economic independence from men, in this article, her melodramatic take on the theme, she describes her newfound happiness upon finding the love of a "real man." She rehearses the familiar image of the butch lesbian as a "failed woman," to employ Sally Munt's phrase.[135] According to her autobiographical essay, she had enjoyed the fame, money, and critical adoration of her professional life, but in her "secret heart, [she] was weeping and wounded because [she] was traveling the wrong road to real love and real happiness."[136] Then, the "miracle" arrived. She explains:

> The miracle came about when I discovered and accepted the one glorious thing which, for so many years, I had bitterly fought with all my heart, mind, and body: the love and tenderness, the true devotion of a man who loved me unselfishly and whose love I could return; the awakening within me of the womanliness I had tried to suppress.[137]

In an ironic understatement, Bentley says that she is no longer married to her savior (a sailor, who calls to mind her "Favorites," a "pansy" chorus dressed as sailors), but she still treasures the precious gift he gave her. In fact, at the time of her writing she was soon to be married again, this time to a writer on the theater. She adds that she "hope[s] and pray[s] this marriage will last."[138] It did not, and her "husband" denied that they were ever married.

Bentley's surprising—albeit histrionic—reversal is a reflection of the conservative viewpoints that had swept the United States by the 1950s. Even as lesbian subcultures were evolving in such places as San Francisco and Buffalo, the lesbian (i.e., the visible butch lesbian) was culturally regarded as a tragic and desolate figure. She was, according to the pulp novels of the era, guaranteed a life of solitude and misery unless she renounced her sinful way of life. Martha Vicinus writes, "The doomed lesbian was a remarkably durable image. By the 1950s everyone knew what a lesbian was; she had been assigned a clearly defined role. Defiance and loneliness marked her life, according to the pulp romances."[139] On one level, the novels offered evidence that lesbians existed and provided a sense of solidarity to lesbians reading the books. But on another level, the novels' emphasis on an ill-fated existence helped to reinscribe heterosexual values.

In February 1954, *Jet*, a popular black magazine, included an article that focused on "the problems of hundreds of women who are trapped in the half-shadow, no-man's-land of the man-woman."[140] The article outlines the deception, which lesbians employ to ensnare unwitting women, and it warns, "The lesbian, like the male homosexual, who stalks a married home is to be considered a dangerous person."[141] Particularly vulnerable to the lesbian's advances, the article claims, are widows, spinsters, lonely women, and "those who have suffered from nervous breakdowns and other mental ills."[142] The essay is not without its hopefulness, though. It contends: "Despite the lesbian's power of persuasion or slyness of approach, she stands a slim chance of debauching a normally sexed woman who is happily married or deeply in love with a man. Studies show that most women feel it is still much nicer to have a man around the house."[143] The author also points to Gladys Bentley's narrative as an example of a "happy ending" for "the lives of strange women." Referring to Bentley's *Ebony* article a year and a half earlier, the author offers the entertainer's "return to womanhood" as proof that "manlike women" can be rescued from their sexually deviate condition.

Bentley's reclaiming of a womanhood that she never admits to having could serve as the content of one of Freud's case analyses, and her article is filled with allusions to Freudian rhetoric. The cause of her "strange" situation, according to the physician she visited, appears to be her failure to pass through the Oedipal complex. After she decided to seek help and to willingly become a woman, he told her : "That's just what I wanted to hear. Now I can tell you what I've known for a very long time. Your sex organs are infantile. They haven't progressed past the stage of those of a fourteen-year-old child."[144] The way out of this "sex underworld in which [she] once lived" was not only the "unselfish" love of a "real" man, but also the "miracle" of science, which consisted of regular injections of female hormones to counteract the excess of male hormones her body produced. The combination of these two elements allowed her to reciprocate the man's love, as well as enjoy "the awakening of the womanliness [she] tried to suppress."

Gladys Bentley's transition (back) to a woman figuratively sets out to show the stability of the gender categories. According to the rhetoric she adopts, they are necessary and truthful if one is to find fulfillment and personal completeness. But in an interesting way, her article subverts her intention as we follow the continually shifting images of her persona. In an effect similar to a fun house of mirrors, Bentley's article juxtaposes pictures of the performer in drag from the 1920s and 1930s with pictures of her in 1952 wearing floral-printed dresses. The reader becomes aware of the instability of the roles Bentley is performing in each shot. Although she claims the "truth" of one role and the happiness it has brought her, her previous role does not seem to foretell misery and shame. On the contrary, posing regally in the early pictures, Bentley appears dignified and independent; while the pictures of Bentley at the time of the writing show her as domestic and dependent. The fluidity of her identity is most cogently revealed in the largest picture, which frames the article. Displaying a scrapbook with photos of herself in top hat and tails, Bentley beams. Looking at the picture of pictures and charting her various personae, the reader is faced with the impossibility of discerning the "real" Gladys Bentley. The endless shifting between what appear to be the boundaries of masculine and feminine, black and white, homosexual and heterosexual produces an unsettling and exciting promise of a category crisis.

Conclusion: "You've Seen Harlem at Its Best"

There's more to Harlem than people suspect,
They spend an evening or two.
You get impressions I'd like to correct;
You don't know nothing, I'm telling you
'Til you've seen gigolos wash their clothes
In a self-respecting nest,
Humming lullabyes instead of hi-de-hi's
You've seen Harlem at its best.

Rolling dice that never win, losing all our rent.
Or marching in the Elks parade,
We would rather run for gin than run for president.
We don't need no park when it comes to petting in the dark.

—"YOU'VE SEEN HARLEM AT ITS BEST"*

The Great Depression brought an unceremonious finale to the entertainment of the Harlem Renaissance. The neighborhood disintegrated further into poverty and destitution as New York's upper crust lost money or turned to new venues for entertainment. The Lafayette Theatre, Harlem Opera House, and many of the nightclubs that flourished in the 1920s went bankrupt or closed by the mid-1930s. The Hamilton Lodge drag balls, a Harlem tradition since the 1870s, ended abruptly in 1939 after a wave of panic over sex crimes seized the nation, and changed the perception of homosexuals from silly oddities and sexual degenerates to dangerous psychopaths.[1] Black people had also lost their exotic appeal for whites. As Langston Hughes wrote, "We were no longer in vogue, anyway, we Negroes. Sophisticated New Yorkers turned to Noel Coward. Colored actors began to go hungry, publishers politely rejected new manuscripts, and patrons found other uses for their money."² National distress and international hostilities of the 1930s and 1940s drastically altered the mood of the country. What was once considered progressive, shocking, or taboo became associated with the destruction of American society and regarded as an issue of national security. Lesbians and gay men, who had been fairly visible in the early decades of the century, slunk back into the closet or declared their change in sexual orientation.

Additionally, the Harlem neighborhood, which had been associated with nightlife and jazz in the popular imagination, became linked with poverty and desperation. Clergy members and neighborhood leaders had voiced their concerns about the social and economic conditions throughout the 1920s, but it was not until an incident in 1935 that the rest of New York and the country officially took notice. On March 19 of that year, sixteen-year-old Lino Rivera was caught stealing a penknife at Kress's Five and Ten Cent store. Rumors spread that Rivera had been beaten and killed at the hands of the police who had been called to the scene. Riots ensued, and by the end of the following day, when order had been fully restored, three people were dead, and there was two million dollars in property damage. Almost immediately Mayor LaGuardia appointed a commission to determine the causes of the riot and help him root out the "long-festering social and economic sore spots."³ And within a week of the riot, the *New York Times* was already declaring that "unrest and rebellion [had] been in the air for a long time" as a result of deplorable housing conditions, the refusal of white merchants in Harlem to hire black employees, and "the deeper problem of racial strains in the life of the city."⁴ The literature and theater that emerged in the second half of the 1930s, particularly as demonstrated by Richard Wright, Langston Hughes, and the Federal Theatre Project, tended to reflect a greater urgency for social and political progress. The arts of the 1920s seemed terribly naive in comparison.

Yet this study will hopefully amend the widely held impression that black performers and performances prior to the 1930s did not make valuable artistic and cultural contributions. Many of the artists of the 1920s were out front in critiquing and refashioning representations of race, gender, class, and sexual orientation, and some even defied social and legal restrictions in order to forge a career in popular entertainment. The various bulldaggers, pansies, and chocolate babies represented here—as well as those who have not yet been reclaimed from the archival trash heap—may not have been completely successful in countering the ingrained moral beliefs equating homosexuality with degeneracy and black women with Lulu Belles, for example, but they should be given their due. While astutely negotiating the social conditions of their time, they crafted complex performances and images that were imbued with individualism and originality.

By way of conclusion, I would like to acknowledge one more performer, not as an afterthought but as a final image, a parting shot, as it were. There was a drag artist of considerable renown at the Ubangi Club, where Gladys Bentley appeared for a number of years. Drawing on the exceedingly alluring image of silent film star Gloria Swanson, the actor whose real name was Walter Winston created the persona "the Sepia Gloria Swanson," and he is credited with beginning a vogue for male impersonators of Broadway and Hollywood starlets.[5] According to Bruce Nugent in a sketch written for the Federal Writers' Project in 1939, Winston had come from Chicago, where he was a frequent winner of the drag balls in that city. Just as Gladys Bentley's stage performance carried over into her everyday life, Winston was rarely ever observed in male attire and lived life like a glamorous movie star. Nugent wrote: "Seldom coming on the street in the daytime, breakfasting when the rest of the world was dining, dining when the rest of the world was taking its final snooze before arising for the day, his public life was lived in evening gowns; his private life in boa-trimmed negligees."[6] People usually referred to "Gloria" with the feminine pronouns *she* and *her,* and with her "swelling and well-modeled bosom" and "chocolate-brown complexion," she was a favorite of the underworld set and a frequent attraction at the Harlem drag balls.

In addition to performing in nightclubs and speakeasies, Sepia Gloria Swanson performed on vaudeville bills that included big names like Fletcher Henderson's band. Wearing a tight corset and tastefully dressed in sequins, fishnet, and furs, the loud and buxom Swanson would dance demurely, raising her skirt just to the knee, and singing risqué songs, such as "Get 'em from the Peanut Man (Hot Nuts)" and her theme song, "Squeeze Me," by Thomas "Fats" Waller. When she appeared at the Harlem Opera House in 1934, Swanson performed a rendition of "I'm a Big Fat Mama with Meat Shaking on My Bones" that caused something of a stir. The lyric calls to mind the home-breaking, man-stealing image of Lulu Belle crossed with the physically imposing, working-class blueswoman. The song takes on an added dimension when sung by a man in glittering drag parodying a white silver screen goddess: "I'm a big fat mama, got the meat shakin' on my bones / I'm a big fat mama, got the meat shakin' on my bones / And every time I shake, some skinny gal loses her home."[7] Sepia Gloria Swanson nearly brought down the house. Augustus Austin, reviewing the show for the *New York Age,* however, was not amused by Swanson's play with cross-racial, cross-gender, and cross-class representations. He found her "'she-male' glorifying act" "repulsive," and he claimed to be physiologically affected by the performance:

> When "Gloria Swanson" made "her" appearance my spirits drooped; when "she" sang "I'm a Big Fat Mama With Meat Shaking on My Bones," I became disgusted; but when "she" showed "her laundry" I had a sinking sensation in the pit of my stomach akin to the feeling one has on his first ocean trip.[8]

By the late 1930s, LaGuardia's tightened legal restrictions made it difficult for Swanson to maintain her public and theatrical lifestyle, and reportedly she had to adopt a male pronoun descriptor, and "masquerade" as a man.

Sadly, the curtain came down a final time for Harlem's most famous female impersonator on April 18, 1940, when Walter Winston died of a cardiac condition that had debilitated him for more than a year. Winston was just thirty-three years old. Purportedly, he had been "rolling in money" as a featured performer in theaters across the East Coast, but he died "practically penniless."[9] Even in death, though, Winston remained a controversial figure, and in an interview after his death his mother indicated both the head wagging and the outpouring of love her son's persona provoked. She said, "Regardless to what people have or will say, I'm more than grateful to the profession and to those friends of Walter's."[10] At the funeral, Reverend W. W. Monroe, who officiated, pointedly addressed the "curiosity seekers" among the congregation, reminding the nearly two hundred people in attendance that "folks who live in glass houses" must refrain from gossip and scorn.[11]

Swanson, along with many of the other performers and performances highlighted in this study, has been largely forgotten. Perhaps their acts had to be seen to be truly appreciated and remembered, but in the pre-civil rights, pre-Stonewall era, they must have been spectacles in themselves. Although we only have fragmentary glimpses of these spectacles, their performances sowed the seeds for future generations to radically envision a society not stratified by classifications based on race, class, gender, and sexual orientation.

Notes

INTRODUCTION

*Epigraph: quoted in Allen Woll, *Black Musical Theatre: From "Coontown" to "Dreamgirls"* (Baton Rouge: Louisiana State University Press, 1989), 76.

1. "The Onlooker: Florence Mills Leads the Way," *Chicago Defender* (November 10, 1923), 12.

2. "Steps toward the Negro Theatre," *The Crisis* (December 1922), 66–68.

3. W. E. B. Du Bois, "Krigwa Players Little Negro Theatre," *The Crisis* (July 1926), 134.

4. Charles S. Johnson, "Editorials," *Opportunity* (August 1926).

5. James V. Hatch, "The Harlem Renaissance," in *A History of African American Theatre,* ed. Errol G. Hill and James V. Hatch (New York: Cambridge University Press, 2003), 215.

6. David Krasner, *A Beautiful Pageant: African American Theatre, Drama, and Performance in the Harlem Renaissance, 1910–1927* (New York: Palgrave, 2002) and Paul Allen Anderson, *Deep River: Music and Memory in Harlem Renaissance Thought* (Durham, NC: Duke University Press, 2001).

7. David Krasner explores the political and theatrical significance of this production in *A Beautiful Pageant* (81–94).

8. *Fast and Furious,* which Brook Atkinson described as "fast, furious, and tiresome in large doses," closed after just seven performances. Atkinson was especially unkind, writing, "When the material is hackneyed, when the performers are fat and clumsy, the animalism of Negro entertainment is lumpish and unwieldy" ("Harlem Fandango," *New York Times* [September 16, 1931], 15).

9. Anthea Kraut, "Between Primitivism and Diaspora: The Dance Performances of Josephine Baker, Zora Neale Hurston, and Katherine Dunham," *Theatre Journal* 55.3 (October 2003): 433–50.

10. Henry Louis Gates, *The Signifying Monkey: A Theory of African-American Literary Criticism* (New York: Oxford University Press, 1988). Explaining this process in African American literature, Gates argues: "Writers Signify upon each other's texts by rewriting the received textual tradition. This can be accomplished by the revision of tropes. This sort of Signifyin(g) revision serves, if successful, to create a space for the revising text. It so alters fundamentally the way we read the tradition, by defining the relation of the text at hand *to* the tradition. The revising text is written in the language of the tradition, employing its tropes, its rhetorical strategies, and its ostensible subject matter, the so-called Black Experience. This mode of revision, of Signifyin(g), is the most striking aspect of Afro-American literary history" (124).

11. "Harlem Facets," *The World Tomorrow* (November 1927), reprinted in *The Col-*

lected Writings of Wallace Thurman: A Harlem Renaissance Reader, ed. Amritjit Singh and Daniel M. Scott III (New Brunswick, NJ: Rutgers University Press, 2003), 35–39.

12. A. B. Christa Schwarz, *Gay Voices of the Harlem Renaissance* (Bloomington: Indiana University Press, 2003), 15.

13. Sterling Brown, "More Odds," *Opportunity* (June 1932). Describing the links between the "masses" and the upper classes, Brown further explained, "Even our 'ritziest' [are] only one and a half removes" from the working class (189).

14. George Hutchinson, *The Harlem Renaissance in Black and White* (Cambridge: Belknap Press of Harvard University Press, 1995), 6.

15. Chauncey, qtd. in Schwarz, *Gay Voices,* 7.

16. See Jill Watts, *Mae West: An Icon in Black and White* (New York: Oxford University Press, 2001), 124–42. The novel became the basis for West's play *The Constant Sinner* (1931), which ran for sixty-four performances on Broadway.

17. See George Chauncey, *Gay New York: Gender, Urban Culture, and the Making of the Gay World, 1890–1940* (New York: Basic Books, 1994).

18. "White Slummer Hit Blow in Report Depicting Conditions in Harlem District," *New York Amsterdam News* (October 16, 1929), clipping in Alexander Gumby Scrapbook Collection, Columbia University Library.

19. In his letter to publisher Alfred A. Knopf, Van Vechten wrote about the upcoming publication of *Nigger Heaven:* "It is necessary to prepare the mind not only of my own public, but of the new public which this book may possibly reach, particularly that public which lies outside of New York. If they see the title, they will ask questions, or read "The New Negro" or something, so that the kind of life I am writing about will not come as an actual shock. To that end, as you know, I have during the past year written countless articles on Negro subjects (I have one in the [*Herald*] Tribune today and two more in proof chez Vanity Fair) and I have seen to it that as many outoftowners as possible saw enough of the life themselves so that they would carry some news of it back to where they came from" (letter dated December 20, 1925, in *Letters of Carl Van Vechten,* ed. Bruce Kellner [New Haven: Yale University Press, 1987], 86–87).

20. "Hint of Police Raids to Clean the Stage," *New York Times* (February 9, 1927), 1.

21. "381 Arrested in a Raid," *New York Times* (May 13, 1927), 28.

22. Qtd. in David Levering Lewis, *When Harlem Was in Vogue* (Oxford: Oxford University Press, 1981), 107–8.

23. Alain Locke, "The Negro Poets of the United States," in *Anthology of Magazine Verse 1926 and Yearbook of American Poetry,* ed. William S. Brathwaite (Boston: Brimmer, 1926), 150.

24. Qtd. in Hutchinson, *Harlem Renaissance,* 220.

CHAPTER 1

*Epigraph: Reprinted in Angela Y. Davis, *Blues Legacies and Black Feminism: Gertrude "Ma" Rainey, Bessie Smith, and Billie Holiday* (New York: Pantheon, 1998), 281–82.

1. Langston Hughes, *The Big Sea: An Autobiography* (New York: Thunder's Mouth Press, 1991; orig. 1940), 228.

2. Mark Helbling, *The Harlem Renaissance: The One and the Many* (Westport, CT: Greenwood Press, 1999).

3. "Social Snapshot," *Inter-State Tattler* (February 15, 1929), 5.

4. "Mme. A'Lelia Walker Entertains Friends," *New York Age* (December 20, 1924), 10.

5. Interview with Joan Nestle, May 21, 1981, transcript in the Mabel Hampton Collection, Lesbian Herstory Archives.

6. Qtd. in Joan Nestle, "'I Lift My Eyes to the Hill': The Life of Mabel Hampton as Told by a White Woman," in *A Fragile Union: New and Selected Writings by Joan Nestle* (San Francisco: Cleiss Press, 1998), 36.

7. The New York tabloid *Broadway Brevities* contained the following blind item (the magazine often only provided the initials of the subject to protect itself from libel and, of course, to make the mystery part of the fun of the gossip), which undoubtedly referred to Joey: "Recently [Mrs. R. W. ——] gave a birthday party to sixty guests, one of the attendant and not unbelievable catastrophes of which was the complete disembowelment—or rather disencandlement—of every candlemaker in the Fifties" (November 1924, 34). Ruby Smith, Bessie Smith's niece, recounted a similar "performer" at a Detroit party. She describes a woman who would "take a cigarette, light it, and puff it with her pussy." She raved, "A real educated pussy" (qtd. in Eric Garber, "A Spectacle in Color: The Lesbian and Gay Subculture of Jazz Age Harlem," in *Hidden from History: Reclaiming the Gay and Lesbian Past,* ed. Martin Bauml Duberman, Martha Vicinus, and George Chauncey, Jr. [New York: NAL Books, 1989], 323).

8. Wallace Thurman, "Where Jazz Was Born," *Birmingham [England] Sunday Mercury* (October 7, 1928), n.p., clipping in Carl Van Vechten Scrapbook Collection, New York Public Library.

9. "High Rents and Overcrowding Responsible for Many of the Ills Suffered by Harlemites," *New York Age* (August 11, 1923), 1.

10. Lemuel F. Parton, "Harlem Becomes a Problem: Economic System Fails to Absorb the Negro, City's Ever-Growing Population" (May 10, 1929), clipping in Alexander Gumby Scrapbook Collection, Columbia University Library.

11. Qtd. in Kathy J. Ogren, *The Jazz Revolution: Twenties America and the Meaning of Jazz* (New York: Oxford University Press, 1989), 83.

12. "Jewish Landlord Tries to Force Sale of Property at Profit by Using Negro Tenants," *New York Age* (December 5, 1925), 2.

13. Herbert Gutman, *The Black Family in Slavery and Freedom, 1750–1925* (New York: Vintage, 1976), 454.

14. Lewis, *Harlem in Vogue,* 108.

15. Gilbert Osofsky, *Harlem: The Making of a Ghetto,* 2nd ed. (Chicago: Elephant Paperbacks, 1996), 135–36.

16. "High Rents and Overcrowding." Similarly, David Levering Lewis writes that "in its 1927 report on 2,326 Harlem apartments, the Urban League found that 48 percent of the renters spent more than twice as much of their income on rent as comparable white New Yorkers. For a four-room apartment (more than half the Urban League's sample), the average monthly rent was $55.70; average family income was about $1,300. The New York white equivalent was $32.43 in rent on a family income of $1,570" (*Harlem,* 108).

17. "New Building on W. 139th St. to Set High Mark for Rental Prices in Harlem," *New York Age* (February 28, 1924), 1.

18. "St. Nicholas Ave. Tenants Wage Fight for Reduction of Alleged Extortionate Rentals for Rooms Opened to Colored," *New York Age* (October 20, 1925), 2.

19. Ibid.

20. Lewis, *Harlem,* 109.

21. Michael Bronski, *The Pleasure Principle: Sex, Backlash, and the Struggle for Gay Freedom* (New York: St. Martin's Press, 1997), 188.

22. Qtd. in Steven Watson, *The Harlem Renaissance: Hub of African-American Culture, 1920–1930* (New York: Pantheon, 1995), 7.

23. Hughes, *The Big Sea,* 373.

24. Ibid., 377.

25. Wallace Thurman, *Negro Life in New York's Harlem* (Girard, Kans: Halderman-Julius Publications, 1928), 43.

26. Thurman, "Where Jazz Was Born."

27. Thurman, *Negro Life,* 41.

28. Ibid., 42.

29. In Alexander Gumby Scrapbook Collection, Columbia University Library, n.p.

30. Card in Mabel Hampton Collection, Lesbian Herstory Archives. In "'I Lift My Eyes to the Hill': The Life of Mabel Hampton as Told by a White Woman" (included in *A Fragile Union,* 23–48), Joan Nestle narrates the life of Mabel Hampton and her relationship with her wife Lillian through letters, documents, and personal interviews. Nestle writes: "Ms. Foster remembers in 1976, two years before her death: 'Forty-four years ago I met Mabel. We was a wonderful pair. I'll never regret it. But she's a little tough. I met her in 1932, September twenty-second. And we haven't been separated since in our whole life. Death will separate us. Other than that I don't want it to end" (38–39).

31. Qtd. in Lewis, *Harlem,* 107–8.

32. Barry Singer, *Black and Blue: The Life and Lyrics of Andy Razaf* (New York: Schirmer Books, 1992), 121.

33. David A. Jasen and Gene Jones, *Spreadin' Rhythm Around: Black Popular Songwriters, 1880–1930* (New York: Schirmer Book, 1998), 391.

34. J. Martin Favor, *Authentic Blackness: The Folk in the New Negro Renaissance* (Durham, NC: Duke University Press, 1999), 13.

35. Ann Douglas, *Terrible Honesty: Mongrel Manhattan in the 1920s* (New York: Farrar, Straus and Giroux, 1995), 426.

36. Carl Van Vechten, *Parties: Scenes from Contemporary New York Life* (Los Angeles: Sun & Moon Press, 1993; orig. 1930), 183.

37. Bronski, *Pleasure Principle,* 269 n. 36.

38. Douglas, *Terrible Honesty,* 106.

39. Thurman, "Where Jazz Was Born."

40. Theophilus Lewis, "Our Informal Night Life," *Inter-State Tattler* (April 5, 1929), 8.

41. "The Slumming Hostess," *New York Age* (November 6, 1926), 4.

42. "Negroes Support Dance-Hall Policy," *New York Times* (June 21, 1926), 5.

43. Edgar M. Grey, "Intimate Glimpses of Harlem," *New York Amsterdam News* (August 26, 1927), 4.

44. Qtd. in David Levering Lewis, *W.E.B. Du Bois: The Fight for Equality and the American Century, 1919–1963* (New York: Henry Holt, 2000), 189.

45. Richard Bruce Nugent, *Gentleman Jigger* (Philadelphia: Da Capo, 2008), 83.

46. "'Rent Parties Are Menace' Says Judge," *New York Amsterdam News* (October 28, 1925), 1.

47. "Prays as Court Frees Him," *New York Times* (November 12, 1926), 25.

48. "250 Taken in Police Raids over Week-End," *New York Amsterdam News* (September 21, 1927), 2.

49. "Drunken Brawls All Too Common," *New York Amsterdam News* (August 15, 1928), 2.

50. "Man Shot with Sawed-Off Gun," *New York Amsterdam News* (June 13, 1928), 1.

51. Qtd. in Burns Mantle, "Realism and the Negro Drama," *New York Daily News* (March 1, 1929), n.p., clipping in Alexander Gumby Scrapbook Collection, Columbia University Library.

52. Lillian Faderman, *Odd Girls and Twilight Lovers: A History of Lesbian Life in Twentieth-Century America* (New York: Columbia University Press, 1991), 68.

53. Kevin J. Mumford, *Interzones: Black/White Sex Districts in Chicago and New York in the Early Twentieth Century* (New York: Columbia University Press, 1997), 178.

54. Chauncey, *Gay New York*, 227.

55. Based on the correspondences between Carl Van Vechten and Langston Hughes, some literary historians have suggested the two men may have been lovers. Emily Bernard, the editor of the published letters, claims that they were not romantically involved because they do not ever discuss sexual attraction to men in their letters. There are, however, possible coded references, such as Van Vechten explaining to Hughes, "There are so many things that one can't talk about in a letter" (June 4, 1925); as well as Hughes's closing remarks, "Lilacs and Pansies to you! Carlo" (May 17, 1925), and "Call Boards and Call Boys to you!" (August 8, 1960). *Remember Me to Harlem: The Letters of Langston Hughes and Carl Van Vechten, 1925–1964*, ed. Emily Bernard (New York: Knopf, 2001).

56. Hampton, 9.

57. The court briefs appeared weekly in the "City News Briefs" section of the *New York Amsterdam News*. These particular briefs are found on the following dates (page numbers in parentheses): June 15, 1929 (4), June 12, 1929 (4), October 23, 1929 (19), and September 11, 1929 (4).

58. See, for example, the "Harlem Court Brief," *New York Amsterdam News* (October 23, 1929), 19. As I explain in the next chapter, Wallace Thurman was arrested for the same crime in 1925.

59. "P.S. Girls Figure in 'Sex Circuses,'" *New York Amsterdam News* (October 23, 1929), 1.

60. Bronski, *Pleasure Principle*, 199.

61. Jeffrey Escoffier, "The Political Economy of the Closet: Notes toward an Economic History of Gay and Lesbian Life before Stonewall," in *Homo Economics: Capitalism, Community, and Lesbian and Gay Life*, ed. Amy Gluckman and Betsy Reed (New York: Routledge, 1997), 125.

62. See Luc Sante, *Low Life: Lures and Snares of Old New York* (New York: Vintage, 1991), 282.

63. Ibid., 283.

64. See, for example, Nicholas de Jongh, *Not in Front of the Audience: Homosexuality on Stage* (New York: Routledge, 1992), 19.

65. *Variety,* February 23, 1927, 1.

66. "Nightclubs and Nudity Ban," *Variety* (April 13, 1927), 38. Smith, who in 1928 was the first Roman Catholic presidential candidate, was a popular four-term governor in New York. Although he was socially liberal and he opposed Prohibition, he was also a skilled politician, who knew that New York's national image would be closely scrutinized if Smith were to take the Democratic nomination.

67. "Manager of Lafayette Theatre and Chorus of Revue Arrested in Drive on Indecent Shows in Greater N.Y.," *New York Age* (April 23, 1927), 2.

68. "New York's Dirtiest Plays," *Variety* (February 2, 1927), 1.

69. Qtd. in Kaier Curtin, *We Can Always Call Them Bulgarians: The Emergence of Lesbian and Gay Men on the American Stage* (New York: Alyson, 1987), 100. Throughout 1927, *Variety* reported on the raids of the "dirt plays" as well as the legislation that followed. For a complete discussion of the controversy surrounding *The Captive* and *The Drag,* see Curtin as well as William Hoffman's *Gay Plays: The First Collection* (New York: Avon, 1979). *The Drag* is anthologized in *Three Plays by Mae West: Sex, The Drag, and The Pleasure Man,* ed. Lillian Schlissel (New York: Routledge, 1997), 95–142.

70. Curtin, *Call Them Bulgarians,* 100.

71. New York of the late 1990s witnessed a similar conservative backlash. In an effort to "clean up" the streets, and improve New York's "quality of life," Mayor Rudolph Giuliani undertook similar conservative steps to rid the city of blatant sexual performances and material. New ordinances forced the closure of adult bookstores, theaters, and strip clubs throughout Manhattan. Ironically, many of these places occupied the Times Square theaters that in the 1920s were deemed the most respectable houses in the city.

72. "Mgrs. Meet Today, Seeking Plan to Head Off Censor," *Variety* (February 27, 1927), 41.

73. Throughout the 1920s, Actors' Equity went to great lengths to distance itself from issues involving homosexuality. In 1928, at the second performance of another Mae West play, *The Pleasure Man,* which also featured cross-dressed men, it too was abruptly closed, and Actors' Equity refused to intervene. The actors in the play were arrested, forcefully removed from the stage by the police, and charged with indecency. Although the charges were eventually dropped after a jury could not reach a decision, rather than defending its union members, Equity responded to the ordeal by reiterating its across-the-board condemnation of "alleged salacious plays." For a detailed account of the legal troubles that faced *The Drag* and *The Pleasure Man,* see Watts, *Mae West.* Watts describes an incident in which the incarcerated gay cast members of *The Pleasure Man* staged a mini-demonstration in prison. Remanded to the Tombs, New York's notoriously harsh prison, the gay men were quite concerned about their safety from the reputably abusive police officers. "However, a visit from [Mae] West reassured them, and *Variety* reported that as a group they 'began chanting felicitations to their colleagues and making merry.' Their demonstration became so disruptive that the guards threatened them with additional charges. They quieted down, but it was clear that for gay cast members, their incarceration carried a political meaning. Finally, after battling the courts into the late

evening of the following day, West secured their freedom" (113–14).

74. These items appear in a regular column called "Tryin' to Find 'Sally' in Our Alley," *Broadway Brevities* (January 1925), 10.

75. *Broadway Brevities* (November 1924), 7.

76. Quotes from "Night No. 11 in Fairy-Land," *Broadway Brevities* (November 1924), 32–36; and "Night No. 13 in Fairy-Land," *Broadway Brevities* (January 1925), 34–40.

77. "Night No. 11 in Fairy-Land," 32.

78. Nathan Irvin Huggins, *Harlem Renaissance* (New York: Oxford University Press, 1971), 56.

79. E. J. Graff, *What Is Marriage For? The Strange Social History of Our Most Intimate Institution* (Boston: Beacon Press, 1999), 240. Graff notes that the drastic rise in divorce caused many commentators in the 1920s to "note that the only way to reduce the divorce rate would be to ban women (not just mothers but all women) from working—an option that no longer seems enforceable or even moral" (240).

80. Ibid. One of the "merry murderesses" in Maurine Watkins's *Chicago*, which opened on Broadway in December 1926, quipped about the chief similarity between murder and suing for divorce, "The *reason* don't count—it's the grounds." Maurine Watkins, *Chicago* (Carbondale: Southern Illinois University Press, 1997; orig. 1927), 26.

81. Qtd. in de Jongh, *Not in Front,* 34.

82. Qtd. in Curtin, *Call Them Bulgarians,* 62.

83. Brooks Atkinson, *Broadway* (New York: Macmillan, 1970), 248.

84. "Zukor Stops 'Captive,'" *Variety* (February 16, 1927), 1.

85. Atkinson, *Broadway,* 248.

86. West, *The Drag,* 124.

87. Qtd. in Richard Helfer, "Mae West on Stage: Themes and Persona," Ph.D. dissertation, City University of New York, 1990, 159. In the same *Parade* interview, West claimed that *The Drag*'s controversy stemmed from the fact that the public was not mature enough yet to see a play that confronted "the problem of homosexuality." Hoping that the play would be socially beneficial, she explained, "The problem is here. It is the duty of the government to at least face this great truth and do something about it. Let them treat it like a disease—like cancer, for instance, discover its causes and if it is curable, cure it" (ibid.). In the 1950s, her view was even less sympathetic toward gay men. In her 1959 autobiography she adopted the Cold War stance that homosexuality was a pernicious threat to American society: "In many ways homosexuality is a danger to the entire social system of western civilization. Certainly a nation should be made aware of its presence—without moral mottoes—and its effects on children recruited to it in their innocence. I had no objection to it as a cult of jaded inverts, or special groups of craftsmen, shrill and involved only with themselves. It was its secret anti-social aspects I wanted to bring into the sun" (Mae West, *Goodness Had Nothing to Do with It* [New York: Prentice Hall, 1959], 94).

88. "Night No. 11 in Fairy-Land," 36.

89. The Pullman Café was somewhat notorious for its intermixture of the races and had been raided at least once for "disorderly conduct" and "improper dancing exhibitions," which included a performance by a female impersonator ("Cabaret Raid Nets 42," *New York Times* [July 9, 1928], 38).

90. Bourne, "Harlem Opera Show Is Pretty Good This Week," *New York Age* (December 1, 1934), 4.

91. Qtd. in Claude McKay's *Home to Harlem* (Boston: Northeastern University Press, 1987; orig. 1928), 36.

92. Carl Van Vechten, *Nigger Heaven* (New York: Alfred A. Knopf, 1926), 12.

93. David Savran, *Communists, Cowboys, and Queers: The Politics of Masculinity in the Work of Arthur Miller and Tennessee Williams* (Minneapolis: University of Minnesota Press, 1992), 109.

94. Hampton, 2.

95. Faderman, *Odd Girls,* 70.

96. Wallace Thurman, *The Blacker the Berry . . .* (New York: Scribner Paperback Fiction, 1996; orig. 1929), 120.

97. Faderman, *Odd Girls,* 78; emphasis added.

98. "Women Rivals for Affection of Another Woman with Knives, and One Has Head Almost Severed from Body," *New York Age* (November 17, 1926), 1.

99. "A Rent Party Tragedy," *New York Age* (December 11, 1926), 4.

CHAPTER 2

*Epigraph: Frank Horne's "Harlem" originally appeared in *The Crisis* (June 1928), 196.

1. Anita Handy, qtd. in "Her Idea Criticized," *Pittsburgh Courier* (March 20, 1926), n.p., in Carl Van Vechten Scrapbook Collection, New York Public Library.

2. Ibid.

3. "They Won't Keep Away," *New York Amsterdam News* (October 23, 1929), n.p., clipping in Alexander Gumby Scrapbook Collection, Columbia University Library.

4. Hutchinson, *Harlem Renaissance,* 2.

5. As David Levering Lewis explains, an instigating factor in Harlem's vogue was the production of Edward Sheldon and Charles MacArthur's *Lulu Belle* in February 1926. Levering writes: He writes: "If the sociology of vogues teaches that single events have complex antecedents, it was, with this qualification, *Lulu Belle* that sent whites straight to Harlem in unprecedented numbers for a taste of the real thing. Their arrival was so sudden that Harlem had to gallop in order to live up to its expectations" (*Harlem,* 164). *Lulu Belle* is explored in depth in chapter 3.

6. Van Vechten, *Nigger Heaven.*

7. "Fire Burns: A Department of Comment" (November 1926), 47.

8. Robert F. Worth, "*Nigger Heaven* and the Harlem Renaissance," *African American Review* 29.3 (Autumn 1995): 465.

9. Bruce Kellner, *Carl Van Vechten and the Irreverent Decades* (Norman: University of Oklahoma Press, 1968), 220–24.

10. "Go Harlem," lyric by Andy Razaf, music by Jimmie Johnson, in Singer, *Black and Blue,* 239.

11. See Michel Foucault, *Discipline and Punish,* trans. Alan Sheridan (New York: Vintage, 1979). For a discussion of the implications of theatrical structure and decorations,

or "*how* theatres mean," see Marvin Carlson's *Places of Performance: The Semiotics of Theatre Architecture* (Ithaca, NY: Cornell University Press, 1989).

12. Van Vechten, *Nigger Heaven*, 149.

13. Lewis, *Harlem*, 188.

14. "Two Harlem Bodies Protest Lynchings," *New York Times* (December 20, 1926), 15.

15. "Romance and Tragedy in Harlem—a Review," *Opportunity* (October 1926), 316–17.

16. Ibid.

17. Review in *The Crisis* (December 1926).

18. Ibid.

19. Ibid.

20. Qtd. in Lester Walton, "Harlem Resents Emphasis on Its Vice—Walton" (October 8, 1927), clipping in Carl Van Vechten Scrapbook Collection, New York Public Library.

21. "Literary Note," *The Messenger* (October 1926), n.p., in Carl Van Vechten Scrapbook Collection, New York Public Library. The black community had rather conflicted feelings toward—to use Zora Neale Hurston's tongue-in-cheek term—Negrotarians. While they supported Blacks in their artistic endeavors, the recipients recognized that the reasons for support were not always so noble. Wallace Thurman wrote: "The Negrotarians have a formula, too. They have regimented their sympathies and fawn around Negroes with a cry in their heart and a superiority bug in their head. It's a new way to get a thrill, a new way to merit distinction in the community . . . this cultivating Negroes" (*Infants of the Spring* [Boston: Northeastern University Press, 1992; orig. 1932], 140.

22. Qtd. in Leon Coleman, *Carl Van Vechten and the Harlem Renaissance: A Critical Assessment* (New York: Garland, 1998), 123.

23. "In 'Nigger Heaven'—Otherwise Harlem, U.S.A.," by Viscountess Weymouth, "who has lately returned from America," *Jamaican Mail* (1929, exact date unspecified), clipping in Carl Van Vechten Scrapbook Collection, New York Public Library.

24. Weymouth, "Nigger Heaven."

25. "'Harlem'—38 and 2: An Approach to Perfection" (February 22, 1929), n.p., review in *Harlem* Clippings File, Billy Rose Theatre Collection, New York Public Library.

26. "Play about Negros Trying for Truth" (March 4, 1929), unidentified clipping, n.p.; Alison Smith, "Other New Plays: God's Chillun," *World* (February 22, 1929), n.p.; and Brooks Atkinson, "Up 'Harlem' Way: Negro Customs, Traits and Acting in a Black-Belt Melodrama—an Idea Lost in Shuffling Entertainment," *New York Times* (March 3, 1929), n.p., reviews in *Harlem* Clippings File, Billy Rose Theatre Collection, New York Public Library. Freda Scott Giles offers a thorough account of the plot, history, and summary of the responses to the play in "Glitter, Glitz, and Race: The Production of *Harlem*," in *Experimenters, Rebels, and Disparate Voices: The Theatre of the 1920s Celebrates American Diversity*, ed. Arthur Gewirtz and James J. Kolb (Westport, CT: Praeger, 2003), 39–46.

27. "'Harlem' Given Clean Bill of Health," *New York Amsterdam News* (June 14, 1929), n.p., *Harlem* Clippings File, Billy Rose Theatre Collection, New York Public Library.

28. "Director of Negro Play, 'Harlem,' Surprises Company That Show Will Close This Saturday," *New York Age* (May 11, 1929), 1.

29. Granville Ganter, "Decadence, Sexuality, and the Bohemian Vision of Wallace Thurman," *MELUS* 28.2 (Summer 2003): 84.

30. "The Browsing Reader," *The Crisis* (July 1929), 238.

31. *Infants of the Spring*, 216, qtd. in David R. Jarraway, "Tales of the City: Marginality, Community, and the Problem of (Gay) Identity in Wallace Thurman's 'Harlem' Fiction," *College English* 65.1 (September 2002): 40.

32. *Jeremiah the Magnificent* is based on the life of Marcus Garvey. The play received a single performance (December 3, 1933, in New York City), and has been published in Thurman's *Collected Writings*, 378–439.

33. The letters are contained in the Thurman Collection in the Beinecke Rare Books and Manuscripts Library, Yale University Library, and have been reprinted in Thurman, *Collected Writings*, 132–63.

34. Letter dated May 7, 1929, in Thurman, *Collected Writings*, 137–39.

35. Thurman, *Collected Writings*, 374.

36. *New York Times* (April 7, 1929), reprinted in Thurman, *Collected Writings*, 371–72.

37. The description and quotations from the play come from Thurman and Rapp's *Harlem: A Melodrama of Negro Life in Harlem,* in Thurman, *Collected Writings*, 313–69. Several previous drafts of the script, including revisions and notes in Thurman's handwriting, are contained in the Thurman Collection in the Beinecke Rare Books and Manuscripts Library, Yale University Library.

38. Rapp and Thurman, *Harlem*, 322.

39. William E. Clark, "Harlem," *New York Age* (March 23, 1929), 6.

40. Theophilus Lewis, "If This Be Puritanism," *Opportunity* (April 1929), 6; Salem Tutt Whitney, "Timely Topics," *Chicago Defender* (April 13, 1929), n.p., *Harlem* Clippings File, Schomburg Center, New York Public Library.

41. Bhabha writes, "For a willingness to descend into that alien territory—where I have led you—may reveal that the theoretical recognition of the split-space of enunciation may open the way to conceptualizing an *inter*national culture, based not on the exoticism of multiculturalism or the *diversity* of cultures, but on the inscription and articulation of culture's *hybridity*. To that end we should remember that it is the 'inter'—the cutting edge of translation and negotiation, the *in-between* space—that carries the burden of the meaning of culture. It makes it possible to begin envisaging national, anti-nationalist histories of the 'people.'" Homi K. Bhabha, *The Location of Culture* (New York: Routledge, 1994), 38–39.

42. Later in the letter, Thurman qualifies his disheartening Broadway experiences by comparing them to what he has encountered in California, where he was unsuccessfully trying to get some screenwriting work: "[New York] is heaven compared to the rest of the country despite certain unpleasant experiences one has. At least people don't stare at you or jump away as if you were a leper. Coming west three people left the observation car in protest to my being there" (letter dated ca. 1929, in *Collected Writings*, 135–37).

43. Rapp and Thurman, *Harlem*, 313.

44. August Strindberg, "Preface to Miss Julie" (1888), reprinted in *Dramatic Theory and Criticism: Greeks to Growtowski,* ed. Bernard F. Dukore (New York: Harcourt Brace Jovanovich, 1974), 573.

45. Una Chaudhuri, *Staging Place: The Geography of Modern Drama* (Ann Arbor: University of Michigan Press, 1995). Chaudhuri explains: "The naturalist stage adumbrates a specific relationship between the performance and the spectator, connecting

them to each other with an ambitious new contract of total visibility, total knowledge. The promise of the well-stocked stage of naturalism is a promise of omniscience, indeed of a transfer of omniscience from dramatist to spectator" (29).

46. Playbill in *Harlem* Clippings File, Billy Rose Theatre Collection, New York Public Library, 15.

47. Zora Neale Hurston, *Mules and Men* (New York: Perennial Library, 1990; orig. 1935), 3.

48. *New York World* (March 3, 1929), n.p., clipping in Alexander Gumby Scrapbook Collection, Columbia University Library, reprinted in Thurman, *Collected Writings,* 66–71.

49. Favor, *Authentic Blackness,* 10.

50. "A Questionnaire," *The Crisis* (February 1926), 165.

51. "'Harlem' as Educational Drama," 1–3, manuscript in Wallace Thurman Collection in the Beinecke Rare Books and Manuscripts Library, Yale University Library; the article is also reprinted in Thurman, *Collected Writings,* 372–73.

52. Handbill for show, qtd. in Osofsky, *Harlem,* 186.

53. "Transplanting Harlem to 42d St.," *New York Times* (March 3, 1929), n.p., clipping in Alexander Gumby Scrapbook Collection, Columbia University Library.

54. C. W. E. Bigsby, *A Critical Introduction to Twentieth-Century American Drama: 1900–1940* (Cambridge: Cambridge University Press, 1982), 156.

55. Rapp and Thurman, *Harlem,* 328.

56. "God's Chillun," *New York Times* (February 21, 1929), n.p.; and "Life in 'Harlem,'" *New York Sun* (February 21, 1929), n.p., reviews in *Harlem* Clippings File, Museum of the City of New York.

57. "'Harlem' Negro Melodrama of Racketeer Sort." Undated and without a source listed, this review is in *Harlem* Clippings File, Museum of the City of New York. Ironically, the critic actually demonstrates the slipperiness of tracing the authenticity in a particular work. He writes, "A valiant attempt at authentic Harlem color, in the vein of disillusion and protest in which the one Negro author of the piece—William Jo[u]rdan Rapp—would appear to be thinking is the sodden picture of the 'rent party.'" Wallace Thurman was the black author of the two. When the review was reprinted in another paper, the error was corrected.

58. "Other New Plays: God's Chillun," *World* (February 22, 1929).

59. As Lady Gregory indicates, the movement was a nationalist effort to unite Ireland and develop a dramatic tradition. In a statement composed by William Butler Yeats, Lady Gregory, and Edward Martyn, which would serve as the basis for the formation of the Abbey Players, they wrote: "We propose to have performed in Dublin in the spring of every year certain Celtic and Irish plays, which whatever be their degree of excellence will be written with a high ambition, and so to build up a Celtic and Irish school of dramatic literature. . . . We will show that Ireland is not the home of buffoonery and of easy sentiment, as it has been represented, but the home of an ancient idealism" (from Lady Gregory's autobiographical *Our Irish Theatre,* and reprinted in *Modern Irish Drama,* ed. John P. Harrington [New York: Norton, 1991], 378). Recent studies have examined these nationalist endeavors as an attempt to replace the British colonial struggle, not with the best interest of the "folk" in mind, but with an agenda imbued with the ideals of its up-

per-class leaders. See Adrian Frazier's *Behind the Scenes: Yeats, Horriman, and the Struggle for the Abbey Theatre* (Berkeley: University of California Press, 1990), and Stephen Tift's "The Parricidal Phantasm: Irish Nationalism and the *Playboy* Riots," in *Nationalisms and Sexualities,* ed. Andrew Parker, Mary Russo, Doris Sommer, and Patricia Yaeger (New York: Routledge, 1992), 313–34.

60. Richardson advocated a "kind of play" that "shows the soul of a people" (qtd. in *Lost Plays of the Harlem Renaissance, 1920–1940,* ed. James V. Hatch and Leo Hamalian [Detroit: Wayne State University Press, 1996], 161). Alain Locke stressed that black writers should follow the example of the Irish Renaissance writers in his introduction to *The New Negro: Voices of the Harlem Renaissance* (New York: Simon and Schuster, 1992; orig. 1925): "Without pretense to their political significance, Harlem has the same rôle to play for the New Negro as Dublin has had for the New Ireland or Prague for the New Czechoslovakia" (7).

61. Rapp and Thurman, *Harlem,* 325.

62. Ibid., 315.

63. Ibid., 316.

64. Locke, "The New Negro," in *The New Negro,* 3.

65. Cornel West, "Black Strivings in a Twilight Civilization," in *The Future of the Race,* ed. Henry Louis Gates, Jr. and Cornel West (New York: Vintage, 1996), 87.

66. Rapp and Thurman, *Harlem,* 323.

67. West, "Black Strivings," 85.

68. Ibid., 87.

69. Rapp and Thurman, *Harlem,* 323.

70. Ibid.

71. W. E. B. Du Bois, *The Souls of Black Folk* (1903), reprinted in *Three Negro Classics,* ed. John Hope Franklin (New York: Avon, 1965), 215.

72. Qtd. in Krasner, *A Beautiful Pageant,* 97.

73. "Opening Nights with Walter Winchell" (February 21, 1929), n.p., clipping in Alexander Gumby Scrapbook Collection, Columbia University Library.

74. Rapp and Thurman, *Harlem,* 316.

75. "'Harlem,' a Melodrama about the Rent-Paying Parties and Gamblers of the Black Belt, with a Large Negro Cast," *New York Evening Post* (February 21, 1929), n.p., clipping in Alexander Gumby Scrapbook Collection, Columbia University Library.

76. Rapp and Thurman, *Harlem,* 337.

77. Richard Lockridge, "Life in 'Harlem,'" *New York Sun* (February 21, 1929), n.p., clipping in the Museum of the City of New York, Theatre Collection.

78. Ibid.

79. Qtd. in Jane C. Desmond, *Staging Tourism: Bodies on Display from Waikiki to Sea World* (Chicago: University of Chicago Press, 1999), 11; emphasis added.

80. Robert Littell, "'Harlem,' a Melodrama about the Rent-Paying Parties and Gamblers of the Black Belt, with a Large Negro Cast," *New York Evening Post* (February 21, 1929), n.p., clipping in Alexander Gumby Scrapbook Collection, Columbia University Library.

81. Atkinson, *Broadway,* 248.

82. Burns Mantle, "Realism and the Negro Drama," *Daily News* (March 1, 1929), n.p., clipping in Alexander Gumby Scrapbook Collection, Columbia University Library.

83. "When White Is Black" (February 21, 1929), n.p., review in *Harlem* Clippings File, Billy Rose Theatre Collection, New York Public Library.

84. "Harlem" (February 21, 1929), n.p., review in *Harlem* Clippings File, Billy Rose Theatre Collection, New York Public Library.

85. As the glossary in the playbill explains, the "Numbers" was "A gambling game peculiar to Harlem; a sort of lottery based on three figures of the daily Clearing House Statement. The banker holds the money bags, pays winners, if any, and allows his runners a commission of all the sums they bring in. . . . Often, when a number of people pick the correct number, a banker disappears. Also, runners sometimes pocket the bets, not turning them over to the banker. The whole business is illegal, so the number entrepreneurs, like the bootleggers, are open to hijacking as they can hardly appeal to the police if their runners and collectors are held up." (Playbill in the *Harlem* Clippings File, Billy Rose Theatre Collection, New York Public Library.)

86. Rapp and Thurman, *Harlem,* 338.

87. Dr. Voodeo and the Hot-Stuff Man do not appear in the published script, but they are billed in the opening-night playbill. The exchange is found in act 3, page 8 in the unpublished (final) manuscript.

88. See, for example, Daniel J. Sharfstein, "The Secret History of Race in the United States," *Yale Law Journal* 112.6 (April 2003): 1473–1509; Patricia A. Williams, *Alchemy of Race and Rights* (Cambridge: Harvard University Press, 1991); A. Leon Higginbotham, *In the Matter of Color: Race and the American Legal Process,* vol. 1, *The Colonial Period* (New York: Oxford University Press, 1978).

89. Daniel Gerould, "The Americanization of Melodrama," in *American Melodrama,* ed. Daniel Gerould (New York: Performing Arts Journal Publications, 1983), 28; Bigsby, *Twentieth-Century American Drama,* 156.

90. Rapp and Thurman, *Harlem,* 369.

91. This quote does not appear in the published script, but it may be found in act 3, page 45 in the unpublished (final) manuscript.

92. Isabel Washington (1909–2008) appeared in the Bessie Smith film *St. Louis Blues,* several nightclub shows, and three Broadway productions before leaving show business to become Mrs. Adam Clayton Powell Jr. in 1933. They were married for twelve years. Many of the *Harlem* reviews list her as "Isabell" Washington, but for the sake of consistency, I have used the preferred "Isabel."

93. Alisa Solomon, *Re-dressing the Canon: Essays on Theater and Gender* (New York: Routledge, 1998), 55.

94. William Jourdan Rapp and Wallace Thurman, "Detouring 'Harlem' to Times Square," *New York Times* (April 7, 1929), x4.

95. Rapp and Thurman, *Harlem,* 369.

96. Bhabha invokes a similar comparison between works by marginalized authors as reflective of the emerging national cultures from which they write. In a postcolonial epoch, the very thought of a "pure," "ethnically cleansed" national identity is absurd. He explains, "The very concepts of homogenous national cultures, the consensual or con-

tiguous transmission of historical traditions, or 'organic' ethnic communities—*as the grounds of cultural comparativism*—are in a profound process of redefinition" (*The Location of Culture*, 5).

97. Solomon, *Re-dressing the Canon*, 57.

98. Rapp and Thurman, *Harlem*, 315.

CHAPTER 3

*Epigraph: "Lulu Belle," words by Leo Robin and music by Richard Myers (authorized by David Belasco and dedicated to Miss Lenore Ulric). Sheet music in Music Collection, New York Public Library at Lincoln Center.

1. "Battle On Among Broadway Elite of the 'Third Sex,'" *Variety* (March 7, 1928), 45, 47.

2. Ibid.

3. George Chauncey argues this point as well in *Gay New York*, 253.

4. David Belasco, "Tomorrow's Stage and the Negro," *Liberty* (August 7, 1926), 18, in Alexander Gumby Scrapbook Collection, Columbia University Library.

5. Edward Sheldon and Charles MacArthur, *Lulu Belle*, in *The Stage Works of Charles MacArthur*, ed. Arthur Dorlag and John Irvine (Tallahassee: Florida State University Foundation, 1974), 44.

6. Ibid.

7. Chauncey, *Gay New York*, 257.

8. John L. Fell and Terkild Vinding, *Stride! Fats, Jimmy, Lion, Lamb, and All the Other Ticklers* (Lanham, MD: Scarecrow Press, 1999), 64. See also Emily Wortis Leider, *Becoming Mae West* (New York: Farrar, Straus and Giroux, 1997), 154.

9. *New York Age* (February 20, 1926), 6.

10. "Hamilton Lodge Ball an Unusual Spectacle," *New York Age* (March 6, 1926), 3.

11. Qtd. in Watson, *Harlem Renaissance*, 136.

12. "My Observations: People of the Half-World and Other Things," *New York Amsterdam News* (April 14, 1934), 6.

13. "Masquerade Ball Draws Over 5,000 People," *New York Amsterdam News* (February 20, 1929), 2.

14. Ibid.

15. "Mere Male Blossoms Out in Garb of Milady at Big Hamilton Lodge Ball," *New York Amsterdam News* (February 19, 1930), 2.

16. "Hamilton Lodge Ball Draws 7,000," *New York Amsterdam News* (March 2, 1932), 2.

17. "Third Sex Hold Sway at Rockland When Hamilton Lodge Holds 65th Masquerade Ball and Dance; Police Arrest Two," *New York Age* (March 4, 1933), 1.

18. Blair Niles, *Strange Brother* (London: Gay Men's Press, 1991; orig. 1931), 210–11.

19. This attitude is similar to the tension between the effeminate-acting and masculine-acting gay men that Esther Newton describes in *Mother Camp: Female Impersonators in America* (Chicago: University of Chicago Press, 1979; orig. 1972), her ethnography of 1960 drag queens. The "masculine," "straight-acting" homosexual is prized over the effeminate or cross-dressed man because, as Newton states, the stereotype of a gay

man is "the stigma of effeminacy." She explains, "Homosexuality is a splotch on the American moral order; it violates the rooted assumption that 'masculinity,' a complex of desirable qualities, is 'natural' for (appropriate to) the male. Masculinity is based on one's successful participation in the male spheres of business, the professions, production, money-making, and action-in-the-world" (2).

20. Charles Henri Ford and Parker Tyler, *The Young and the Evil* (New York: Masquerade Books, 1996; orig. 1933), 152.

21. Ethel Waters with Charles Samuels, *His Eye Is on the Sparrow* (New York: Da Capo, 1992; orig. 1951), 150.

22. "Hamilton Lodge Ball Draws 7,000," 2.

23. "Snow and Ice Cover Streets as Pansies Blossom Out at Hamilton Lodge's Dance," *New York Amsterdam News* (February 28, 1934), 2.

24. "Gracious Me! Dear, 'Twas To-oo Divine," *New York Amsterdam News* (March 7, 1936), 8.

25. "6,000 at Harlem Pansy Dance," *Atlantic World* (March 11, 1932), 2. The "(?)" appears in the original article.

26. "Hamilton Lodge Ball Draws 7,000," 2.

27. Ibid.

28. Among Bonnie Clark's New York credits include the Lafayette Theatre musical revue *Get Set* (1923), which featured Ethel Waters, and *Triple-A Plowed Under* (1936), a WPA Living Newspaper production at Broadway's Biltmore Theatre.

29. "3,000 Attend Ball of Hamilton Lodge," *New York Amsterdam News* (March 1, 1933), 2.

30. Ibid.

31. "Gracious Me!" 8. Chauncey also discusses the black/white rivalry in *Gay New York* (263).

32. Hughes, *The Big Sea*, 208.

33. "Strange 'Third' Sex Flooding Nation, Writer Reveals," *Pittsburgh Courier* (March 19, 1932), 6.

34. "Gracious Me!" 8.

35. "Strange 'Third' Sex," 6.

36. Theophilus Lewis, "Dissension on the Left," *The Messenger* (March, 1926), 85.

37. Arthur Hornblow, "Mr. Hornblow Goes to the Play," *Theatre* (April 1926), 15; James Weldon Johnson, *Black Manhattan* (New York: Da Capo, 1991; orig. 1930), 205. *Variety* (April 28, 1926) reprinted black intellectual W. E. B. Du Bois's praise for the white actors from the black journal *The Crisis:* "I knew, of course, that Miss Ulric was white. The exaggerated dialect fixes the racial status of the doctor, I was in doubt as to the prizefighter, and the lover absolutely deceived me. I was sure he was colored." The *Variety* reporter added: "The 'lover' is played by Henry Hull. This tribute coming from Dr. Du Bois as to Hull's characterization is without a precedent among white theatricals" (72).

38. Hubert H. Harrison, "The Significance of 'Lulu Belle,'" *New York Amsterdam News* (July 28, 1926), 11.

39. References to the play and the editors' introduction come from MacArthur, *Stage Works*, 3–75.

40. "Wages of Sin in Four Acts," *New York Times* (February 10, 1926), 20.

41. In "The Spirit of Flesh: Wedekind's Lulu," *Modern Language Review* 79.2 (April 1984): 336–55, J. L. Hibberd argues that *Lulu* was written with the intent of pointing out the dehumanizing effect of Christian values and civic laws. The character of Lulu represents the opposite stance. Hibberd explains, "She is body, matter, instinct; she is irrational and antisocial; she is beauty, the triumph of nature, the spirit of flesh" (346).

42. Sheldon and MacArthur, *Lulu Belle*, 20.

43. Ibid., 21.

44. Ibid.

45. Ibid., 28.

46. Ibid.

47. Hazel V. Carby, "Policing the Black Woman's Body in an Urban Context," *Critical Inquiry* 18.4 (Summer 1992): 738–55.

48. Ibid., 741.

49. Ibid., 747. In *Ain't I a Woman*, bell hooks also outlines the historical basis for the portrayal of black women as degenerate and threats to the race. She points out the "competition" engendered between black and white women entering the work arena early in the century. According to hooks, white women workers enforced segregation so that they wouldn't catch a "private," "Negro" disease, which was a result from black women's sexual promiscuity. See bell hooks, *Ain't I a Woman: Black Women and Feminism* (Boston: South End Press, 1981), 131–33.

50. "The Task of Negro Womanhood," in Locke, *The New Negro*, 379.

51. Ruth Dennis, "Lulu Belles—All?" *New York Amsterdam News* (March 24, 1926), 5.

52. "Battle On Among Broadway Elite."

53. The connection Dennis makes in "Lulu Belles—All?" to "rotten theatricals" is a familiar argument. Throughout history, the theater has been considered a repository of sin and vice, and dramatic literature is viewed as the instigator. Actresses have traditionally taken a great deal of reproach, for they have often been regarded as whores who offer their bodies up for display (and sometimes more) to the paying public. See Jonas Barish's *The Anti-Theatrical Prejudice* (Berkeley: University of California Press, 1981), and Kristina Straub's *Sexual Suspects: Eighteenth-Century Players and Sexual Ideology* (Princeton: Princeton University Press, 1992).

54. Dennis, "Lulu Belles—All?" 5.

55. Sheldon and MacArthur, *Lulu Belle*, 51.

56. Watson, *Harlem Renaissance*, 134.

57. Qtd. in Chauncey, *Gay New York*, 254.

58. Ibid., 255.

59. See the *Variety* front-page article, "Lukor Stops 'Captive'" (February 16, 1927), which details the events surrounding the arrest of the show's twelve cast members on indecency charges. Faderman mentions this event in *Odd Girls* (66), and Kaier Curtin discusses the play in his *Call Them Bulgarians*.

60. "New York City Police Report: Commercialized Amusement, February 24, 1928," in *We Are Everywhere: A Historical Sourcebook of Gay and Lesbian Politics*, ed. Mark Blasius and Shane Phelan (New York: Routledge, 1997), 228.

61. Ibid.

62. Chauncey develops this comparison quite fully in *Gay New York*. He explains that the two groups also had in common an ability to be "sexually exploited" by men without compromise to their manhood. He writes: "The belief that fairies could be substituted for female prostitutes—and were virtually interchangeable with them—was particularly prevalent among men in the bachelor subculture whose opportunities for meeting 'respectable' women were limited by the moral codes, gender segregation, or unbalanced sex ratios of their ethnic cultures" (83).

63. "Colored Impersonator Tries Kiss Cop—60 Days," *Variety* (April 21, 1926), 11.

64. Undated review in *Lulu Belle* Clipping File, Museum of the City of New York.

65. Ibid.

66. Sheldon and MacArthur, *Lulu Belle*, 55–56.

67. Thurman, *The Blacker the Berry*, 105.

68. Ibid.

69. Ibid., 110.

70. "Tomorrow's Stage and the Negro: The Producer of 'Lulu Belle' Makes a Discovery and a Prophecy," *Liberty* (August 7, 1926), 18, in Alexander Gumby Collection, Columbia University Library.

71. Ibid.

72. Ibid., 21.

73. Ibid.

74. Ibid., 23.

75. Harrison, "Significance of 'Lulu Belle,'" 11.

76. Evelyn Mason, "Mr. Belasco's 'Lulu Belle,' as Seen by Miss Evelyn Mason," *New York Amsterdam News* (March 3, 1926), 11.

77. "The Theatre: 'Lulu Belle,'" *The Crisis* (May 1926), n.p., clipping in Alexander Gumby Scrapbook Collection, Columbia University Library.

78. "Oddments and Remainders," *New York Herald Tribune* (February 21, 1926), n.p., in Carl Van Vechten Scrapbook Collection, New York Public Library.

79. Ibid.

80. Of course, Ulric's comments echo the arguments behind the naturalistic movement developing in the nineteenth century. One of the principal theorists behind it, Émile Zola, claimed that the theater's true power could only be tapped by presenting "life as it is" on stage. In regard to depiction of "real people on stage," Zola wanted the stage to be a scientific laboratory for examining how individuals react in certain situations. He wanted "the surroundings to determine the characters, and . . . characters to act according to the logic of facts, combined with the logic of their own temperament" ("Naturalism on the Stage," in Dukore, *Dramatic Theory and Criticism*, 711). Just as Ulric saw the educational and enlightening possibilities of the true-to-life Lulu Belle, Zola explained that the development of naturalism in the theater would allow audiences to "see . . . that the highest and most useful lessons will be taught by depicting what is, and not by oft-dinned generalities, nor by airs of bravado, which are chanted merely to tickle our ears" (718).

81. Elsie McCormack, "Looking at the Star," undated, unidentified source in *Lulu Belle* Clippings File, Museum of the City of New York.

82. "Society Shocked by Belasco Play; Revision Asked," *Daily Mirror* (January 28, 1926), n.p.

83. " 'Lulu Belle' Replete in Vulgarisms," n.p., clipping in Alexander Gumby Scrapbook Collection, Columbia University Library.

84. Monroe Mason, "Boston Bans Belasco Play," *New York Amsterdam News* (April 4, 1928), n.p., clipping in Alexander Gumby Scrapbook Collection, Columbia University Library.

85. Hornblow, "Mr. Hornblow Goes," 15.

86. Ibid.

87. Clipping in Carl Van Vechten Scrapbook Collection, New York Public Library.

88. Qtd. in Mel Watkins, *On the Real Side: Laughing, Lying, and Signifying—the Underground Tradition of African-American Humor That Transformed American Culture, from Slavery to Richard Pryor* (New York: Simon and Schuster, 1994), 209.

89. From an interview with George Sylvester Vierick, "Harlem's Emotional Beauty Charms 'Einstein of Sex,' " *Chicago Herald and Examiner* (December 3, 1931), n.p., in Carl Van Vechten Scrapbook Collection, New York Public Library.

90. Bruce Nugent explained that homosexuality was generally tolerated within the Harlem Renaissance. In an interview with Thomas Wirth, he said: "I have never been in what they call 'the closet.' It has *never* occurred to me that it was anything to be ashamed of, and it never occurred to me that it was anybody's business but mine. . . . There was a great admixture—the mixture of blacks and whites during that particular two or three years. Whites making p-i-l-g-r-i-m-a-g-e-s to black Harlem, *doing* the cabarets or Clinton Moore's private parties. Whites being able to mingle freely in every way, including sexual, with blacks. Blacks suddenly having the freedom to have white sex partners. . . . Blacks [were] very sought-after for everything, from cabarets, to *everything*" (interview in *Gay Rebel of the Harlem Renaissance: Selections from the Work of Richard Bruce Nugent,* ed. Thomas H. Wirth (Durham, NC: Duke University Press, 2002), 268, 270.

91. "63 Seized in Club Raid," *New York Times* (January 30, 1928), 25.

92. Van Vechten also records going to drag balls, and he frequently went to the Clam House to see Gladys Bentley perform. Giving a sense of the exhausting nightlife he led, a rather typical entry from February 15, 1929 includes: "I went to a drag in Harlem with Harry, Hal, Emily, Virgil [Thomson] and [indecipherable], we picked up Eadie and went to the Lenox Ave Club where I danced with Louis Cole in drag. And then to Pods and Jerrys. Home at 7:30 A.M.—Saw millions of people I know" (Carl Van Vechten Papers, New York Public Library).

93. "Citizens Claim That Lulu Belle Club on Lenox Avenue Is Notorious Dive," *New York Amsterdam News* (February 15, 1928).

94. Niles, *Strange Brother,* 97.

95. Ibid., 272.

96. Sheldon and MacArthur, *Lulu Belle,* 75.

CHAPTER 4

*Epigraph: sung by Ethel Waters in the Arthur Schwartz and Howard Dietz musical revue *At Home Abroad* (1935). Lyric reprinted with permission of Paul Schwartz on behalf of Arthur Schwartz Music Publishing and Alfred Publishing Co., Inc. "Hottentot Potentate" is available on the original cast recording of the musical (sound restoration and mastering by Elliston Cavell [Los Angeles: AEI, 1999]). The song is also available on *Ethel Waters: On Stage and Screen, 1925–1940* (New York: Sony Music Entertainment, 1989). I am deeply appreciative of Charles Kloth, who first introduced me to this song.

1. Display advertisement, *New York Times* (February 19, 1926), 19.

2. "Play 'Degrades' Her Race, and Star Refuses to Act," interview reported in the *Amsterdam News* (February 17, 1926), n.p., clipping in Florence Mills Scrapbook in the Schomburg Center.

3. In "Lulu Belles—All?" Ruth Dennis asks: "Was 'Lulu Belle' actually based on the life of Florence Mills? is a query which has been asked continuously since the play of that name startled theatergoers. Denials have been forthcoming from Miss Mills and others repeatedly. But so true to life is this play that 'Lulu Belle' seems typical of the average Negro girl" (*Amsterdam News,* March 24, 1926, 5). In an entertainment editorial, the *Amsterdam News* spoke out against the link between Lulu Belle and Florence Mills, claiming that it was a disgraceful publicity stunt pulled by Lew Leslie. (March 3, 1926, 5). On Mills's death, however, Drusilla Dunjee Houston in the *America's News Magazine,* a black newspaper, implied that her early death was a result of her sexual lifestyle. She wrote, "Many women of grace and personality could do the thing that she was doing and win the homage of kings, but true women will not prostitute the higher things within them to use the beauties of the body for the less sacred service of attracting men." ("The Death of Florence Mills, Its Meaning," [December 17, 1927], n.p., clipping in Alexander Gumby Scrapbook Collection, Columbia University Library.)

4. Waters, *Eye on the Sparrow,* 187. Waters parodied Baker in another musical revue as well. In the hit 1933 Irving Berlin show *As Thousands Cheer,* she sang "Harlem on My Mind." In his 1967 liner notes for *Ethel Waters: On Stage and Screen, 1925–1940,* Miles Kreuger described the impression she made in this show: "On the satiric side, she portrayed the ultra-chic darling of Parisian society, Josephine Baker, who drips with diamonds, attends all the best parties, but rather wistfully longs for the lost lusts of the old days, with Harlem on her mind" (rprt. New York: Sony Music Entertainment, 1989).

5. Thomas Van Dycke, "'Africana' at Daly's Theatre," *New York World Telegram* (July 12, 1927), n.p., *Africana* Clippings File, Billy Rose Theatre Collection, New York Public Library.

6. Hughes, *The Big Sea,* 223. For the history and significance of *Shuffle Along* and its influence on the development of the black musical revue, see, for instance, Krasner, *A Beautiful Pageant;* Bernard L. Peterson, Jr., *A Century of Musicals in Black and White* (Westport, CT: Greenwood Press, 1993); Woll, *Black Musical Theatre;* and Helen Armistead-Johnson, "Blacks in Vaudeville: Broadway and Beyond," *American Popular Entertainment: Papers and Proceedings of the Conference on the History of Popular Entertainment,* ed. Myron Matlaw (Westport, CT: Greenwood Press, 1979).

7. Krasner, *A Beautiful Pageant,* 287.

8. Brooks Atkinson, "When the Black Gals Dance," *New York Times* (October 23, 1930), n.p., clipping in Alexander Gumby Scrapbook Collection, Columbia University Library.

9. Huggins, *Harlem Renaissance,* 261.

10. In his article about the chitlin circuit, Henry Louis Gates, Jr. points to the historical links between the TOBA shows and the modern equivalent of plays like *My Grand-*

mother Prayed for Me and *Beauty Shop*. Gates writes that in these plays, "All the very worst stereotypes of the race are on display, larger than life. Here in this racially sequestered space, a black audience laughs uninhibitedly, whereas the white folks would have engendered a familiar anxiety: *Will they think that's what we're really like?* ("The Chitlin Circuit," printed in *African American Performance and Theater History*, edited by Harry J. Elam, Jr. and David Krasner [New York: Oxford University Press, 2001], 142).

11. Theophilus Lewis, *The Messenger* (June 1927). Essay reprinted in Allen Woll, *Dictionary of the Black Theatre: Broadway, Off-Broadway, and Selected Harlem Theatre* (Westport, CT: Greenwood Press, 1983), 200.

12. "Stage and Public," *New York Amsterdam News* (March 28, 1928), 20. The editorial page of the paper said that the argument recalls the "old question as to which came first, the hen or the egg. Does the stage develop the public taste, or does the public taste develop the stage? Generally the public, like a young girl, does not know what it wants till it sees it." The editorial concludes with the statement, "Whichever came first, the production or the public demand for it, the stage has always reflected its time" (20).

13. Peterson, *Century of Musicals*, 108.

14. Lester Walton, "Negroes' Dream Realized as Race Plays Broadway," *New York World* (November 23, 1924), n.p., clipping in Alexander Gumby Scrapbook Collection, Columbia University Library.

15. Woll, *Black Musical Theatre*, 111.

16. Qtd. in Johnson, *Black Manhattan*, 197–98. "Hannah from Savannah" was first performed by Aida Overton Walker in the original production of *The Sons of Ham* in 1900. Contemporary publicity materials attempted to form an artistic lineage between Mills and Walker by asserting that Walker taught the up-and-coming star the song. As Bill Egan explains, the story, while enchanting, is not true. At the time that Mills was rehearsing the show, Aida Overton Walker, along with Bert Williams and her husband George Walker, was performing their latest show, *In Dahomey*, in London (Bill Egan, *Florence Mills: Harlem Jazz Queen* [Lanham, MD: Scarecrow Press, 2004], 6).

17. Bricktop (Ada Smith Ducongé) with James Haskins, *Bricktop* (New York: Atheneum Press, 1983), 54–56.

18. Theophilus Lewis, "Florence Mills—an Appreciation," *Inter-State Tattler* (November 11, 1927), n.p., in Florence Mills Clippings File, Schomburg Center, New York Public Library.

19. Qtd. in Martin Bauml Duberman's *Paul Robeson* (New York: Alfred K. Knopf, 1988), 584 n. 11. Duberman notes that Robeson once referred to Mills as "the greatest Negro artist he has ever heard" (584 n. 11).

20. "'Flo' Mills First of Race to Headline at the Palace," *Chicago Defender* (June 27, 1925), 6.

21. Johnson, *Black Manhattan*, 200.

22. Irene Kuhn of the *New York Daily Mirror*, for example, wrote: "Never before in the history of Harlem has there been such a funeral. Never have the emotional colored people been so moved. Never have they sung their spirituals, and their heart-swelling hymns of sorrowful mourners, with such evident heart-break." She goes on to describe the emotional outbursts of people in the church, and adds: "But Juanita Stinnett, a pal of Flo Mills, provided the high drama. She sang 'Florence,' a song dedicated to Flo Mills,

and written especially for her funeral. The girl sang the song through bravely. She began to break at the last few lines and she, too, fainted and was carried out crying hysterically: 'Florence, Oh Florence.'" (November 7, 1927, n.p., clipping in Alexander Gumby Scrapbook Collection, Columbia University Library).

23. "Scores Collapse at Mills Funeral" (November 7, 1927), n.p., unidentified clipping in Alexander Gumby Scrapbook Collection, Columbia University Library.

24. The poem is reprinted in Henry T. Sampson, *Blacks in Blackface: A Source Book on Early Black Musical Shows* (Metuchen, NJ: Scarecrow Press, 1980), 104. Barry Singer reports that Razaf recorded the song himself on November 4, 1927, for Columbia Records, accompanied by J. C. Johnson on piano and Eddie King on organ (*Black and Blue*, 185–86).

25. Johnson, *Black Manhattan*, 197.

26. Bill Egan's "Dixie Dreams" and "The Great White Way" chapters in *Florence Mills* offer a very detailed account of the show's development and the responses it received. See also Allen Woll's chapter "*Dixie to Broadway: Lew Leslie and the Black Revues*" in *Black Musical Theatre* (94–113).

27. Tony Langston, "Florence Mills Heads Great Review [*sic*]," *Chicago Defender* (August 23, 1924), 6.

28. Alexander Woollcott, "Rhapsody in Brown Presented," *New York Sun* (October 30, 1924), n.p., clipping in Alexander Gumby Scrapbook Collection, Columbia University Library.

29. Gilbert Gabriel, *Telegram and Evening Mail* (October 30, 1924), n.p., clipping in Alexander Gumby Scrapbook Collection, Columbia University Library.

30. Heywood Broun, *New York World* (October 30, 1924), n.p., clipping in Alexander Gumby Scrapbook Collection, Columbia University Library.

31. Percy Hammond, *Herald Tribune* (October 30, 1924), n.p.; Alan Dale, *American* (October 30, 1924), n.p.; and Alexander Woollcott, *New York Sun* (October 30, 1924), n.p., clippings in Alexander Gumby Scrapbook Collection, Columbia University Library.

32. Randolph Edmonds, "Not Many of Your People Come Here: A Discussion of Segregation in the Theatre," *The Messenger* (March 1928), 70.

33. David Levering Lewis writes, "But Harlem would never have been on white New York's extra-curricular itinerary had it not been for the Broadway musical. . . . Whatever their shortcomings, the musicals sent more and more whites from the theatre Uptown to Lenox and Seventh avenues" (*Harlem*, 167).

34. "Dixie Dreams," lyric by Grant Clarke and Roy Turke, music by George W. Meyer and Arthur Johnston, published by Irving Berlin, Inc., 1924. Sheet music in Music Collection, New York Public Library of the Performing Arts.

35. Eric Lott, *Love and Theft: Blackface Minstrelsy and the American Working Class* (New York: Oxford University Press, 1993), 187.

36. E. W. Osborne, quoted in "N.Y. Critics Hail Flossie Mills as a Genius," *Baltimore Afro-American* (November 8, 1924), n.p., in Florence Mills Clippings File, Schomburg Center, New York Public Library.

37. Qtd. in Egan, *Florence Mills* 110.

38. Qtd. in Woll, *Black Musical Theatre*, 103.

39. Langston Hughes, "The Negro Artist and the Racial Mountain" (1926), in *The*

Norton Anthology of African American Literature, ed. Henry Louis Gates, Jr. and Nellie Y. McKay, 2nd ed. (New York: Norton, 2004), 1311–14.

40. Zora Neale Hurston, "How It Feels to Be Colored Me" (1928), in Gates and McKay, *Norton African American Literature,* 1032. Hurston was actually fascinated in theatrical presentations of "blackness," and in 1932 staged a dance concert called *The Great Day.* The evening featured a performance of reconstructed Bahamian dances in a revue she referred to as a "concert in the raw," "natural," and "untampered with" view of the African American folk. (For a fascinating account of this event, see Anthea Kraut, "Everybody's Fire Dance: Zora Neale Hurston and American Dance History," *The Scholar and Feminist Online* 3.2 [Winter 2005], http://www.barnard.columbia.edu/sfon line/hurston/printakr.htm).

41. J. Martin Favor argues a similar thesis in *Authentic Blackness.*

42. Qtd. in Woll, *Black Musical Theatre,* 110.

43. "'Dixie to Broadway' Drawing fine; 'Runnin' Wild' on Final Week," *Chicago Defender* (August 30, 1924), 6.

44. The remark is in response to Mills's performance of this number in the *Plantation Revue,* which played at the Lafayette Theatre in Harlem. The show played there for two weeks prior to its London and Paris engagements. "About Things Theatrical," *New York Amsterdam News* (February 20, 1924), 8.

45. Qtd. in Samuel A. Hay, *African American Theatre: An Historical and Critical Analysis* (Cambridge: Cambridge University Press, 1994), 18.

46. Qtd. in Woll, *Black Musical Theatre,* 110.

47. Roger Didier (née P. L. Prattis), "Dixie to Broadway," *Opportunity* (November 1924), 345–46.

48. Alain Locke, "The New Negro" (1925), in Gates and McKay, *Norton African American Literature,* 984–93.

49. Ibid., 988.

50. Qtd. in "Florence Mills Turned Down Offer to Appear in Ziegfeld Follies," *Chicago Defender* (August 23, 1924), 8.

51. "Florence Mills," *New York Amsterdam News* (November 9, 1927), 20. The following week the same page wrote, "One other incident concerning Florence Mills before we close the chapter; one which proves almost conclusively that she not only typified the spirit and personality of her race, but that she had pride of race, and confidence in her race. Soon after she returned from Europe she placed her legal affairs in the hands of a young Negro attorney, Ralph Mizelle, who was her husband's commanding officer during the World War, and they are in his hands now. A little incident, indeed, but one which far too many Negroes would have neglected doing when they were sitting on 'top of the world'" ("Pride of Race," *New York Amsterdam News* [November 16, 1927], 20).

52. The show had a book by Walter De Leon, Tom Howard, Lew Leslie, and Sydney Lazarus; music by George W. Meyer and Arthur Johnston; lyrics by Grant Clarke and Roy Turke; and the show was staged and conceived by Lew Leslie. (Credits from *Dixie to Broadway* playbill, Billy Rose Theatre Collection, New York Public Library for the Performing Arts.)

53. Allen Woll points out in a note that the striking resemblance to Ziegfeld is rather deliberate: "Acute observers should have noticed that this song was at best an homage to,

but more likely a retread of, a classic Irving Berlin number called 'Mandy.' The song first appeared in a World War I all-soldier show *Yip, Yip, Yaphank* in 1918 and later in the 1919 edition of the *Ziegfeld Follies*. In a similar sex-switch strategy, Marilyn Miller played minstrel George Primrose" (*Black Musical Theatre*, 104n.).

54. "Mandy Make Up Your Mind," lyric by Grant Clarke and Roy Turke, music by George W. Meyer and Arthur Johnston, published by Irving Berlin, Inc., 1924. Sheet music in Music Collection, New York Public Library of the Performing Arts. Mills's performance in this number left a lasting imprint on her public. The image of the star wearing a full tuxedo proved so enduring that after her death, Lew Leslie included an act in his *Blackbirds of 1928* featuring a woman similarly dressed as homage to Mills.

55. George Jean Nathan, "Colored Actress Given the Palm by George Jean Nathan, Yah!" *New York Telegram* (incorrectly dated April 16, 1931), n.p., Florence Mills Clippings File, Schomburg Center, New York Public Library.

56. Unidentified author, *American*, Florence Mills Clippings File, Schomburg Center, New York Public Library.

57. Qtd. in Woll, *Black Musical Theatre*, 107.

58. As Bill Egan states, the "overtly antiracist references have been edited out in more recent performances" (*Florence Mills*, 113).

59. Qtd. in Woll, *Black Musical Theatre*, 108.

60. Florence Mills, "The Soul of the Negro" *Sun-Chronicle* (London), reprinted in the *New York Amsterdam News* (November 24, 1926), 10.

61. Qtd. in "Jewish Song Writers," undated and unattributed newspaper clipping, Florence Mills Scrapbook, Schomburg Center.

62. Locke, "The New Negro," 991–92.

63. Reported in the *London Star* (December 12, 1926), n.p., clipping in Florence Mills Scrapbook, Schomburg Center.

64. Nathan, "Colored Actress."

65. Theophilus Lewis, "Theatre," *Messenger* (January 1925), 18, 62.

66. Mills, "Soul of the Negro," 10.

67. *Amsterdam News* (August 10, 1927), 10.

68. Ibid.

69. Nathan, "Colored Actress."

70. Johnson, *Black Manhattan*, 199.

71. Brooks Atkinson, "Beatrice Lillie and Ethel Waters in a Musical Travelogue Entitled 'At Home Abroad,'" *New York Times* (September 20, 1935), 17.

72. Van Vechten, *Letters*, October 23, 1950, 244. Carl Van Vechten remained a tremendous admirer of Waters for most of his life. In a letter dated December 14, 1932, to Blanche Knopf, the wife of publisher Alfred, he wrote: "I have long believed that Ethel Waters and Langston [Hughes] had more genius than any others of their race in this country and I think Langston will in the end have as wide a success as Ethel" (129).

73. Waters, *Eye on the Sparrow*, 71–72.

74. William Gardner Smith, "Phylon Profile, XXI: Ethel Waters," *Phylon* (circa 1950), in Alexander Gumby Scrapbook Collection, Columbia University Library, 115–16.

75. Rebecca A. Bryant, "Shaking Things Up: Popularizing the Shimmy in America," *American Music* 20:2 (Summer 2002): 168–87.

76. Krasner, *A Beautiful Pageant*, 75–76.

77. Waters, *Eye on the Sparrow*, 125.

78. Ibid., 124.

79. Music and lyric by Clarence Williams and Spencer Williams. Recorded in 1923 or 1924. *Bessie Smith: The Complete Recordings, Vol. 1* (New York: Columbia/Legacy, 1991).

80. Music and lyric by Papa Charlie Jackson. Recorded in 1926. *The Incomparable Ethel Waters* (New York: Sony, 2003).

81. Johnson, *Black Manhattan*, 210.

82. Smith, "Phylon Profile," 116.

83. "The Triumph of Vulgarity," *New York Amsterdam News*, reprinted from the *Chicago Bee* (August 4, 1926), n.p., clipping in Alexander Gumby Scrapbook, Columbia University Library.

84. "Ethel Waters Opens with 'Africana' at Daly's Amid Riot of Barbaric Splendor," *Amsterdam News* (July 13, 1927), 11.

85. Rowland Field, "Africana" (July 11, 1927), n.p., *Africana* Clippings File, Billy Rose Theatre Collection, New York Public Library.

86. Henry T. Sampson reprints the numbers from the program in his *Blacks in Blackface*, and several of Waters's numbers were recorded, which are available on *The Chronological Ethel Waters, 1926–1929* (France: Classics Records, 1993). These include "I'm Coming Virginia," "My Special Friend is Back in Town," "Weary Feet," "Smile!" and "Take Your Black Bottom Outside." She also sang her signature song, "Dinah," at the loud vocal request of Carl Van Vechten on opening night, and this song is available on *The Chronological Ethel Waters, 1931–1934* (France: Classics Records, 1993).

87. The *Amsterdam News* reported a week after its opening: "True, there were some things which some of us thought 'passe' in the show, but it is good to see that those very things were withdrawn the very next night and at this writing there have been many additions which cannot help but enhance the production" ("Many Changes in 'Africana,'" July 20, 1927, 7).

88. Qtd. in Bide Dudley, "Africana" review, *New York Mirror* (July 12, 1927), n.p., *Africana* Clippings File, Billy Rose Theatre Collection, New York Public Library.

89. Walter Winchell, "Opening Nights with Walter Winchell: Muddy (Ethel) Waters," *New York Graphic* (July 12, 1927), n.p., clipping in the Billy Rose Theatre Collection, New York Public Library.

90. Robert Garland, "Well—What of It?" *New York Evening Telegram*, undated and unpaginated clipping in Alexander Gumby Scrapbook Collection, Columbia University Library.

91. J. A. Rodgers, "Ethel Waters Selected as First Subject from Pen of Gifted Writer and Author," *New York Amsterdam News* (November 27, 1929), n.p., clipping in Alexander Gumby Scrapbook Collection, Columbia University Library.

92. "Ethel Waters a Hit in Negro Revue, 'Africana,' at Daly's," *New York Herald Tribune* (July 12, 1927), n.p., clipping in the Billy Rose Theatre Collection, New York Public Library.

93. Field, "Africana."

94. "Prancin,'" *New York World-Telegram* (July 12, 1927), n.p., clipping in the Billy Rose Theatre Collection, New York Public Library.

95. "Black and Tan Revues," *The Dance Magazine,* no author (September 1927). Clipping in Alexander Gamby Scrapbook Collection, Columbia University Library.

96. Interview with Harriet Underhill, "Two Ladies Who Would Be Great," *New York Herald Tribune* (July 17, 1927), clipping in Alexander Gumby Scrapbook Collection, Columbia University Library.

97. Waters, *Eye on the Sparrow,* 215.

98. *Law Leslie's Blackbirds of 1930* program, in the Billy Rose Theatre Collection, New York Public Library.

99. Percy Hammond, "Glorifying the American Negro," *New York Tribune* (October 23, 1930), clipping in the Billy Rose Theatre Collection, New York Public Library.

100. Richard Lockridge, "Black and Brown," *New York Sun* (October 23, 1930), clipping in the Billy Rose Theatre Collection, New York Public Library.

101. Gates, *Signifying Monkey,* 113.

102. Theophilus Lewis, *The Messenger* (May 1926), n.p., in Florence Mills Clippings File, Schomburg Center, New York Public Library.

103. Charles Darnton, "The New Play," *Evening World* (October 23, 1930), n.p., in the *Blackbirds of 1930* Clippings File, Billy Rose Theatre Collection, New York Public Library.

104. Ibid.; Lockridge; *New Yorker* (November 1, 1930), 26, articles in the *Blackbirds of 1930* Clippings File, Billy Rose Theatre Collection, New York Public Library.

105. The lyric is reprinted in Barry Singer's *Black and Blue,* 194–95. Ethel Waters recorded the song on August 21, 1928, for Columbia, and it is available on *Ethel Waters, 1926–1929* (Classics Records, 1993).

106. Singer, *Black and Blue,* 194.

107. Jasen and Jones, *Spreadin' Rhythm Around,* 355.

108. Lyric reprinted in Singer, *Black and Blue,* 249.

109. Woll, *Black Musical Theatre,* 145.

110. Davis, *Blues Legacies,* 44.

111. Hazel Carby, "It Just Be's Dat Way Sometime: The Sexual Politics of Women's Blues," *Radical America* 20.4 (June–July 1986), 9–22. See also Paula Giddings, *When and Where I Enter: The Impact of Black Women on Race and Sex in America* (New York: Morrow, 1984); Cheryl Wall, "Whose Sweet Angel Child? Blues Women, Langston Hughes, and Writing during the Harlem Renaissance," in Arnold Rampersad, *Langston Hughes: The Man, His Art, and His Continuing Influence,* ed. C. James Trotman (New York: Garland, 1995); and Michele Wallace, *Invisibility Blues: From Pop to Theory* (New York: Verso, 1990).

112. Davis, *Blues Legacies,* 44, 46.

113. Singer, *Black and Blue,* 179–80.

114. E. F. M., "Testing the Wings of the 'Blackbirds,'" *New York Times,* undated, unpaginated article in the *Blackbirds of 1930* Clippings File, Billy Rose Theatre Collection, New York Public Library.

115. Watkins, *On the Real Side,* 52.

116. Giles Oakley, *The Devil's Music: A History of the Blues* (New York: Harcourt Brace Jovanovich, 1976), 36–40.

117. Gates, *Signifying Monkey,* 121.

118. Darnton, "The New Play."

119. Whitney Bolton, "Put 'At Home Abroad' on 'See' List: Lillie, Powell and Waters Are Tops!" *New York Telgraph* (September 21, 1935), n.p.; Brooks Atkinson re-review, *New York Times* (October 27, 1935); n.p., clippings in *At Home Abroad* Scrapbook, Billy Rose Theatre Collection, New York Public Library.

120. Atkinson, "Beatrice Lillie and Ethel Waters in a Musical Travelogue."

121. Percy Hammond, "At Home Abroad" review, *New York Tribune* (September 20, 1935), n.p., clipping in *At Home Abroad* Scrapbook, Billy Rose Theatre Collection, New York Public Library.

122. In a 1966 essay, Harlem Renaissance writer Sterling Brown condemned the images of "exotic primitives whose dances—the Charleston, the 'black bottom,' the 'snake hips,' the 'walking the dog'—were tribal rituals; whose music with wa-wa trumpets and trombones and drum batteries doubled for tom-toms; whose chorus girls with bunches of bananas girding their shapely middles nurtured tourists' delusions of the 'Congo creeping through the black" ("A Century of Negro Portraiture in American Literature," *The Massachussetts Review* (Winter 1966): 73–96. Quote appears on page 83.

123. Kelcey Allen, "At Home Abroad" review, *Women's Wear Daily* (September 20, 1935), n.p., clipping in *At Home Abroad* Scrapbook, Billy Rose Theatre Collection, New York Public Library; Atkinson, "Beatrice Lillie and Ethel Waters in a Musical Travelogue."

124. See opening epigraph to chapter 4.

125. Hazel V. Carby, *Race Men* (Cambridge: Harvard University Press, 1998), 77–78.

126. "'At Home Abroad' Offered in Boston," *New York Times* (September 4, 1935), 22.

127. Qtd. in Felicia R. Lee, "An Encore for Black Vaudeville," *New York Times* (February 10, 1999), E1, 6.

128. Waters, *Eye on the Sparrow,* 149.

129. Qtd. in Chauncey, *Gay New York,* 288.

130. Ibid.

131. For an excellent analysis of this trend, particularly in the MGM and Twentieth-Century Fox film musicals, see Sean Griffin's "The Gang's All Here: Generic versus Racial Integration in the 1940s Musical," *Cinema Journal* 42:1 (Autumn 2002): 21–45.

132. Woll, *Black Musical Theatre,* 193.

133. She was only the second black actress to receive this prestigious honor—Hattie McDaniel had been nominated and won for *Gone with the Wind* in 1939.

CHAPTER 5

*Epigraph: recorded August 8, 1928 for OKeh Race Records. Song available on *Maggie Jones, volume 2, and Gladys Bentley: Complete Recorded Works in Chronological Order* (Vienna: Document Records, 1995).

1. Qtd. in Watts, *Mae West,* 92.

2. Schwarz, *Gay Voices,* 9.

3. Marcus Wright, "The Talk of the Town," *New York Age* (December 22, 1934), 4. Richard Bruce Nugent provides a colorful sketch of "Gloria Swanson," née Mr. Winston. After incurring the wrath of the police in Chicago, Winston moved to New York in the early 1930s and "had little trouble finding employment in a popular night spot on 134th

Street in Harlem. There he reigned regally, entertaining with his 'hail-fellow-well-met' freedom, so perfect a woman that frequently clients came and left never suspecting his true sex. He sang bawdy parodies and danced a little, all very casually and quite impersonally, lifting modestly to just above the knee his perennial net and sequins or his velvet-trimmed evening-gown skirts, displaying with professional coyness a length of silk-clad limb" (222). "On 'Gloria Swanson,'" reprinted in Nugent, *Gay Rebel*, 221–23.

4. Wilbur Young, "Gladys Bentley," from *Biographical Sketches: Negroes of New York* (Schomburg Center, New York Public Library: WPA Writers Program, 1939), 1.

5. As Lillian Faderman explains, this kind of wedding among lesbian couples was not unheard of in Harlem of the 1920s and early 1930s. A lesbian wedding was often a grand affair, which included bridesmaids and attendants. Faderman states, "Real marriage licenses were obtained by masculinizing a first name or having a gay male surrogate apply for a license for the lesbian couple" (*Odd Girls,* 73).

6. "Night Club Notes" (March 14, 1936), 11.

7. The Washboard Serenaders were a well-known jazz group that recorded on the Victor label. In 1930, Bentley recorded "Kazoo Man" with them.

8. "Washboard Serenaders Feature at Opera House," *New York Age* (September 15, 1934), 4.

9. Hughes, *The Big Sea,* 225.

10. "Holds Hall Book Obscene," *New York Times* (November 17, 1928), 6.

11. "Shaw and Wells Rap Seizure of Sex Novel," *New York Times* (October 6, 1928), 6.

12. Qtd. in Gillian Whitlock, "'Everything Is out of Place': Radclyffe Hall and the Lesbian Literary Tradition," *Feminist Studies* 13.3 (Autumn 1987): 559.

13. Qtd. in "Holds Hall Book Obscene," 6.

14. "Police Seize Novel by Radclyffe Hall," *New York Times* (January 12, 1929), 3.

15. Ibid.

16. Qtd. in Schwarz, *Gay Voices,* 13.

17. Lillian Faderman and Ann Williams state, "The saddest piece of irony in Hall's noble gesture was that she—perhaps more than Kraft-Ebing, Ellis, Freud—helped to wreak confusion in young women who, knowing themselves to love other women and having no other role models but Stephen Gordon, learned through Hall's novel that if they were really lesbians they were not women but members of a third sex, and that they need not expect joy or fulfillment in this world" ("Radclyffe Hall and the Lesbian Image," *Conditions* 1 [April 1977]: 32).

18. The number is listed in Ken Jessamy's review of the *Brevities in Bronze,* "Club Revue Is Entertaining and Brilliant," *New York Amsterdam News* (April 3, 1937), 16.

19. The autobiography was never published. She announced that the book was forthcoming when she appeared on Groucho Marx's *You Bet Your Life* (filmed April 1958 and broadcast on May 15, 1958). The episode (#57-34) was released on DVD on *You Bet Your Life: The Best Episodes.* (DVD Produced by Paul Brownstein, Shout Factory and National Broadcast Company, 2004.)

20. Gladys Bentley, "I Am a Woman Again," *Ebony* (August 1952), 97.

21. Radclyffe Hall, *The Well of Loneliness* (New York: Anchor, 1990; orig. 1928), 12–13.

22. Ibid., 12.

23. William Hannibal Thomas, *The American Negro: What He Is, What He Was, and*

What He May Become (1901), qtd. in Anne Stavney, "'Mothers of Tomorrow': The New Negro Renaissance and the Politics of Maternal Representation," *African American Review* 32.4 (Winter 1998): 535.

24. Bentley, "I Am a Woman," 95.

25. Hall, *The Well of Loneliness*, 73.

26. Bentley, "I Am a Woman," 96.

27. Jeannetta H. Foster, *Sex Variant Women in Literature*, 1956. New York: Naiad Press, 1985; Lillian Faderman, *Surpassing the Love of Men: Romantic Friendship and Love Between Women from the Renaissance to the Present*. New York: Quill Books, 1981; Esther Newton, "The Mythic Mannish Lesbian: Radclyffe Hall and the New Woman," *Signs* (Summer 1984): 557–75; Margot Gayle Backus, "Sexual Orientation in the (Post) Imperial Nation: Celticism and Inversion Theory in Radclyffe Hall's *The Well of Loneliness*: *Tulsa Studies in Women's Literature* (Autumn 1996): 253–66; Judith Halberstam, "A Writer of Misfits: John Radclyffe Hall and the Discourse of Inversion," in *Female Masculinity* (Durham: Duke University Press, 1998): 75–110; and Laura Green, "Radclyffe Hall's *The Well of Loneliness* and Modernist Fictions of Identity," *Twentieth-Century Literature* 49.3 (2003): 277–97.

28. In particular, see George Chauncey, Jr., "From Sexual Inversion to Homosexuality: Medicine and the Changing Conception of Female Deviance," *Salmagundi* 59 (Winter 1983): 136–37.

29. Green, "Hall's *Well of Loneliness*," 279.

30. Hall, *The Well of Loneliness*, 18.

31. Ibid., 21.

32. Bentley, "I Am a Woman," 96.

33. Heike Bauer, "Richard von Krafft-Ebing's *Psychopathia Sexualis* as Sexual Sourcebook for Radclyffe Hall's *The Well of Loneliness*," *Critical Survey* 15.3 (2003): 27.

34. Hall, *The Well of Loneliness*, 204.

35. Bentley, "I Am a Woman," 96.

36. Hall, *The Well of Loneliness*, 204–5.

37. Bentley, "I Am a Woman," 96.

38. Esther Newton, "The Mythic Mannish Lesbian: Radclyffe Hall and the New Woman," *Signs* 9.4 (Summer 1984): 574.

39. Richard von Krafft-Ebing, *Psychopathia Sexualis,* trans. Franklin S. Klaf (New York: Bell Publishing Co., 1965; orig. 1886), 262.

40. Hall, *The Well of Loneliness*, 79.

41. Bentley, "I Am a Woman," 93.

42. See, for instance, Sheldon Harris, *Blues Who's Who* (New York: Da Capo, 1981), 43; and John Wilby, liner notes for *Gladys Bentley: Complete Recorded Works in Chronological Order* (Vienna: Document Records, 1995).

43. Eric Garber, "Gladys Bentley: The Bulldagger Who Sang the Blues," *Out/Look* (Spring 1988), 55.

44. Bentley, "I Am a Woman," 94.

45. The eight songs that Bentley recorded for OKeh Records are available on *Gladys Bentley: Complete Recorded Works in Chronological Order* (Vienna: Document Records, 1995). According to the credits on *The Complete Blues Sessions of Gladys Bentley and*

Mary Dixon, Bentley herself wrote "Ground Hog Blues," "Worried Blues," and "How Much Can I Stand?"; the composers of the other songs are, characteristically of the 1920s, unclear. "How Long—How Long Blues" was written by Carr; "Moanful Wailin' Blues" and "Wild Geese Blues" were by Louis; "Red Beans and Rice" was by Fuller; and the composer of "Red Beans and Rice" is unknown. The lyrics are from my own transcription.

46. Her records were advertised in the *Chicago Defender* (September 29, 1928), and the *New York Amsterdam News* ran a quarter-page advertisement on September 26, 1928, announcing her as a "New Blues Star" (2).

47. Davis, *Blues Legacies,* 119.

48. Nghana tamu Lewis pursues a similar argument in her essay "In a Different Chord: Interpreting the Relations among Black Female Sexuality, Agency, and the Blues," *African American Review* 37.4 (Winter 2003): 599–609. In addition to looking at the songs of (later) blueswomen, Billie Holiday, Mari Evans, and Natalie Cole, Lewis explores the "metasexual dimensions" of the blues through an examination of the Langston Hughes's blues poetry.

49. Paul Oliver, *Blues Fell This Morning: Meaning in the Blues,* 2nd ed. (Cambridge: Cambridge University Press, 1990), 185.

50. Harrison, *Black Pearls.*

51. Qtd. in ibid., 81.

52. Qtd. in Davis, *Blues Legacies,* 28–29.

53. Qtd. in Davis, *Blues Legacies,* 27.

54. Marybeth Hamilton, "Sexuality, Authenticity and the Making of the Blues Tradition," *Past and Present* 169 (November 2000): 143.

55. Recording on *Sissy Man Blues: 25 Authentic Straight and Gay Blues and Jazz Vocals* (Mojo Records, 1996).

56. Recording on *Sissy Man Blues.*

57. "Nevertheless, from the time I can remember anything," Bentley writes, "even when I was a toddling, I never wanted a man to touch me" ("I Am a Woman," 96).

58. Ann DuCille, "Blues Notes on Black Sexuality: Sex and the Texts of Jessie Fauset and Nella Larsen," *Journal of the History of Sexuality* 3 (January 1993): 426.

59. Johnson, *Black Manhattan,* 228.

60. W. C. Handy, *Father of the Blues* (New York: Da Capo, 1991; orig. 1941), 231.

61. Amiri Baraka (LeRoi Jones), *Blues People: The Negro Experience in White America and the Music That Developed from It* (New York: Morrow Quill Paperbacks, 1963), 17.

62. As Ann Douglas writes, one must be cautious in attempting to locate an "authentic" blackness in the blues. The form was influenced both by the effects of black oppression and by white commodification. Douglas writes, "If their rhythms and vocal techniques, their call-and-answer patterns, were Negro and African in origin, their marketing and the needs from which they came were American and mongrel. Only blacks could have written the blues, but they could not have written them in an all-black world" (*Terrible Honesty,* 391).

63. As Alisa Solomon points out, the definition of this term is quite broad, and may in fact include, as Alisa Solomon points out, drag kings, transsexuals, and "soft butches" (*Re-Dressing the Canon: Essays on Theater and Gender* [New York: Routledge, 1997], 167).

64. Judith Halberstam, *Female Masculinity* (Durham, NC: Duke University Press, 1998), 59. Rather than a parody of a culturally inscribed definition of maleness, the butch lesbian, according to Halberstam, comprises "multiple" masculinities, and rather than perceiving her as "lacking" femininity and *real* masculinity, the butch shows the possibility of "gender variance," or "female masculinity." See also Carmen Mitchell's "Creations of Fantasies / Constructions of Identities: The Oppositional Lives of Gladys Bentley," in *The Greatest Taboo: Homosexuality in Black Communities* (Los Angeles: Alyson Books, 2001), 211–25. Mitchell examines Bentley's "fluctuating" personae as a means of exploring the "construction, actualization, and subsequent pathologizing and regulation" of a black lesbian identity in Western culture (212).

65. "Bentley at Opera House," *New York Age* (April 27, 1935), 4.

66. Young, "Gladys Bentley," 1–2.

67. Lott, *Love and Theft*, 146.

68. Marjorie Garber, *Vested Interests: Cross-Dressing and Cultural Anxiety* (New York: Routledge, 1992). Garber writes, "By 'category crisis' I mean a failure of definitional distinction, a borderline that becomes permeable, that permits of border crossings from one (apparently distinct) category to another: black/white, Jew/Christian, noble/bourgeois, master/servant, master/slave. The binarism male/female, one apparent ground of distinction (in contemporary eyes, at least) between 'this' and 'that,' 'him' and 'me,' is itself put in question or under erasure in transvestism, and a transvestite figure, or a transvestite mode, will always function as a sign of overdetermination—a mechanism of displacement from one blurred boundary to another" (16).

69. Qtd. in Eric Garber, "Gladys Bentley," 55.

70. Recordings of blues songs in the 1920s, while flirting with the taboo, tended to be far less explicit than this parody. Still, as Marybeth Hamilton, explains, the blues "sexual song," which had been suppressed by proponents of the blues as a form of African American folk music, was not uncommon among performers in brothels and juke joints. Jelly Roll Morton's "Winin' Boy Blues" is but one example:

I had a gal, I had her in the grass
I had the bitch, had her in the grass (× 2)
One days [sic] she got scared and a snake ran up her big ass,
I'm the winin' boy don't deny my name

I had that bitch, had her on the stump (× 3)
I fucked her till her pussy stunk
I'm the winin' boy, don't deny my name
(Qtd. in Hamilton, "Sexuality," 145)

71. Edgar M. Grey, "Harlem after Dark: Lax Law Enforcement in Harlem Attracted Cabarets to Harlem," *New York Amsterdam News* (April 6, 1927), 16.

72. Charles G. Shaw, *Nightlife: Vanity Fair's Intimate Guide to New York after Dark* (New York: John Day Company, 1931), 76.

73. Qtd. in Garber, "Gladys Bentley," 56.

74. Hughes, *The Big Sea*, 225–26. In a 1945 column, Hughes recalled Bentley, along

with Hanna Sylvester, Billy Mitchell, and Jackie Mabley, as among the most commanding nightclub presences without amplification. "Those people could sing so loud a mike
would have made the patrons deaf. And they could entertain so well you would remember them for months after you had seen and heard them" ("Too 'Too' Artistic Entertainers," *Chicago Defender* [November 17, 1945], 14).

75. Qtd. in Garber, "Gladys Bentley," 56.

76. "I Am a Woman Again," 94.

77. Van Vechten, *Parties*, 33. As Garber points out, Bentley also appears as a character
in Clement Wood's novel *Deep River* (1931), and Blair Niles's *Strange Brother* (1931). In
the latter work she is represented as Sybil, a large, black cabaret pianist with a "deep
man's voice," who performs at a club called the Lobster Pot (a takeoff on the Clam
House, where Bentley performed). The narrator describes Sybil as a grotesque, "clumsy
figure," "whose hands passed with such incredible speed up and down the piano." Regardless of Sybil's grotesquerie, one of the characters claims her performance is "sheer
genius . . . nothing but sheer genius!" (Niles, *Strange Brother*, 41–42).

78. November 10, 1929, diary entry, Carl Van Vechten Diaries, New York Public Library.

79. December 5 and December 29, 1929, diary entries. Van Vechten mentions seeing
Bentley at parties or at the Clam House in the following diary entries of 1929 and 1930:
April 25, May 4, November 17, November 27, and December 28, 1929; January 4, January
12, January 19, January 25, February 2, February 9, April 19, April 20, April 22, May 2, and
May 24, 1930.

80. Louis Sobol, the *New York Graphic*, n.p., undated clipping in Carl Van Vechten
Scrapbook Collection, New York Public Library.

81. "Today on the Radio," *New York Times* (February 11, 1930), 31. Appearances were
weekly until April 8, 1930.

82. "New York Cops Hit Vulgar Dance in Cafes," *Chicago Defender* (March 17, 1934),
5.

83. Lyric reprinted in Ed Cray's *The Erotic Muse: Bawdy American Songs* (Urbana:
University of Illinois Press, 1999), 52.

84. "Cops Hit Vulgar Dance."

85. "New York Police's War on Cafes Ends," *Chicago Defender* (April 7, 1934), 8.

86. "Gladys Bentley and Her Entertainers," *New York Amsterdam News* (April 7, 1934),
6.

87. Chauncey, *Gay New York*, 78. Chauncey writes, "The sailor, seen as young and
manly, unattached, and unconstrained by conventional morality, epitomized the bachelor subculture in the gay cultural imagination" (78).

88. Vere E. Johns, "Lafayette Theatre," *New York Age* (April 14, 1934), 5.

89. Ibid.

90. "Theatricals," *New York Age* (April 14, 1934), 5.

91. The *Amsterdam News* reported that famed black musician and composer W. C.
Handy went to the club accompanied by a white couple "with the intention of hearing a
special rendition of songs he had written." The group was denied entrance, and the article states, "Mixed parties usually are told to shun the club to avoid embarrassment"
("Cotton Club Takes Round in Ban Fight" [February 13, 1937], 1). Roi Ottley reported a

similar situation nearly three years before in his column when an African American fellow invited three white friends to Harlem and was refused admittance to the Ubangi Club, as "mixed parties" were "positively barred from the premises." They met with a similar fate at the Cotton Club ("This Hectic Harlem," *New York Amsterdam News* [September 8, 1934], 9).

92. "Night Club Notes," *New York Times* (October 24, 1936), 22.

93. "Night Club Notes," *New York Times* (October 17, 1936), 20.

94. "Hollywood to Harlem," *Brooklyn Daily Eagle* (June 12, 1936), n.p.; *New York Evening Journal* (January 23, 1937), n.p., clippings in Gladys Bentley File, Billy Rose Theatre Collection, New York Public Library.

95. Marcus Wright, "The Talk of the Town," *New York Age* (June 30, 1934), 4.

96. Lou Layne, "Showmanship Is King at Apollo," *New York Age* (July 13, 1935), 4.

97. "Monster Breakfast Dance," advertisement, *New York Amsterdam News* (December 14, 1935), 4.

98. "Bentley at Opera House," *New York Age* (April 27, 1935), 4.

99. "Night Club Notes," *New York Times* (October 17, 1936), 20; and "Night Club Notes," *New York Times* (October 24, 1936), 22.

100. "5 A.M.," *New York Post* (March 16, 1936), n.p., clipping in Gladys Bentley File, Billy Rose Theatre Collection, New York Public Library; "Night Club Notes," *New York Times* (October 24, 1936), 22.

101. Joe Bostic, "Seeing the Show," *New York Age* (April 25, 1936), 8.

102. Joe Bostic, "Seeing the Show," *New York Age* (August 15, 1936), 8.

103. Marcus Wright, "The Talk of the Town," *New York Age* (May 12, 1934), 5.

104. Young, "Gladys Bentley," 2.

105. Archie Seale, "Man about Harlem," *New York Age* (August 1, 1936), 8.

106. Qtd. in Garber, "Gladys Bentley," 58.

107. Hughes, *The Big Sea,* 225.

108. Ken Jassamy, "Club Revue Is Entertaining and Brilliant," *New York Amsterdam News* (April 3, 1937), 16.

109. April 3, 1937, untitled article in Ubangi Club Clippings File, Billy Rose Theatre Collection, New York Public Library.

110. April 17, 1937. Untitled article in Ubangi Club Clippings File, Billy Rose Theatre Collection, New York Public Library.

111. *New York World Telegram,* April 17, 1937.

112. "Night Clubs," *New York Times* (October 24, 1936), 22.

113. "Night-Club Notes," *New York Times* (May 8, 1937), 22.

114. "Business Records," *New York Times* (February 16, 1938), 36; "Business Records," *New York Times* (August 9, 1938), 31.

115. Louis Calta, "News of the Night-Clubs," *New York Times* (January 23, 1944), X6. According to the announcement, the Ubangi Club, which is dubbed the "emporium of sepian entertainment," contained music and lyrics by Donald Heywood, the composer-lyricist of several black Broadway revues, including the Ethel Waters vehicle *Africana,* and who contributed material for many of Gladys Bentley's floor shows.

116. James V. Hatch, introduction to Hatch and Hamalian, *Lost Plays,* 17.

117. "Harlem Runs Wild," *Nation* (April 3, 1935), 382–83.

118. Episode #57-34 from DVD release of *You Bet Your Life: The Best Episodes;* transcription of the interview is mine.

119. Garber, "Gladys Bentley," 59.

120. Advertisement in *San Francisco Life* (December 1942), clipping from the Virtual Museum of the City of San Francisco. Site maintained 1995–2004, http://www.sfmuseum.org/hist10/mona.html.

121. Excelsior Label, 1945.

122. "Gladys Bentley Opened Thursday at Tondaleyos," *New York Amsterdam News* (September 30, 1944), B9.

123. "Ziggy, Page, Bentley, Tab, Others On Bill," *New York Amsterdam News* (May 12, 1945), B9.

124. Recorded June 9, 1952, in Hollywood. The song is available on *Dexter Gordon, Wardell Gray: Citizens Bop* (Black Lion, 1997).

125. On *Boogie Blues: Women Sing and Play Boogie Woogie.* Rosetta Records, 1983, available in the Schomburg Center, New York Public Library.

126. Alfred Duckett, "The Third Sex," *Chicago Defender* (March 2, 1957), 7.

127. Ibid.

128. The obituary in the *Los Angeles Sentinel* states that Bentley was ordained, but she never received her ordination papers, which "were delivered to her mother, Mrs. Mary C. Bentley, after her death. A copy will be buried with her." (A. S. Doc Young, "Death Takes Gladys Bentley" [January 21, 1960], C1.)

129. Bentley's burial record on file at Lincoln Memorial Park, 16701 Central Avenue, Carson, CA 90746.

130. "Voice of Broadway," *Washington Post, Times Herald* (March 6, 1960), G7.

131. Savran, *Cowboys, Communists, and Queers,* 7.

132. For instance, historian Lee Edelman explains that the nation's concerted efforts "to control homosexual behavior" after World War II "responded to the widespread perception of gay sexuality as an alien infestation, and unnatural because un-American practice, resulting from the entanglement with foreign countries—and foreign nationals—during the war." ("Tearooms and Sympathy, or, The Epistemology of the Water Closet," in Parker et al., *Nationalisms and Sexualities,* 269.)

133. Bentley, "I Am a Woman," 94.

134. Ibid.

135. Sally R. Munt, *Butch/Femme: Inside Lesbian Gender* (London: Cassell, 1998), 3.

136. Bentley, "I Am a Woman," 93.

137. Ibid., 94.

138. Ibid., 98.

139. Martha Vicinus, " 'They Wonder to Which Sex I Belong': The Historical Roots of the Modern Lesbian Identity," in *Homosexuality, Which Homosexuality?* ed. Anja van Kooten Niekark and Theo ven der Meer (Amsterdam: An Dekker/Schorer, 1989), 189.

140. "Women Who Pass for Men," *Jet* (February 1954), reprinted in *The Persistent Desire: A Femme-Butch Reader,* ed. Joan Nestle (Boston: Alyson, 1992), 98–101.

141. Ibid., 100.

142. Ibid.

143. Ibid., 101.

144. Ibid. Halberstam states that historically lesbianism is equated with a woman's failed attempt to pass through puberty. She writes in *Female Masculinity:* "We could say that tomboyism is tolerated as long as the child remains prepubescent; as soon as puberty begins, however, the full force of gender conformity descends upon the girl. Gender conformity is pressed onto all girls, not just tomboys, and this is where it becomes hard to uphold the notion that male femininity presents a greater threat to social and familial stability than female masculinity" (6).

CONCLUSION

*Epigraph: "You've Seen Harlem at Its Best," music by Jimmy McHugh, lyrics by Dorothy Fields. Recorded by Ethel Waters, March 30, 1934. Available on *Ethel Waters, 1931–1934* (France: Classics Records, 1993).

1. See Chauncey, *Gay New York,* 359.

2. Hughes, *The Big Sea,* 334.

3. "Harlem Riot Laid to Economic Ills," *New York Times* (March 26, 1935), 5.

4. Rose C. Field, "Harlem Riot Attributed to Many Economic Ills," *New York Times* (March 24, 1935), E11.

5. "Impersonator a Wow at 101," *New York Amsterdam News* (January 22, 1938), 17.

6. Bruce Nugent, "Gloria Swanson," from *Biographical Sketches,* 1. The sketch has been published in *Gay Rebel,* 221–23.

7. Qtd. in Baraka, *Blues People,* 92.

8. Augustus Austin, "Fletcher Henderson's Band Pleases at Opera House," *New York Age* (September 1, 1934), 4.

9. "'Gloria Swanson,' Impersonator, Dies," *New York Amsterdam News* (April 27, 1940), 1.

10. Maurice Dancer, "'Gloria Swanson' Buried in Harlem," *Chicago Defender* (May 4, 1940), 21.

11. "'Gloria Swanson,' Impersonator, Dies," 1.

Bibliography

MANUSCRIPTS AND ARCHIVES

Beinecke Rare Book and Manuscript Library, Yale University, Wallace Thurman Papers
Billy Rose Theatre Collection, New York Public Library, New York City
    Africana clippings file
    Appearances clippings file
    At Home Abroad clippings file
    Gladys Bentley clippings file
    Blackbirds of 1928 clippings file
    Blackbirds of 1930 clippings file
    Brevities in Bronze clippings file
    Broadway Brevities (monthly periodical)
    The Chip Woman's Fortune clippings file
    Dixie to Broadway clippings file
    Harlem clippings file
    Lulu Belle clippings file
    Ubangi Club clippings file
Borough of Manhattan Municipal Court Records, New York City
Columbia University Library, New York City, Alexander Gumby Scrapbook Collection
Institute of Jazz Studies, Rutgers University, Newark, New Jersey
Lesbian Herstory Archives, New York City, Mabel Hampton Papers
Lincoln Memorial Park Burial Records, Carson, California
Museum of the City of New York, New York City
    Africana clippings file
    Dixie to Broadway clippings file
    Lulu Belle clippings file
    Florence Mills clippings file
    Ethel Waters clippings file
New York Public Library Rare Books and Manuscript Division, New York City
Carl Van Vechten Diaries, Letters, and Scrapbooks
Richard Bruce Nugent Papers, Thomas Wirth, executor, Elizabeth, New Jersey
Schomburg Center for Research in Black Culture, New York Public Library, New York
    City
    Glenn Carrington Papers
    Alberta Hunter Papers
    Ada "Bricktop" Smith Papers
    WPA Writers Program
    Marvin Smith Personal Papers and Photographs, New York City

NEWSPAPERS AND PERIODICALS

Atlanta Daily World, 1935–50
Chicago Defender, 1920–30
The Crisis, 1920–35
Inter-State Tattler, 1920–30
Los Angeles Sentinel 1934–60
Messenger, 1920–30
Negro World, 1920–30
New York Age, 1920–39
New York Amsterdam News, 1920–39
New York Times, 1920–60
Pittsburgh Courier, 1920–39
Variety, 1920–39

PRIMARY SOURCES AND RECORDINGS

Anderson, Garland. *Appearances*. In *Black Theater USA: Forty-Five Plays by Black Americans, 1847–1974*, ed. James V. Hatch, Ted Shine, consultant. New York: Free Press, 1974.

Bentley, Gladys. "I Am a Woman Again." *Ebony* (August 1952), 92–98.

Bentley, Gladys. *Maggie Jones, volume 2, and Gladys Bentley: Complete Recorded Works in Chronological Order*. Vienna: Document Records, 1995.

Bricktop (Ada Smith Ducongé) with James Haskins. *Bricktop*. New York: Atheneum, 1983.

Club Verboten: "The Music That Dared Not Speak Its Name." Chatsworth, CA: DCC Compact Classics, 1997.

Du Bois, W. E. B. "Krigwa Players Little Theatre: The Story of a Little Theatre Movement." *The Crisis* (June 1926).

Du Bois, W. E. B. "Paying for Plays." *The Crisis* (July 1926).

Du Bois, W. E. B. *The Souls of Black Folk*. In *Three Negro Classics*, ed. John Hope Franklin. New York: Avon, 1965; orig. 1903.

Fauset, Jessie. "The Negro in Art: How Shall He Be Portrayed?" *The Crisis* (June 1926).

Freud, Sigmund. *Dora: An Analysis of a Case of Hysteria*. New York: Collier Books, 1963.

Freud, Sigmund. *Three Essays on the Theory of Sexuality*. Trans. and ed. James Strachey. New York: Basic Books, 1962.

Grimké, Angelina W. "'Rachel' the Play of the Month: The Reason and the Synopsis." *The Competitor* (January 1926).

Hall, Radclyffe. *The Well of Loneliness*. New York: Anchor, 1990; orig. 1928.

Haskell, Arnold L. "Further Studies in Ballet: Negro Dancing." *Dancing Times* (January 1930).

Hughes, Langston. *The Big Sea*. New York: Thunder's Mouth Press, 1991; orig. 1940.

Hughes, Langston. *Five Plays by Langston Hughes*. Ed. Webster Smalley. Bloomington: Indiana University Press, 1963.

Hughes, Langston, and Zora Neale Hurston. *Mule Bone: A Comedy of Negro Life*. Ed. George Houston Bass and Henry Louis Gates, Jr. New York: Harper Perennial, 1991.

Johnson, James Weldon. *The Autobiography of an Ex-Coloured Man*. New York: Vintage, 1989; orig. 1927.

Johnson, James Weldon. *Black Manhattan*. New York: Da Capo, 1991; orig. 1930.

Larsen, Nella. *Quicksand* and *Passing*. Ed. Deborah E. McDowell. New Brunswick, NJ: Rutgers University Press, 1986; orig. 1928 and 1929.

Levinson, André. "The Negro Dance under European Eyes." *Theatre Arts Monthly* (April 1927).

Lewis, Theophilus. "Actors Smashed Barriers with Undeniable Talent: Famous Names Grace Roster of Who Paced Theatre Progress." *Philadelphia Courier* (1950).

Lewis, Theophilus. "Main Problems of the Negro Theater." *The Messenger* (July 1926).

Lewis, Theophilus. "Reflections of an Alleged Dramatic Critic." *The Messenger* (June 1927).

Lewis, Theophilus. "Survey of the Negro: No. II." *The Messenger* (September 1926).

Lewis, Theophilus. "Variation 0137 of Monologue No. 8." *The Messenger* (February 1927).

Locke, Alain. "Art or Propaganda?" *Harlem* (November 1928), 12–13.

Locke, Alain. "Broadway and the Negro Drama." *Theater Arts* (October 1941), 745–52.

Locke, Alain. "The New Negro." In *The New Negro: Voices of the Harlem Renaissance*, ed. Alain Locke. New York: Simon and Schuster, 1992; orig. 1925.

Locke, Alain. "Steps toward the Negro Theatre." *The Crisis* (December 1922), 66–68.

McKay, Charles. *Home to Harlem*. Boston: Northeastern University Press, 1987; orig. 1928.

Niles, Blair. *Strange Brother*. London: Gay Men's Press, 1991; orig. 1931.

Nugent, Richard Bruce. *Gentleman Jigger*. Philadelphia: Da Capo, 2008.

O'Neill, Eugene. *All God's Chillun Got Wings*. In *Nine Plays*. New York: Modern Library, 1923.

O'Neill, Eugene. *The Emperor Jones*. In *Nine Plays*. New York: Modern Library, 1923.

Richardson, Willis. *The Chip Woman's Fortune*. In *The Roots of African American Drama: An Anthology of Early Plays, 1858–1938*, ed. Leo Hamalian and James V. Hatch. Detroit: Wayne State University Press, 1991.

Rogers, J. A. "What Are We, Negroes or Americans?" *The Messenger* (August 1926).

Sheldon, Edward, and Charles MacArthur. *Lulu Belle*. In *The Stage Works of Charles MacArthur*, ed. Arthur Dorlag and John Irvine. Tallahassee: Florida State University Foundation, 1974.

Sissy Man Blues: 25 Authentic Straight and Gay Blues and Jazz Vocals. New York: Mojo Records, 1996.

Smith, Bessie. *Empty Bed Blues*. London: Living Era Records, 1996.

Spence, Eulalie. "Negro Art Players in Harlem." *Opportunity* (December 1928).

Thurman, Wallace. *The Blacker the Berry . . .* New York: Scribner Paperback Fiction, 1996; orig. 1929.

Thurman, Wallace. *The Collected Writings of Wallace Thurman: A Harlem Renaissance Reader*. Ed. Amritjit Singh and Daniel M. Scott III. New Brunswick, NJ: Rutgers University Press, 2003.

Thurman, Wallace. "Cordelia the Crude." *Fire!!: A Quarterly Devoted to Younger Negro Artists* 1.1 (November 1926): 5–6.

Thurman, Wallace. *Infants of the Spring*. Boston: Northeastern University Press, 1992; orig. 1930.

Thurman, Wallace. *Negro Life in New York's Harlem*. Girard, Kans.: Halderman-Julius Publications, 1928.

Van Vechten, Carl. *Letters of Carl Van Vechten*. Ed. Bruce Kellner. New Haven: Yale University Press, 1987.

Van Vechten, Carl. *Nigger Heaven*. New York: Alfred A. Knopf, 1926.

Van Vechten, Carl. *Parties: Scenes from Contemporary New York Life*. Los Angeles: Sun and Moon Press, 1993; orig. 1930.

Van Vechten, Carl. "Prescription for the Negro Theatre." *Vanity Fair* (October 1925): 46, 92, 98.

Waters, Ethel. *The Chronological Ethel Waters, 1926–1929*. Classics Records, 1993.

Waters, Ethel. *The Chronological Ethel Waters, 1931–1934*. Classics Records, 1993.

Waters, Ethel. *Ethel Waters: On Stage and Screen*. New York: Sony Music Special Products, 1989.

Waters, Ethel. *An Introduction to Ethel Waters: Her Best Recordings, 1921–1940*. Best of Jazz Records, 1994.

Waters, Ethel, with Charles Samuels. *His Eye Is on the Sparrow*. New York: Da Capo, 1992; orig. 1950.

West, Mae. *Goodness Had Nothing to Do with It*. New York: Prentice Hall, 1959.

"Women Who Pass for Men." *Jet* (February 1954). Reprinted in *The Persistent Desire: A Femme-Butch Reader,* ed. Joan Nestle. Boston: Alyson, 1992.

SECONDARY SOURCES

Abramson, Doris E. "The Great White Way: Critics and the First Black Playwrights on Broadway." *Educational Theatre Journal* 28 (March 1976): 45–55.

Ackerman, Robert John. *Heterogeneities: Race, Gender, Class, Nation, and State*. Amherst: University of Massachusetts Press, 1996.

Anderson, Addell Austin. "The Ethiopian Arts Theatre." *Theatre Survey* 33.2 (November 1992): 132–43.

Anderson, Jervis. *This Was Harlem: A Cultural Portrait, 1900–1950*. New York: Farrar, Straus and Giroux, 1981.

Anderson, Paul Allen. *Deep River: Music and Memory in Harlem Renaissance Thought*. Durham, NC: Duke University Press, 2001.

Appiah, K. Anthony, with Amy Gutman. *Color Conscious: The Political Morality of Race*. Princeton: Princeton University Press, 1996.

Appiah, K. Anthony, and Henry Louis Gates, Jr., eds. *Identities*. Chicago: Chicago University Press, 1995.

Armistead-Johnson, Helen. "Blacks in Vaudeville: Broadway and Beyond." In *American Popular Entertainment: Papers and Proceedings of the Conference on the History of American Popular Entertainment,* ed. Myron Matlaw. Westport, CT: Greenwood Press, 1979.

Armistead-Johnson, Helen. "*Shuffle Along:* Keynote of the Harlem Renaissance." In *The Theatre of Black Americans: A Collection of Critical Essays,* ed. Erroll Hill. New York: Applause Theatre Books, 1980.

Atkinson, Brooks. *Broadway*. New York: Macmillan, 1970.

Awkward, Michael. *Negotiating Difference: Race, Gender, and the Politics of Positionality.* Chicago: University of Chicago Press, 1995.

Babuscio, Jack. "Camp and the Gay Sensibility." In *Camp Grounds: Style and Sexuality,* ed. David Bergman. Amherst: University of Massachusetts Press, 1993.

Baker, Houston A., Jr. *Modernism and the Harlem Renaissance.* Chicago: University of Chicago Press, 1987.

Baker, Roger. *Drag: A History of Female Impersonation in the Performing Arts.* New York: New York University Press, 1994.

Banes, Sally. "Will the Real . . . Please Stand Up? An Introduction to the Issue." *TDR* 34 (Winter 1990): 21–27.

Barish, Jonas. *The Anti-Theatrical Prejudice.* Berkeley: University of California Press, 1981.

Bascom, Lionel C. *A Renaissance in Harlem: Lost Voices of an American Community.* New York: Avon, 1999.

Baudrillard, Jean. *Simulacra and Simulation.* Trans. Shiela Faria Glaser. Ann Arbor: University of Michigan Press, 1981.

Bauer, Heike. "Richard von Krafft-Ebing's *Psychopathia Sexualis* as Sexual Sourcebook for Radclyffe Hall's *The Well of Loneliness.*" *Critical Survey* 15.3 (2003): 23–38.

Bennett, Susan. *Theatre Audiences: A Theory of Production and Reception.* New York: Routledge, 1990.

Bergman, David, ed. *Camp Grounds: Style and Sexuality.* Amherst: University of Massachusetts Press, 1993.

Bernard, Emily, ed. *Remember Me to Harlem: The Letters of Langston Hughes and Carl Van Vechten, 1925–1964.* New York: Knopf, 2001.

Bhabha, Homi K. *The Location of Culture.* New York: Routledge, 1994.

Bigsby, C. W. E. *A Critical Introduction to Twentieth-Century Drama: 1900–1940.* Cambridge: Cambridge University Press, 1982.

Blau, Herbert. *The Audience.* Baltimore: John Hopkins University Press, 1990.

Blount, Marcellus, and George Cunningham, eds. *Representing Black Men.* New York: Routledge, 1995.

Bogle, Donald. *Brown Sugar: Eighty Years of America's Black Female Superstars.* New York: Harmony, 1980.

Bontemps, Arna Wendell, ed. *The Harlem Renaissance Remembered.* New York: Dodd, Mead, 1972.

Boorstin, Daniel J. *The Image: A Guide to Pseudo-events in America.* New York: Vintage, 1986; orig. 1961.

Booth, Michael, ed. *Hiss the Villain: Six English and American Melodramas.* New York: Benjamin Blom, 1967.

Borden, Anne. "Heroic 'Hussies' and 'Brilliant Queers': Genderracial Resistance in the Works of Langston Hughes." *African American Review* 28.3 (Fall 1994): 333–45.

Bordman, Gerald. *American Musical Revue: From "The Passing Show" to "Sugar Babies."* New York: Oxford University Press, 1978.

Bradby, David, Louis James, and Bernard Sharratt, eds. *Performance and Politics in Popular Drama: Aspects of Popular Entertainment in Theatre, Film and Television, 1800–1976.* Cambridge: Cambridge University Press, 1980.

Bratton, Jacky, Jim Cook, and Christine Gledhill, eds. *Melodrama: Stage, Picture, Screen.* London: British Film Institute, 1994.

Bronski, Michael. *The Pleasure Principle: Sex, Backlash, and the Struggle for Gay Freedom.* New York: St. Martin's Press, 1998.

Brooks, Peter. "Melodrama, Body, Revolution." In *Melodrama: Stage, Picture, Screen,* ed. Jacky Bratton, Jim Cook, and Christine Gledhill. London: British Film Institute, 1994.

Brooks, Peter. *The Melodramatic Imagination: Balzac, Henry James, Melodrama, and the Mode of Excess.* New Haven: Yale University Press, 1976.

Butler, Judith. *Bodies That Matter: On the Discursive Limits of "Sex."* New York: Routledge, 1993.

Butler, Judith. *Gender Trouble: Feminism and the Subversion of Identity.* New York: Routledge, 1990.

Byrd, Rudolph P., ed. *Generations in Black and White: Photographs by Carl Van Vechten from the James Weldon Johnson Memorial Collection.* Athens: University of Georgia Press, 1993.

Carby, Hazel V. "It Just Be's Dat Way Sometime: The Sexual Politics of Women's Blues." *Radical America* 20.4 (June–July 1986): 9–22.

Carby, Hazel V. "The Quicksands of Representation: Rethinking Black Cultural Politics." In *Reading Black, Reading Feminist,* ed. Henry Louis Gates, Jr. New York: Meridian, 1990.

Carby, Hazel V. *Race Men.* Cambridge: Harvard University Press, 1998.

Carby, Hazel V. *Reconstructing Womanhood: The Emergence of the Afro-American Woman Novelist.* New York: Oxford University Press, 1987.

Carlson, Marvin. *Deathtraps: The Postmodern Comedy Thriller.* Bloomington: Indiana University Press, 1993.

Carlson, Marvin. "The Haunted Stage: Recycling and Reception in the Theatre." *Theatre Survey* 35 (May 1994): 5–18.

Carlson, Marvin. *Places of Performance: The Semiotics of Theatre Architecture.* Ithaca, NY: Cornell University Press, 1989.

Case, Sue Ellen, Philip Brett, and Susan Leigh Foster, eds. *Cruising the Performative: Interventions into Representation of Ethnicity, Nationality, and Sexuality.* Bloomington: Indiana University Press, 1995.

Case, Sue Ellen, Philip Brett, and Susan Leigh Foster, eds. *Feminism and Theatre.* London: Routledge, 1988.

Castle, Gregory. "Staging Ethnography: John M. Synge's *Playboy of the Western World* and the Problem of Cultural Translation." *Theatre Journal* 49.3 (October 1997): 265–86.

Champagne, John. *The Ethics of Marginality: A New Approach to Gay Studies.* Minneapolis: University of Minnesota Press, 1995.

Chaudhuri, Una. *Staging Place: The Geography of Modern Drama.* Ann Arbor: University of Michigan Press, 1995.

Chauncey, George. *Gay New York: Gender, Urban Culture, and the Making of the Gay Male World, 1890–1940.* New York: Basic Books, 1994.

Chauncey, George. "From Sexual Inversion to Homosexuality: Medicine and the Changing Conception of Female Deviance." *Salmagundi* 59 (Winter 1983): 114–46.

Chinoy, Helen Krich. "Art versus Business: The Role of Women in American Theatre." In *A Sourcebook of Feminist Theatre and Performance: On and Beyond the Stage,* ed. Carol Martin. London: Routledge, 1996.

Cockrell, Dale. *Demons of Disorder: Early Blackface Minstrels and Their World.* Cambridge: Cambridge University Press, 1997.

Cohen, Cathy J. "Punks, Bulldaggers, and Welfare Queens: The Radical Potential of Queer Politics?" *GLQ: A Journal of Lesbian and Gay Studies* 3 (1997): 437–65.

Cone, James H. *The Spirituals and the Blues: An Interpretation.* New York: Seabury, 1972.

Cooper, Wayne F. *Claude McKay, Rebel Sojourner in the Harlem Renaissance: A Biography.* Baton Rouge: Louisiana State University Press, 1987.

Crenshaw, Kimberle. "Whose Story Is It Anyway? Feminist and Antiracist Appropriations of Anita Hill." In *Race-ing Justice, En-gendering Power: Essays on Anita Hill, Clarence Thomas, and the Construction of Social Reality,* ed. Toni Morrison. New York: Pantheon, 1992.

Curtin, Kaier. *We Can Always Call Them Bulgarians: The Emergence of Lesbian and Gay Men on the American Stage.* New York: Alyson, 1987.

Davis, Angela Y. *Blues Legacies and Black Feminism: Gertrude "Ma" Rainey, Bessie Smith, and Billie Holiday.* New York: Pantheon, 1998.

Davis, Angela Y. *Women, Race, and Class.* New York: Random House, 1981.

Davis, Tracy C. "Performing and the Real Thing in the Postmodern Museum." *TDR* 39.3 (Fall 1995): 15–40.

Davy, Kate. "Fe/male Impersonation: The Discourse of Camp." In *Critical Theory and Performance,* ed. Janelle G. Reinelt and Joseph R. Roach. Ann Arbor: University of Michigan Press, 1992.

Davy, Kate. "Outing Whiteness: A Feminist/Lesbian Project." *Theatre Journal* 47 (May 1995): 189–206.

Dawidoff, Robert. "The Kind of Person You Have to Sound Like to Sing 'Alexander's Ragtime Band." In *Prehistories of the Furture: The Primitivist Project and the Culture of Modernism,* ed. Elazar Barkan and Ronald Bush. Stanford: Stanford University Press, 1995.

Debord, Guy. *The Society of the Spectacle.* Trans. Donald Nicholson-Smith. New York: Zone Books, 1994.

De Jongh, Nicholas. *Not in Front of the Audience: Homosexuality on Stage.* New York: Routledge, 1992.

De Lauretis, Teresa. "Eccentric Subjects: Feminist Theory and Historical Consciousness." *Feminist Studies* 16.1 (Spring 1990): 115–50.

De Lauretis, Teresa. "Sexual Indifference and Lesbian Representation." In *Performing Feminisms,* ed. Sue-Ellen Case. Baltimore: Johns Hopkins University Press, 1990.

Desmond, Jane C. *Staging Tourism: Bodies on Display from Waikiki to Sea World.* Chicago: Chicago University Press, 1999.

Diamond, Elin. "Brechtian Theory / Feminist Theory: Toward a Gestic Feminist Criticism." *TDR* 32 (Spring 1988): 82–94.

Diamond, Elin. "Mimesis, Mimicry, and the 'True-Real.'" In *Acting Out: Feminist Performance,* ed. Janelle G. Reinelt and Joseph R. Roach. Ann Arbor: University of Michigan Press, 1993.

Diamond, Elin. *Unmaking Mimesis*. London: Routledge, 1997.

Dickerson, Glenda. "The Cult of True Womanhood: Toward a Womanist Attitude in African-American Theatre." In *Performing Feminisms: Feminist Critical Theory and Theatre*, ed. Sue Ellen Case. Baltimore: Johns Hopkins University Press, 1990.

Dolan, Jill. *The Feminist Spectator as Critic*. Ann Arbor: University of Michigan Press, 1991.

Dolan, Jill. *Presence and Desire: Essays on Gender, Sexuality, Performance*. Ann Arbor: University of Michigan Press, 1993.

Douglas, Ann. *Terrible Honesty: Mongrel Manhattan in the 1920s*. New York: Noonday Press, 1995.

DuCille, Ann. "Blues Notes on Black Sexuality: Sex and the Texts of Jessie Fauset and Nella Larsen." *Journal of the History of Sexuality* 3 (January 1993): 418–44.

Duberman, Martin Bauml. *Paul Robeson*. New York: Knopf, 1988.

Dyer, Richard. *Heavenly Bodies: Film Stars and Society*. New York: St. Martin's Press, 1986.

Dyer, Richard. *The Matter of Images: Essays on Representations*. London: Routledge, 1993.

Egan, Bill. *Florence Mills: Harlem Jazz Queen*. Lanham, MD: Scarecrow Press, 2004.

Engle, Ron, and Tice L. Miller, eds. *The American Stage: Social and Economic Issues from the Colonial Period to the Present*. Cambridge: Cambridge University Press, 1993.

Erenberg, Lewis A. *Steppin' Out: New York Nightlife and the Transformation of American Culture, 1890–1930*. Westport, CT: Greenwood Press, 1981.

Escoffier, Jeffrey. "The Political Economy of the Closet: Notes toward an Economic History of Gay and Lesbian Life before Stonewall." In *Homo Economics: Capitalism, Community, and Lesbian and Gay Life*, ed. Amy Gluckman and Betsy Reed. New York: Routledge, 1997.

Faderman, Lillian. *Odd Girls and Twilight Lovers: A History of Lesbian Life in Twentieth-Century America*. New York: Columbia University Press, 1991.

Faderman, Lillian, and Ann Williams. "Radclyffe Hall and the Lesbian Image." *Conditions* 1 (April 1977): 32.

Favor, J. Martin. *Authentic Blackness: The Folk in the New Negro Renaissance*. Durham, NC: Duke University Press, 1999.

Fell, John L., and Terkild Vinding. *Stride! Fats, Jimmy, Lion, Lamb, and All the Other Ticklers*. Lanham, MD: Scarecrow Press, 1999.

Ferris, Lesley, ed. *Crossing the Stage: Controversies on Cross-Dressing*. New York: Routledge, 1993.

Fine, Michelle, Mun Wong, Lois Weis, and Linda Powell, eds. *Off White: Readings on Society, Race, and Culture*. New York: Routledge, 1996.

Fjellman, Stephen M. *Vinyl Leaves: Walt Disney World and America*. Boulder: Westview Press, 1992.

Floyd, Samuel A., Jr., ed. *Black Music in the Harlem Renaissance: A Collection of Essays*. New York: Greenwood Press, 1990.

Foucault, Michel. *Discipline and Punish*. Trans. Alan Sheidan. New York: Vintage, 1979.

Fraden, Rena. "Critical Directions: Toward a National Negro Theatre." In *Blueprints for a Black Theatre, 1935–1939*. Cambridge: Cambridge University Press, 1994.

Frankenberg, Ruth. *White Women, Race Matters: The Social Construction of Whiteness.* Minneapolis: University of Minnesota Press, 1993.

Frazier, Adrian. *Behind the Scenes: Yeats, Horniman, and the Abbey Theatre.* Berkeley: University of California Press, 1990.

Fuss, Diana. "Freud's Fallen Women: Identification, Desire, and 'A Case of Homosexuality in a Woman.'" In *Fear of a Queer Planet: Queer Politics and Social Theory,* ed. Michael Warner. Minneapolis: University of Minnesota Press, 1993.

Fuss, Diana. *Identification Papers.* New York: Routledge, 1995.

Gaines, Jane. "Fire and Desire: Race, Melodrama, and Oscar Michaux." In *Melodrama: Stage, Picture, Screen,* ed. Jacky Bratton, Jim Cook, and Christine Gledhill. London: British Film Institute, 1994.

Garber, Eric. "A Spectacle in Color: The Lesbian and Gay Subculture of Jazz Age Harlem." In *Hidden from History: Reclaiming the Gay and Lesbian Past,* ed. Martin Duberman, Martha Vicinus, and George Chauncy, Jr. New York: Meridian, 1990.

Garber, Eric. "Gladys Bentley: The Bulldagger Who Sang the Blues." *Out/Look* (Spring 1988), 52–61.

Garber, Marjorie. *Vested Interests: Cross-Dressing and Cultural Anxiety.* New York: Routledge, 1992.

Gates, Henry Louis, Jr., ed. *Reading Black, Reading Feminist: A Critical Anthology.* New York: Meridian, 1990.

Gates, Henry Louis, Jr. *The Signifying Monkey: A Theory of African-American Literary Criticism.* Oxford: Oxford University Press, 1988.

Giddings, Paula. *When and Where I Enter: The Impact of Black Women on Race and Sex in America.* New York: Bantam, 1984.

Gilroy, Paul. *The Black Atlantic: Modernity and Double Consciousness.* Cambridge: Harvard University Press, 1993.

Gerould, Daniel, ed. *American Melodrama.* New York: Performing Arts Journal Publications, 1983.

Gerould, Daniel, ed. *Melodrama.* New York: New York Literary Forum, 1980.

Giles, Freda Scott. "Glitter, Glitz, and Race: The Production of *Harlem.*" In *Experimenters, Rebels, and Disparate Voices: The Theatre of the 1920s Celebrates American Diversity,* ed. Arthur Gewirtz and James J. Kolb. Westport, CT: Praeger, 2003.

Giles, Freda Scott. "*The Star of Ethiopia:* A Contribution toward the Development of Black Drama and Theater in the Harlem Renaissance." In *The Harlem Renaissance: Revaluations,* ed. Amritjit Singh, William S. Shiver, and Stanley Brodwin. New York: Garland, 1989.

Gordon, Allan M. "Interactions between Art and Music during the Harlem Renaissance." In *Black Music in the Harlem Renaissance: A Collection of Essays,* ed. Samuel A. Floyd, Jr. New York: Greenwood Press, 1990.

Graff, E. J. *What Is Marriage For? The Strange Social History of Our Most Intimate Institution.* Boston: Beacon Press, 1999.

Graziano, John. "Black Musical Theater and the Harlem Renaissance Movement." In *Black Music in the Harlem Renaissance: A Collection of Essays,* ed. Samuel A. Floyd, Jr. New York: Greenwood Press, 1990.

Green, Jeffrey P. "The Negro Renaissance and England." In *Black Music in the Harlem Renaissance: A Collection of Essays,* ed. Samuel A. Floyd, Jr. New York: Greenwood Press, 1990.

Green, Laura. "Radclyffe Hall's *The Well of Loneliness* and Modernist Fictions of Identity." *Twentieth-Century Literature* 49.3 (Fall 2003): 277–97.

Griffin, Sean. "The Gang's All Here: Generic versus Racial Integration in the 1940s Musical." *Cinema Journal* 42.1 (Autumn 2002): 21–45.

Grimsted, David. *Melodrama Unveiled: American Theater and Culture, 1800–1850.* Chicago: University of Chicago Press, 1968.

Gubar, Susan. *Racechanges: White Skin, Black Face in American Culture.* New York: Oxford University Press, 1997.

Gutman, Herbert. *The Black Family in Slavery and Freedom, 1750–1925.* New York: Vintage, 1976.

Halberstam, Judith. "Between Butches." In *Butch/Femme: Inside Lesbian Gender,* ed. Sally Munt. London: Cassell, 1998.

Halberstam, Judith. *Female Masculinity.* Durham, NC: Duke University Press, 1998.

Hamalian, Leo, and James V. Hatch. *The Roots of African American Drama: An Anthology of Early Plays, 1858–1938.* Detroit: Wayne State University Press, 1991.

Hamilton, Marybeth. "Sexuality, Authenticity and the Making of the Blues Tradition." *Past and Present* 169 (November 2000): 132–60.

Harrington, John P., ed. *Modern Irish Drama.* New York: Norton, 1991.

Harris, Laura Alexandra. "Queer Black Feminism: The Pleasure Principle." *Feminist Review* 54 (Autumn 1996): 3–30.

Harrison, Daphne Duval. *Black Pearls: Blues Queens of the 1920s.* New Brunswick, NJ: Rutgers University Press, 1988.

Hart, Lynda. *Fatal Women: Lesbian Sexuality and the Mark of Aggression.* Princeton: Princeton University Press, 1994.

Haskins, Jim. *Black Theater in America.* New York: Thomas Y. Crowell, 1982.

Haskins, Jim. *The Cotton Club.* New York: Random House, 1977.

Hatch, James V. "Here Comes Everybody: Scholarship and Black Theatre History." In *Interpreting the Theatrical Past,* ed. Thomas Postlewait and Bruce A. McConachie. Iowa City: University of Iowa Press, 1989.

Hatch, James V. "Some African Influences on the Afro-American Theatre." In *The Theatre of Black Americans: A Collection of Critical Essays,* ed. Erroll Hill. New York: Applause Theatre Books, 1980.

Hatch, James V., and Leo Hamalian, eds. *Lost Plays of the Harlem Renaissance, 1920–1940.* Detroit: Wayne State University Press, 1996.

Hatch, James V., ed., and Ted Shine, consultant. *Black Theater USA: Forty-Five Plays by Black Americans, 1847–1974.* New York: Free Press, 1974.

Hay, Samuel A. *African American Theatre: An Historical and Critical Analysis.* Cambridge: Cambridge University Press, 1994.

Hemenway, Robert. *Zora Neale Hurston: A Literary Biography.* Urbana: University of Illinois Press, 1977.

Hibberd, J. L. "The Spirit of Flesh: Wedekind's Lulu." *Modern Language Review* 79.2 (April 1984): 336–55.

Hill, Errol. "The Hyers Sisters: Pioneers in Black Musical Comedy." In *The American Stage: Social and Economic Issues from the Colonial Period to the Present*, ed. Ron Engle and Tice L. Miller. Cambridge: Cambridge University Press, 1993.

Hill, Errol, ed. *The Theatre of Black Americans: A Collection of Critical Essays*. New York: Applause Theatre Books, 1980.

Hill, Errol, and James V. Hatch, eds. *A History of African American Theatre*. New York: Cambridge University Press, 2003.

Hoffman, William M., ed. *Gay Plays: The First Collection*. New York: Avon, 1979.

Holloway, Joseph E. *Africanisms in American Culture*. Bloomington: Indiana University Press, 1990.

hooks, bell. *Ain't I a Woman: Black Women and Feminism*. Boston: South End Press, 1981.

hooks, bell. "Representing Whiteness." In *Yearning: Race, Gender, and Cultural Politics*. Boston: South End Press, 1990.

Huggins, Nathan Irvin. *The Harlem Renaissance*. New York: Oxford University Press, 1971.

Huggins, Nathan Irvin, ed. *Voices of the Harlem Renaissance*. New York: Oxford University Press, 1976.

Hurewitz, Daniel. "When 'The Life' Was in Vogue: Touring the Harlem Renaissance." In *Stepping Out: Nine Walks through New York City's Gay and Lesbian Past*. New York: Henry Holt, 1997.

Hutcheon, Linda. *A Theory of Parody: The Teaching of Twentieth-Century Art Forms*. New York: Methuen, 1985.

Hutchinson, George. *The Harlem Renaissance in Black and White*. Cambridge: Belknap Press of Harvard University Press, 1995.

Hutchinson, George. "Mediating 'Race' and 'Nation': The Cultural Politics of *The Messenger*." *African American Review* 28 (Winter 1994): 531–48.

Jones, LeRoi (Amiri Baraka). *Blues People: Negro Music in White America*. New York: William Morrow, 1963.

Julien, Isaac. "Black Is, Black Ain't: Notes on De-essentializing Black Identities." In *Black Popular Culture: A Michele Wallace Project*, ed. Gina Dent. Seattle: Bay Press, 1992.

Kellner, Bruce, ed. *The Harlem Renaissance: A Historical Dictionary for the Era*. Westport, CT: Greenwood Press, 1984.

Kellner, Bruce. *Keep A Inchin' Along*. Westport, CT: Greenwood Press, 1979.

King, Deborah. "Multiple Jeopardy, Multiple Consciousness: The Context of a Black Feminist Ideology." In *Black Women in America: Social Science Perspectives*, ed. Micheline R. Malston, Elisabeth Mudimbe-Boyi, Jean F. O'Barr, and Mary Wyer. Urbana: University of Illinois Press, 1990.

Krafft-Ebing, Richard von. *Psychopathia Sexualis*. Trans. Franklin S. Klaf. New York: Bell, 1965; orig. 1886.

Krasner, David. *A Beautiful Pageant: African American Theatre, Drama, and Performance in the Harlem Renaissance*. New York: Palgrave MacMillan, 2002.

Krasner, David. "Parody and Double Consciousness in the Language of Early Black Musical Theatre." *African American Review* 29.2 (Summer 1995): 317–23.

Krasner, David. *Resistance, Parody, and Double Consciousness in African American Theatre, 1895–1910*. New York: St. Martin's Press, 1997.

Krasner, David. "Whose Role Is It Anyway? Charles Gilpin and the Harlem Renaissance." *African American Review* 29.3 (Fall 1995): 483–96.

Kraut, Anthea. "Between Primitivism and Diaspora: The Dance Performances of Josephine Baker, Zora Neale Hurston, and Katherine Dunham." *Theatre Journal* 55.3 (October 2003): 433–50.

Kraut, Anthea. "Everybody's Fire Dance: Zora Neale Hurston and American Dance History." *Scholar and Feminist Online* 3.2 (Winter 2005). http://www.barnard.columbia .edu/sfonline/hurston/printakr.htm.

Leider, Emily Wortis. *Becoming Mae West*. New York: Farrar, Straus and Giroux, 1997.

Lentrichia, Frank, and Thomas McLaughlin. *Critical Terms for Literary Study*. Chicago: University of Chicago Press, 1990.

Levine, Lawrence. *Black Culture and Black Consciousness: Afro-American Thought from Slavery to Freedom*. New York: Oxford University Press, 1977.

Levine, Lawrence. *High Brow / Low Brow: The Emergence of Cultural Hierarchy in America*. Cambridge: Harvard University Press, 1988.

Lewis, David Levering. "Harlem My Home." In *Harlem Renaissance: Art of Black America*. New York: Studio Museum in Harlem, 1987.

Lewis, David Levering, ed. *The Portable Harlem Renaissance Reader*. New York: Viking, 1994.

Lewis, David Levering. *When Harlem Was in Vogue*. New York: Oxford University Press, 1979.

Lewis, Nghana tamu. "In a Different Chord: Interpreting the Relations among Black Female Sexuality, Agency, and the Blues." *African American Review* 37.4 (Winter 2003): 599–609.

Lieb, Sandra. *Mother of the Blues: A Study of Ma Rainey*. Amherst: University of Massachusetts Press, 1981.

Livingston, Robert Eric. "Decolonizing the Theatre: Césaire, Serreau and the Drama of Negritude." In *Imperialism and Theatre: Essays on World Theatre, Drama, and Performance*, ed. J. Ellen Gainor. London: Routledge, 1995.

Loney, Glenn, ed. *Musical Theatre in America*. Westport, CT: Greenwood Press, 1981.

Long, Richard A. "Interactions between Writers and Music during the Harlem Renaissance." In *Black Music in the Harlem Renaissance: A Collection of Essays*, ed. Samuel A. Floyd, Jr. New York: Greenwood Press, 1990.

Lott, Eric. *Love and Theft: Blackface Minstrelsy and the American Working Class*. New York: Oxford University Press, 1993.

Madsen, Axel. *The Sewing Circle: Hollywood's Greatest Secret: Female Stars Who Loved Other Women*. New York: Birch Lane Press, 1995.

Mahone, Sydné, ed. *Moon Marked and Touched by Sun: Plays by African-American Women*. New York: Theatre Communications Group, 1994.

Malone, Jacqui. *Steppin' on the Blues: The Visible Rhythms of African American Dance*. Urbana: University of Illinois Press, 1996.

Marks, Carole, and Diana Edkins. *The Power of Pride: Stylemakers and Rulebreakers of the Harlem Renaissance*. New York: Crown, 1999.

Martin, Wendy. "'Remembering the Jungle': Josephine Baker and Modernist Parody." In *Prehistories of the Future: The Primitivist Project and the Culture of Modernism*, ed. Elazar Barkan and Ronald Bush. Stanford: Stanford University Press, 1995.

Marx, Groucho. *You Bet Your Life* (filmed April 1958 and broadcast on May 15, 1958). Episode #57-34 on DVD on *You Bet Your Life: The Best Episodes*. Produced by Paul Brownstein. Shout Factory and National Broadcast Company, 2004.

Matlaw, Myron, ed. *American Popular Entertainment: Papers and Proceedings of the Conference on the History of American Popular Entertainment*. Westport, CT: Greenwood Press, 1979.

McConachie, Bruce, and Daniel Friedman, eds. *Theatre for the Working-Class Audiences in the United States, 1830–1980*. Westport, CT: Greenwood Press, 1985.

Mercer, Kobena. *Welcome to the Jungle: New Positions in Black Cultural Studies*. New York: Routledge, 1994.

Mitchell, Carmen. "Creation of Fantasies / Constructions of Identities: The Oppositional Lives of Gladys Bentley." In *The Greatest Taboo: Homosexuality in Black Communities*, ed. Delroy Constantine-Simms. Los Angeles: Alyson, 2001.

Mizejewski, Linda. *Ziegfeld Girl: Image and Icon in Culture and Cinema*. Durham, NC: Duke University Press, 1999.

Molette, Carlton W., and Barbara Molette. *Black Theatre, Premise and Presentation*. Bristol, IN: Wyndam Hall Press, 1986.

Mordden, Ethan. *Make Believe: The Broadway Musical in the 1920s*. New York: Oxford University Press, 1997.

Morrison, Toni, ed. *Race-ing Justice, En-gendering Power: Essays on Anita Hill, Clarence Thomas, and the Construction of Social Reality*. New York: Pantheon, 1992.

Mumford, Kevin J. *Interzones: Black/White Sex Districts in Chicago and New York in the Early Twentieth Century*. New York: Columbia University Press, 1997.

Munt, Sally R., ed. *Butch/Femme: Inside Lesbian Gender*. London: Cassell, 1998.

Murphy, Brenda. *American Realism and American Drama, 1880–1940*. Cambridge: Cambridge University Press, 1987.

Nero, Charles I. "Re/Membering Langston: Homophobic Textuality and Arnold Rampersad's *Life of Lanston Hughes*." In *Queer Representations: Reading Lives, Reading Cultures*, ed. Martin Duberman. New York: New York University Press, 1997.

Nero, Charles I. "Toward a Black Gay Aesthetic: Signifying in Contemporary Black Gay Culture." In *Brother to Brother: New Writings by Black Gay Men*, ed. Essex Hemphill and Joseph Beam. Boston: Alyson, 1991.

Nestle, Joan. "Flamboyance and Fortitude: An Introduction." In *The Persistent Desire*, ed. Joan Nestle. Boston: Alyson, 1992.

Newton, Esther. *Mother Camp: Female Impersonators in America*. Chicago: University of Chicago Press, 1972.

Newton, Esther. "The Mythic Mannish Lesbian: Radclyffe Hall and the New Woman." In *Hidden from History: Reclaiming the Lesbian and Gay Past*, ed. Martin Duberman, Martha Vicinus, and George Chauncy, Jr. New York: Meridan, 1990.

Newton, Esther. "Role Models." In *Camp Grounds: Style and Sexuality*, ed. David Bergman. Amherst: University of Massachusets Press, 1993.

Newton, Judith, and Deborah Rosenfelt. *Feminist Criticism and Social Change: Sex, Class, and Race in Literature and Culture*. New York: Methuen, 1985.

Nielsen, Aldon L. *Writing between the Lines: Race and Intertextuality*. Athens: University of Georgia Press, 1994.

North, Michael. *The Dialect of Modernism: Race, Language, and Twentieth-Century Literature.* New York: Oxford University Press, 1994.

O'Connor, Patrick J. "Discovering the Rich Differences in the Blues: The Rural and Urban Genres." *The Midwest Quarterly: A Journal of Contemporary Thought* (Autumn 1991): 28–42.

Ogren, Kathy J. *The Jazz Revolution: Twenties America and the Meaning of Jazz.* New York: Oxford University Press, 1989.

Oliver, Paul. *Blues Fell this Morning: Meaning in the Blues.* 2nd ed. Cambridge: Cambridge University Press, 1990.

Oliver, Paul. *Raunchy Business, Hot Nuts & Lollypops.* Liner notes. New York: Sony Music Entertainment, 1991.

Osofsky, Gilbert. *Harlem: The Making of a Ghetto.* 2nd ed. Chicago: Elephant Paperbacks, 1996; orig. 1971.

Patton, Cindy. "Tremble, Hetero Swine!" In *Fear of a Queer Planet: Queer Politics and Social Theory,* ed. Michael Warner. Minneapolis: University of Minnesota Press, 1993.

Pellegrini, Ann. *Performance Anxieties: Staging Psychoanalysis, Staging Race.* New York: Routledge, 1997.

Perkins, Kathy A., ed. *Black Female Playwrights: An Anthology of Plays before 1950.* Bloomington and Indianapolis: Indiana University Press, 1990.

Perry, Margaret. *The Harlem Renaissance: An Annotated Bibliography and Commentary.* New York: Garland, 1982.

Peterson, Bernard L., Jr. *A Century of Musicals in Black and White: An Encyclopedia of Musical Stage Works By, About, or Involving African-Americans.* Westport, CT: Greenwood Press, 1993.

Peterson, Bernard L., Jr. "Willis Richardson: Pioneer Playwright." In *The Theatre of Black Americans: A Collection of Critical Essays,* ed. Erroll Hill. New York: Applause Theatre Books, 1980.

Peterson, Jane T. "Pride and Prejudice: The Demise of the Ethiopian Art Theatre." *Theatre History Studies* 14 (June 1994): 141–49.

Phelan, Peggy. *Mourning Sex: Performing Public Memories.* London: Routledge, 1997.

Phelan, Peggy. *Unmarked: The Politics of Performance.* New York: Routledge, 1993.

Phelan, Shane. "Public Discourse and the Closeting of Butch Lesbians." In *Butch/Femme: Inside Lesbian Gender,* ed. Sally Munt. London: Cassell, 1998.

Quick, Andrew. "Approaching the Real: Reality Effects and the Play of Fiction." *Performance Research: On Illusion* 1. 3 (Autumn 1996): 12–22.

Rampersad, Arnold. *The Life of Langston Hughes.* Vol. 1, *1902–1941: I, Too, Sing America* New York: Oxford University Press, 1986.

Reinelt, Janelle G., and Joseph R. Roach, eds. *Critical Theory and Performance.* Ann Arbor: University of Michigan Press, 1992.

Riis, Thomas. *Just Before Jazz: Musical Theater in New York, 1890–1915.* Washington, DC: Smithsonian Institute Press, 1989.

Robertson, Pamela. *Guilty Pleasures: Feminist Camp from Mae West to Madonna.* Durham, DC: Duke University Press, 1996.

Robinson, Amy. "It Takes One to Know One: Passing and Communities of Common Interest." *Critical Inquiry* 20.4 (Summer 1994): 715–36.

Ross, Andrew. "Uses of Camp." In *Camp Grounds: Style and Sexuality,* ed. David Bergman. Amherst: University of Massachusetts Press, 1993.

Rubin, Gayle. "Of Catamites and Kings: Reflections on Butch, Gender, and Boundaries." In *The Persistent Desire: A Femme-Butch Reader,* ed. Joan Nestle. Boston: Alyson, 1992.

Sampson, Henry T. *Blacks in Blackface: A Source Book on Early Black Musical Shows.* Metuchen, NJ: Scarecrow Press, 1980.

Sanders, Leslie Catherine. *The Development of Black Theater in America: From Shadows to Selves.* Baton Rouge: Louisiana State University Press, 1988.

Sante, Luc. *Low Life: Lures and Snares of Old New York.* New York: Vintage, 1992.

Savran, David. *Communists, Cowboys, and Queers: The Politics of Masculinity in the Work of Arthur Miller and Tennessee Williams.* Minneapolis: University of Minnesota Press, 1992.

Savran, David. *A Queer Sort of Materialism: Recontextualizing American Theater.* Ann Arbor: University of Michigan Press, 2003.

Schechner, Richard. "Victor Turner's Last Adventure." In *The Anthropology of Performance,* by Victor Turner. New York: PAJ Publications, 1987.

Schiffman, Jack. *Harlem Heyday: A Pictorial History of Modern Black Show Business and the Apollo Theatre.* Buffalo: Prometheus Books, 1984.

Schneider, Rebecca. *The Explicit Body in Performance.* New York: Routledge, 1997.

Schwarz, A. B. Christa. *Gay Voices of the Harlem Renaissance.* Bloomington: Indiana University Press, 2003.

Scott, Freda L. "Black Drama and the Harlem Renaissance." *Theatre Journal* 37 (December 1985): 426–40.

Sinclair, Abiola. "The Image of Black Women in Minstrelsy." *Black History Magazine* (Fall 1998), 53–55.

Singer, Barry. *Black and Blue: The Life of Andy Razaf.* New York: Schirmer Books, 1992.

Singh, Amritjit, William S. Shiver, and Stanley Brodwin, eds. *The Harlem Renaissance: Revaluations.* New York: Garland, 1989.

Smith, Bill. "Vaudeville: Entertainment of the Masses." In *American Popular Entertainment: Papers and Proceedings of the Conference on the History of American Popular Entertainment,* ed. Myron Matlaw. Westport, CT: Greenwood Press, 1979.

Smith, Cecil, and Glenn Litton. *Musical Comedy in America.* New York: Theatre Arts Books, 1981.

Smith-Rosenberg, Carroll. "Discourses of Sexuality and Sujectivity: The New Woman, 1870–1936." In *Hidden from History: Reclaiming the Gay and Lesbian Past,* ed. Martin Duberman, Martha Vicinus, and George Chauncy, Jr. New York: Meridian, 1989.

Solomon, Alisa. "It's Never Too Late to Switch: Crossing toward Power." In *Crossing the Stage: Controversies on Cross-Dressing,* ed. Lesley Ferris. New York: Routledge, 1993.

Solomon, Alisa. *Re-dressing the Canon: Essays on Theater and Gender.* New York: Routledge, 1997.

Sontag, Susan. "Notes on 'Camp.'" In *Against Interpretation.* New York: Farrar, Straus and Giroux, 1966.

Spencer, Jon Michael. "The Black Church and the Harlem Renaissance." *African American Review* 30.3 (Fall 1996): 453–59.

Spencer, Jon Michael. *Blues and Evil.* Knoxville: University of Tennessee Press, 1993.

Spencer, Jon Michael. *The New Negroes and Their Music: The Success of the Harlem Renaissance.* Knoxville: University of Tennessee Press, 1997.

Spillers, Hortense. "Mama's Baby, Papa's Maybe: An American Grammar Book." *Diacritics* 17 (Summer 1987): 65–81.

Staples, Robert. "The Myth of Black Macho: A Response to Angry Black Feminists." *Black Scholar* (March–April 1979): 24–32.

Stavney, Anne, "'Mothers of Tomorrow': The New Negro Renaissance and the Politics of Maternal Representation." *African American Review* 32.4 (Winter 1998): 533–61.

Stearns, Marshall, and Jean Stearns. *Jazz Dance: The Story of American Vernacular Dance.* New York: Macmillan, 1968.

Stephens, Judith L. "Anti-lynch Plays by African American Women: Race, Gender, and Social Protest in American Drama." *African American Review* 26 (Summer 1992): 329–39.

Straub, Kristina. *Sexual Suspects: Eighteenth-Century Players and Sexual Ideology.* Princeton: Princeton University Press, 1992.

Thompson, Sister M. Francesca, O.S.F. "The Lafayette Players, 1915–1932." In *The Theatre of Black Americans: A Collection of Critical Essays*, ed. Erroll Hill. New York: Applause Theatre Books, 1980.

Toll, Robert. *Blacking Up: The Minstrel Show in Nineteenth-Century America.* New York: Oxford University Press, 1974.

Toll, Robert. *On with the Show.* New York: Oxford University Press, 1976.

Toll, Robert. "Show Biz in Blackface: The Evolution of the Minstrel Show as a Theatrical Form." In *American Popular Entertainment: Papers and Proceedings of the Conference on the History of American Popular Entertainment,* ed. Myron Matlaw. Westport, CT: Greenwood Press, 1979.

Turner, Darwin T. "Langston Hughes as Playwright." In *The Theatre of Black Americans: A Collection of Critical Essays,* ed. Erroll Hill. New York: Applause Theatre Books, 1980.

Turner, Victor. *The Anthropology of Performance.* New York: Performing Arts Journal Publications, 1987.

Turner, Victor. *From Ritual to Theatre: The Human Seriousness of Play.* New York: Performing Arts Journal Publications, 1982.

Van Notten, Eleonore. *Wallace Thurman's Harlem Renaissance.* Amsterdam: Rodopi, 1994.

Vicinus, Martha. "'They Wonder to Which Sex I Belong': The Historical Roots of the Modern Lesbian Identity." In *Homosexuality, Which Homosexuality?* ed. Anja van Kooten Niekark and Theo ven der Meer. Amsterdam: An Dekker/Schorer, 1989.

Vorlicky, Robert. *Act Like a Man.* Ann Arbor: University of Michigan Press, 1995.

Waldron, Edward. *Walter White and the Harlem Renaissance.* Port Washington, NY: Kennikat Press, 1978.

Wall, Cheryl A. "Whose Sweet Angel Child? Blues Women, Langston Hughes, and Writing during the Harlem Renaissance." In Arnold Rampersad, *Langston Hughes: The Man, His Art, and His Continuing Influence,* ed. C. James Trotman. New York: Garland, 1995.

Wall, Cheryl A. *Women of the Harlem Renaissance.* Bloomington: University of Indiana Press, 1995.

Wallace, Michele. *Invisibility Blues: From Pop to Theory.* New York: Verso, 1990.

Wallace, Michele. "Variations on Negation and the Heresy of Black Feminist Creativity." In *Reading Black, Reading Feminist: A Critical Anthology,* ed. Henry Louis Gates, Jr. New York: Meridian, 1990.

Warner, Michael, ed. *Fear of a Queer Planet: Queer Politics and Social Theory.* Minneapolis: University of Minnesota Press, 1993.

Watkins, Mel. *On the Real Side: Laughing, Lying, and Signifying—the Underground Tradition of African-American Humor That Transformed American Culture, from Slavery to Richard Pryor.* New York: Simon and Schuster, 1994.

Watson, Steven. *The Harlem Renaissance: Hub of African-American Culture, 1920–1930.* New York: Pantheon, 1995.

Watts, Jill. *Mae West: An Icon in Black and White.* New York: Oxford University Press, 2001.

West, Cornel. *Keeping Faith: Philosophy and Race in America.* New York: Routledge, 1993.

West, Cornel. *Race Matters.* New York: Vintage, 1994.

West, Ron. "Others, Adults, Censored: The Federal Theatre Project's Black Lysistrata Cancellation." *Theatre Survey* 37.2 (November 1996): 93–113.

Weston, Kath. "Do Clothes Make the Woman?: Gender, Performance Theory, and Lesbian Eroticism." *Genders* 17 (Fall 1993): 1–21.

White, Shane, and Graham White. *Stylin': African American Expressive Culture from Its Beginnings to the Zoot Suit.* Ithaca, NY: Cornell University Press, 1998.

Whitlock, Gillian. "'Everything Is out of Place': Radclyffe Hall and the Lesbian Literary Tradition." *Feminist Studies* 13.3 (Autumn 1987): 554–82.

Wilshire, Bruce. *Role Playing and Identity: The Limits of Theatre as Metaphor.* Bloomington: Indiana University Press, 1982.

Wilson, Garff B. *Three Hundred Years of American Drama and Theatre: From Ye Bare and Ye Cubb to Chorus Line.* Englewood Cliffs: Prentice-Hall, 1982.

Wittke, Carl. *Tambo and Bones: A History of the American Minstrel Stage.* Westport, CT: Greenwood Press, 1930.

Woll, Allen. *Black Musical Theatre: From "Coontown" to "Dreamgirls."* Baton Rouge: Louisiana State University Press, 1989.

Woll, Allen. *Dictionary of the Black Theatre: Broadway, Off-Broadway, and Selected Harlem Theatre.* Westport, CT: Greenwood Press, 1983.

Young, Lola. *Fear of the Dark: Race, Gender, and Sexuality in the Cinema.* New York: Routledge, 1995.

Young, Wilbur. "Gladys Bentley." In *Biographical Sketches: Negroes of New York.* Schomburg Collection, New York Public Library: WPA Writers Program, 1939.

DISSERTATIONS

Anderson, Lisa Marie. "Icons, Myths, and Reflections: Images of African-American Women in American Theatre and Film." University of Washington, 1995.

Anderson, Paul Allen. "From Spirituals to Swing: Harlem Renaissance Intellectuals, the Folk Inheritance, and the Prospects of Jazz." Cornell University, 1997.

Austin, Addell Patricia. "Pioneering Black Authored Dramas: 1924–1927." Michigan State University, 1987.

Belcher, Fannin S. "The Place of the Negro in the Evolution of the American Theatre, 1767–1940." Yale University, 1945.

Burdine, Warren Buster, Jr. "The Evolution of Images of African-American Characters in the American Commercial Musical." City University of New York, 1991.

Helfer, Richard. "Mae West on Stage: Themes and Persona." City University of New York, 1990.

Henderson, Dorothy Faye. "Georgia Douglas Johnson: A Study of Her Life and Literature." Florida State University, 1995.

McCoy, Beth Ann. " 'Do I Look Like This or This?': Race, Gender, Class, and Sexuality in the Novels of Jessie Fauset, Carl Van Vechten, Nella Larsen, and F. Scott Fitzgerald." University of Delaware, 1995.

Monroe, John Gilbert. "A Record of the Black Theatre in New York City: 1920–1929." University of Texas at Austin, 1980.

Scott, Freda L. "Five African-American Playwrights on Broadway, 1923–1929." City University of New York, 1990.

Vick, Marsha Cook. "African-American Drama on Broadway, 1923–1955: The Construction of Black Subjectivity." University of North Carolina at Chapel Hill, 1996.

Index

Page numbers in italics refer to figures.

249

Printed and bound by CPI Group (UK) Ltd, Croydon, CR0 4YY

09/06/2025

14685638-0004